andyfre
and
petegr

Punkmonk

New Monasticism and the Ancient Art of Breathing

Regal

From Gospel Light
Ventura. California. U.S.A.

Published by Regal Books
From Gospel Light
Ventura, California, U.S.A.
Printed in the U.S.A.

Library of Congress Cataloging-in-Publication Data
Freeman, Andy, 1969-
  Punk monk : new monasticism and the ancient art of breathing / Andy Freeman with Pete Greig.
    p. cm.
  Includes bibliographical references.
  ISBN 978-0-8307-4368-1 (trade paper)
  1. Spiritual life—Christianity. 2. Prayer—Christianity. 3. Monastic and religious life.
4. Christian life. 5. Freeman, Andy, 1969- 6. Greig, Pete. I. Greig, Pete. II. Title.
  BV4501.3.F739 2007
  255—dc22

                                                                2007002091

1 2 3 4 5 6 7 8 9 10 / 10 09 08 07

I dedicate this book to Mum and Dad. Love you both.
Thanks for being there.
ANDY FREEMAN

I dedicate this book to the BCC boys in Kansas City,
the Heasley clan in Ibiza
and the Lägels in "Bilder" Ramsdorf.
PETE GREIG

𝔓𝔲𝔫𝔨ᴍᴏɴᴋ

𝔓𝔲𝔫𝔨: (pə̄ngk) *n.* 1. slang. a. A young person, especially a member of a rebellious counterculture group. b. An inexperienced young man. 2. Dry, decayed wood that can be used as tinder. 3. A follower of "Punk Rock."[1]

ᴍᴏɴᴋ: (mə̄ngk) *n.* A male religious living in a cloister and devoting himself to contemplation and prayer and work.[2]

The restoration of the church will surely come from a sort of new monasticism which has in common with the old only the uncompromising attitude of a life lived according to the Sermon on the Mount in the following of Christ. I believe it is now time to call people together to do this.

Dietrich Bonhoeffer

Taken from a letter written to his brother, Karl-Friedrich Bonhoeffer, on January 14, 1935

Contents

SECTION ONE

Roots: Punks, Monks and the Birth of Boiler Rooms

SECTION TWO

Rhythms: The Ancient Art of Breathing

acknowledgments

This book has been born and raised in the 24-7 Prayer community, a group of friends who are precious to us and to whom we want to express enormous thanks.

Our specific thanks are due to Karen, David, Jonathan, Lucy, Jessica and Daniel Freeman and also to Samie, Hudson and Daniel Greig. Thanks for allowing us to take over kitchen tables, studies and living rooms with papers, books and computers. Thanks for freely giving up time so that we could write.

I'd like to mention the Boiler Room team in Reading particularly—thank you so much. To Pete "Wardy" Ward for faithfulness and sheer hard work; to Terri for continued wisdom and your Jesus-focused vision; to Annie for years of amazing kindness and support; to Lorraine for taking on the impossible job and succeeding. Thanks also to all who have been part of our team over the years: Danutia, Gemma, Josh, Andrew, Becky, Ruth, Heather and Sarah.

Thank you to Malc and Penny Peirce—this story is as much yours as anybody else's and so many of the changed lives of the Forbury young people came from your obedience and hard work.

Finally, thanks go to Steph Heald, Helen Monkton, Jon Peterson, Dan and Carrie Heyward, Andy Wilson and Aleke Dekker for your input and advice during the writing of the book. Your words have been invaluable to us.

Colonies of Heaven

Pete Greig

How do we begin to keep in time with the deep
pulsations of Eternity
and establish colonies of heaven in a society
that is profoundly earthborn,
materialistic and secular? One way is by
establishing communities
which embrace many of the disciplines . . . found in the
Celtic and Anglo-Saxon monastarium.

IAN BRADLEY[1]

Punk Monk is mainly the story of Andy Freeman's remarkable journey of discovery, which began with the initial explosion of 24-7
prayer rooms in 1999 and has led to the establishment of small,
contemporary, monastic communities around the world today.

Of course, Andy's stories, like mine, are far less exciting than
those of our heroes and predecessors on the monastic way—people
like Saint Patrick of Ireland, Saint Francis of Assisi and the modern-
day martyr Dietrich Bonhoeffer. But at least we have stories to
tell—we come to this book as practitioners rather than theorists.
Our prayer is that *Punk Monk* might encourage and equip many
others to establish their own communities of Christ-centered,
mission-minded prayer as centers of blessing both for Jesus Himself
and for those who do not yet know Him: "For my house will be

called a house of prayer for all nations" (Isa. 56:7).

The author Dr. Leonard Sweet believes that "the future belongs to the storytellers and the connectors."[2] If he's right and the telling of stories and the connecting of people can somehow shape tomorrow's world, then to that end we offer this book as our contribution to a much larger conversation.

The Discovery of Prayer

When a publisher first approached me more than five years ago and asked me to write a book about the emergence of the 24-7 Prayer movement, I questioned his sanity. "Who's going to want to read a book about a prayer movement?" I asked. "Especially one they've probably never even heard of!" However, the last time I checked, *Red Moon Rising* had been translated into German, Slovakian and Finnish, and there's apparently even an audio version for the blind. It's also been granted the ultimate rock and roll accolade of being banned from certain bookstores in America!

I suspect one reason for this unexpected interest is the fact that the story describes the truly extraordinary things God can somehow do through ordinary people like me and my friend Andy Freeman. We're like the Napoleon Dynamites of Christendom, only less funny. Most people can relate. I'm often approached by people who say words to the same affect: "Pete," they say, "*Red Moon Rising* made me realize that if God can use someone as untalented and boring as you and your friends, then He must surely be able to do something pretty spectacular through me and my friends." When I get this kind of encouragement, it's always hard to know whether to smile or wipe the tears from my eyes.

No one was more surprised than me when our little prayer room on the south coast of England began self-seeding around the world. I often tried to make sense of it. Why was this crazy idea of night-and-day prayer catching on? What was God doing? Why were people from Belgium to Brazil suddenly so hungry to pray that they were even willing to sacrifice sleep night after night just to sit with God alone in a dedicated room? Was there some big heavenly switch that we would eventually trigger if we prayed hard enough and long enough? As I tried to make sense of the perplexing phenomenon of which I had somehow become an intrinsic part, God began to show me that prayer is more important than I had ever realized. I admit that I had always viewed it merely as a boring, but important, power source for getting God's will done on Earth, a bit like jumper cables for your car when nothing else will work. If you pray with enough faith (and "in the name of Jesus") out will pop the occasional miracle in the form of a vanishing wart, a friend who wants to become a Christian or a parking space in town at 4 P.M. on Christmas Eve.

But in biblical times, Jesus revealed a different, deeper dimension to prayer. One day, when Mary chose to sit at His feet while her sister Martha impersonated a headless chicken let loose in the kitchen, Jesus said, "Martha, Martha . . . you are worried and upset about many things, but only one thing is needed. Mary has chosen what is better" (Luke 10:41-42). Contrary to appearances, it was poor, hardworking Martha who was wasting her time that day and not Mary as she relaxed with Jesus.

As I watched the explosion of 24-7, I began to realize that prayer is not just about making "stuff" happen—it's also simply about waiting at the feet of Jesus. This, He says—dismissing the clutter of things we confuse with Christianity—is the "one thing needed."

Waiting Room

A few months after the encounter with Mary and Martha and prior to His ascension, Jesus commanded His disciples to wait in Jerusalem (see Acts 1:4). We know that while they waited, they spent their time in prayer. It can't have been easy for them to wait: They had just witnessed Christ's resurrection from the dead and must surely have been bursting to tell people!

They had also just been given "all authority in heaven and earth" by Jesus Himself, which is an awful lot of authority by anyone's standards. And they had been commissioned in no uncertain terms to go out and proclaim the gospel to the whole world (see

Matt. 28:16-20). These were men on a mission with some very serious work to do—yet having commanded them to *Go*, Jesus cau-
tioned that they must first *Wait*. Accordingly, the disciples hid
themselves away in their 24-7 prayer room and it was there, as they
prayed obediently in that Upper Room, that the Holy Spirit came
upon them with such power that they were propelled out onto the
streets to preach. The Church was born in a day.

Prayer is undoubtedly productive! Just as the intimacy of lovers
may result in the conception, gestation and eventual birth of new
life, so prayer begins in intimacy and often produces miraculous
fruit. As 24-7 prayer rooms multiplied and thousands of people
began praying like never before, we watched in wonder as prayer
gave birth to mission and to wonderful justice initiatives, to vibrant
creativity, to salvations, to writing and music, to the renewing of tired
vision and, perhaps inevitably, to many new communities with a
passion to pray.

Why "New Monasticism"?

People often ask me where I see the 24-7 Prayer movement heading and, when they do, I invariably mutter just two cryptic words:
"Boiler Rooms." As Andy Freeman explains in this book, Boiler
Rooms are communities that are centered on a disciplined rhythm
of prayer and committed to the outward and upward practices of
creativity, hospitality, learning, mission and justice. It's not exactly a new idea, of course. The Boiler Room model is derived from
the descriptions of the Early Church in the book of Acts who "all
joined together constantly in prayer" (Acts 1:14) while preaching
the gospel (see Acts 2:14), teaching the Scriptures (see Acts 2:42)
and caring sacrificially for the poor (see Acts 2:45).

We've also been deeply inspired by the ancient Celtic Christian
communities that combined prayer and mission so successfully
more than a thousand years ago. Their monastic settlements (called
muintir) shaped the culture of northern Europe and evangelized the
British Isles more effectively than any other mission before or since.

In his book *How the Irish Saved Civilization*, Thomas Cahill describes the profound transformation brought by Saint Patrick's

29-year mission to Ireland. Arriving as a teenage slave, Patrick beheld a country dominated by superstition and druidical paganism. But by the time he died, Patrick left behind a Christian nation:

> Patrick's gift to the Irish was his Christianity . . . which transformed Ireland into something new, something never seen before—a Christian culture, where slavery and human sacrifice became unthinkable, and warfare, though impossible for humans to eradicate, diminished markedly.[3]

As I studied the lives of Celtic saints like Patrick in Ireland, Aidan in Lindisfarne, Columba in Iona and Columbanus across France, Switzerland and Italy, I was deeply inspired to see the way that their prayer lives had shaped modern civilization. Many modern British and Irish towns and cities, I discovered, actually originated as places of prayer! For instance, there are today literally hundreds of places in England, Scotland, Wales and Ireland with names that begin with the prefix "Kil," derived from the word "cell," which refers to a hermit's place of prayer. Ironically, these towns and cities grew up around a solitary intercessor or a small group of friends who had decided to abandon the bustling centers of civilization in order to pray. Gradually, others must have relocated to join them, causing monastic communities to evolve or to be planted more deliberately. Many of these prayer settlements continued to grow in size and influence, developing their own economies and cultures and thereby attracting many to build houses nearby where they could benefit from the monastic education, trade, medical provision and preaching.

I am fascinated by the way those Celtic apostles expressed the gospel. Where we prioritize Sunday meetings, they planted entirely alternative societies! While we tend to try to build communities around *programs*, the Celtic evangelists congregated around *prayer*. Having given most of my adult life to Christian leadership and particularly to church planting along fairly traditional lines, I began to wonder whether there might be keys for our contemporary, postmodern culture hidden away in the lives of these ancient, pre-modern saints.

Bringing the Past into the Future

People often encounter God in extraordinary ways during seasons of 24-7 prayer, which tend to run nonstop for a week or a month at a time. As a result, people often don't want these times of prayer to end, and they dream of establishing permanent houses of prayer in which an unceasing chorus of worship and intercession can rise to God every minute of every hour of every day of every month of every year.

When this idea was first put to me, I was initially wary as I don't believe we have to take the scriptural descriptions of unceasing prayer in such a literal way, and I certainly don't ascribe intrinsic merit to the act of merely clocking up units of prayer. I guess I was also wary of creating Christian ghettoes in which people could dis-associate themselves from "the world" in order to spend every waking moment in an unreal, rarefied atmosphere. But then I recalled the precedent of those remarkable Celtic settlements and wondered, with growing excitement, whether we could perhaps try to combine the various aspects of prayer, work and mission that had proved so effective more than a thousand years ago. We can't assume that the Celtic Christians thought like we do—they did not—but we can, as one author puts it, "look to them for ideas and a framework for doing mission and ministry in our time."[4]

However, Boiler Rooms would probably have remained merely an idea cloistered away in my imagination if Andy Freeman had not picked up the vision and run with it in his home town of Reading (pronounced "Redding") just outside London. When he did, we quickly discovered that Boiler Rooms were much, much harder to be involved in and yet much more fruitful than we had ever expected. Some people came close to burnout while others came closer to Jesus than ever before. Andy is always quick to list our many mistakes, but there have also been many wonderful encouragements as we have given ourselves to lifestyles of Christ-centered, mission-minded prayer. Consequently, the Boiler Room vision quickly spread and there are now many similar communities all over the world, in the unlikeliest places. We're still very much making it up as we go along, but we have done a great deal of thinking over the last five years and much of that wisdom is woven into the narrative of this book.

Billy Graham was once accused of trying to set the Church back 50 years and he famously retorted that he would rather set the Church back 2,000 years to the explosive days of its inception. Boiler Rooms look back to the Early Church and our allegiance is foundationally to Scripture, which means that we reject those aspects of monasticism that seem to us to be extra-biblical, such as the tendency in certain traditions toward extreme asceticism, spiritual elitism or unhealthy, isolated introversion. We also recognize, however, the wealth of biblical wisdom outworked dynamically in so many expressions of Christian community down the ages: In the *Catholic* tradition we have learned much from the Franciscans and Benedictines. In the *Protestant* tradition we have learned from Zinzendorf and the Moravian community at Herrnhut, from Dietrich Bonhoeffer's dreams for the Confessing Brethren, from Francis Schaeffer and from missional theologians such as Lesslie Newbigin. And we have also learned from the Desert Fathers of Egypt and their Celtic disciples—a spirituality that predated the Catholic/Protestant divide.

The culture of the ancient Celtic peoples can provoke a great deal of nostalgia, evidenced by the number of New Age stores selling "Celtic" trinkets, "Celtic" music and "Celtic" jewelry. If you like such stuff, that's fine—but the romance of lilting accents and Irish mists has little to contribute to the pressing challenges confronting us in postmodern culture. Just as a driver needs to check his rearview mirror regularly, we need to keep glancing back to observe the past, but only because we are focused on the future and moving at top speed.

You'll find that Andy and I are not particularly nostalgic for the apparent serenity of our Celtic past. As the title of this book perhaps suggests, you are more likely to find us listening to the

music of Radiohead, Nirvana or The Clash than that of Irish fiddles
and pan-pipes. Our fascination with yesterday's Christian communities is driven not by a yearning for an age gone by, but by a love for
our own brave new world. We're drawn to explore monasticism by
two thoroughly contemporary and deeply urgent concerns: the call
to *mission* at a time when the Church is in sharp decline, and the
call to a *deeper life* at a time when society is more complex and frenetic than ever before.

What Is Meant by "The Ancient Art of Breathing"?

Gandhi, the great Indian pacifist, told American missionary Charles
F. Andrews, "The trouble with you Americans is that you start doing
before being." It's a charge to which we must all plead guilty.

The monastic traditions have a great deal to teach us about
how to live balanced and sustainable lives, oscillating naturally
between work and recreation, outward mission and inward prayer.
We often describe this rhythmic interaction between giving and
receiving, doing and being in terms of *breathing*. It's a useful, biblical metaphor that we explore throughout this book. In their communal rules of life, the ancients show us how to live with greater
humanity. They reveal that we must not fail to inhale the breath of
God (by which we were created and without which we die) through
disciplined prayer and meditation upon Scripture. And having
inhaled God's breath, we may breathe out His life in loving mission, acts of mercy, celebratory worship and generous hospitality.

All 24-7 communities seek to balance the inward breath of
prayer with the outward breath of social engagement. For this reason, they tend to be situated in "the thick of the action," wherever
we can find the poor and the lost. As I write, Boiler Room communities are being established among partygoers in Ibiza and among
liberal arts students in Madison, Wisconsin. We're reaching out to
prostitutes and pimps in Mexico and to neo-Nazi teenagers in East
Germany. In downtown Kansas City, a 24-7 community is seeking
to live prayerfully beside an adult-video shop. In Seville, Spain, a
small group is praying three times a day in a shop they have rented

for the purpose. And in Reading, as this book describes, we planted our first Boiler Room in a disused pub in part for swearing, puking, vodka-swilling "Goths."

In all these contexts, it's a wonderful challenge to seek to love our neighbors as we love ourselves! Breathing in makes us breathe out, and breathing out makes us breathe in and we find ourselves living life the way we were created to be.

Introducing the (Other) Author

An introduction is a place for establishing the core themes of a book, and, having introduced the idea of "new monasticism" and the metaphor of "breathing" described in our subtitle, it only remains for me to introduce my coauthor, who has written the majority of this book. Andy and I have worked together on this project as we have worked together on Boiler Rooms over several years, but you will notice that the majority of the narrative is his—where I have written a chapter, my authorship is made clear.

How do I describe Andy Freeman? Well, he's one of the kindest people I know, and yet, you might not notice him in a crowded room. To me (and he'll hate me for saying it) Andy Freeman is like a walking, talking outworking of the Beatitudes. Meek? Yup. Hungry for righteousness? Without a doubt. Poor in spirit? He thinks he is. A peacemaker? Invariably. And so, as Jesus promised, Andy is being blessed and raised up by God.

Recently he was invited to preach in Canterbury Cathedral with Archbishop Rowan Williams by his side—not bad for a lad who was turned down for ordination and rejected repeatedly for youth work positions in various Anglican churches! Andy has become one of my closest friends and, as we have traveled together over recent years, I have lost count of the number of people in many different places who have quietly thanked him for influencing their lives or leading them to Jesus or discipling their youth group leader. Andy seems to leave a trail of changed lives behind him wherever he goes, yet most of the time he flies under the radar and avoids the limelight. While I hold forth at the dinner table,

Andy will often be washing dishes in the kitchen, getting deep beneath the skin of the person who's wielding the tea towel.

I was once asked to speak at a particular event in Canada but couldn't make it, so I asked Andy to go instead. The organizer later admitted that he had been secretly disappointed to get Andy rather than me, because he (incorrectly) perceived me to be more influential in the 24-7 movement and because Andy wasn't particularly known for his preaching. Oblivious to these dynamics, Andy (who had only recently obtained his first passport) landed in Canada and found himself staying in the home of the organizer. Immediately, Andy did what Andy always does and began to get to know the organizer's family, playing with the kids, helping with the chores and sitting up late into the night talking with exceptional levels of vulnerability and insight, but mostly just listening. Between these times he dutifully attended the meetings he was required to attend and preached when he was required to preach.

Some of the talks were, no doubt, better than others, but by the end of the week when it was time for Andy to leave, every single one of the leaders' children cried and asked him to stay. That, to me, is more a mark of Christian leadership than the exalted ability to fill an auditorium with words. As I said, Andy is a walking, talking outworking of the Beatitudes, and if that doesn't qualify him to write the majority of this book, then I don't know what does!

For Punks, Monks . . . and People Like Us

Punk Monk picks up a key part of the 24-7 story where *Red Moon Rising* left off. In response to a brief description of the Reading Boiler Room in the final chapter of *Red Moon Rising*, people have often said, "Now, tell me more about these 'boiler thingies.' That last chapter was tantalizing!"

Well, whether you're reading this because you want to know more about "these boiler thingies" or simply because you like stories about the extraordinary things God can do through ordinary people like us, we've written *Punk Monk* as an invitation to experiment, explore and connect (please don't feel you have to replicate our model). And whether you're a punk, a monk, neither or both, we'd love it if our journey should somehow, someday intertwine with yours.

> *As we progress in this way of life and in faith, we shall run*
> *on the path of God's commandments, our hearts overflowing*
> *with the inexpressible delight of love.*
> RULE OF SAINT BENEDICT, PROLOGUE: 49

You also, like living stones, are being built into a spiritual house to be a holy priesthood, offering spiritual sacrifices acceptable to God through Jesus Christ (1 Peter 2:5).

Roots:
Punks, Monks and the Birth of Boiler Rooms

Adventures in the Formative Years of the Boiler Room Movement

Chapter 1

Revolution: Evolution

*The kingdom of heaven is like a mustard seed, which a man
took and planted in his field. Though it is the smallest of
all your seeds, yet when it grows, it is the largest of garden plants and
becomes a tree, so that the birds of the air come
and perch in its branches.*

MATTHEW 13:31-32

*True progress quietly and persistently moves
along without notice.*

SAINT FRANCIS OF ASSISI[1]

*Don't you know? They're talkin' bout a revolution—
It sounds like a whisper.*

TRACY CHAPMAN[2]

It had been a long night and I was back in my room, stereo on and
sitting in the dark. I laughed as I remembered the moment when
my friend Owen had arrived in his newly purchased leather trousers.
The girls thought they were great and Owen got lots of attention,
but they were not for me. Mascara and crimped hair maybe. But
leather trousers? No way.

It had been another night knocking back beers at my local
Goth basement club. "On the Rocks" got its name from the cave-
like décor and mysterious underground feel. I never knew whether
or not it was a real cave—though its location in leafy suburbia makes

it unlikely. I was 17 and my life was more and more about parties, friends and, yes, the odd bit of manly makeup. I loved On the Rocks for the music. Bands like The Mission, The Cult and Killing Joke had punctuated my evening and I had loved thrashing around in the club's heady Saturday night atmosphere in my jeans, studded belt, DM boots and eyeliner.

But now, back home, I was forced to face the fact that although life was full of fun and discovery, it was also full of painful questions. Sitting in the dark of my bedroom listening to *War* by U2 playing through my headphones, I sensed that Bono had something I lacked.

I wasn't a Christian. I hadn't grown up going to church, and I was dismissive of religion. However, I had a sense that something was drawing me in. I now look back and realize that God had spoken to me on a number of occasions, long before I acknowledged His existence. There was the time sitting on a mountain in Austria when I was suddenly overwhelmed by the majesty of what I could see. I began to cry. There were dreams I had as a child, promising me I was loved. And there was this evening, too, listening to U2. I was an activist, always had been, but that wasn't enough to make my life meaningful. I loved having fun, but the music couldn't be everything. Deep down I knew I was actually pretty low and unhappy. I had tried to be many things to many people in order to be loved, but there wasn't the peace and purpose I desired. I wanted more.

I glanced across at my desk and at the books piled on the corner. At the top was *The Imitation of Christ* by Thomas à Kempis. I had taken it out of the school library for a history project on my friend Barry's (a Christian) recommendation. It sat there unread, but for some reason—it was a bizarre thing to do at midnight—I picked it up and began to read.

> *Without love, the outward work is of no value; but whatever*
> *is done out of love, be it ever so little, is wholly fruitful.*
> *For God regards the greatness of love that prompts a man,*
> *rather than the greatness of achievement.*
> THOMAS À KEMPIS, *THE IMITATION OF CHRIST* [3]

I know now that something significant happened to me that night. It felt like some sort of new start, even though I didn't know what sort of start it was. It was an elusive, yet peaceful, place that I found, reading there in my room. Maybe that night the little idealistic misfit boy finally began to grow up. In Austria looking at mountains and in On the Rocks dancing to The Cure, through ancient writers like Thomas à Kempis and modern-day rock stars like Bono—God was speaking to me, calling me, whispering my destiny.

The next track kicked in: "New Year's Day." Bono's lyrics, describing New Year's Day 1981 when Russian tanks rolled into Warsaw's streets to crush the revolutionary protests of Lech Walesa's Solidarity Movement, stirred me: "We can break through, though torn in two, we can be one."[4] In hindsight, we know that nothing would resist the coming revolution in Poland. (Just as my heart could not resist its coming spiritual revolution.)

Poland's historic journey to freedom had begun only 18 months earlier, in a historic gathering and through an unlikely hero.

A Bright Morning in Warsaw

In the weary city of Warsaw, an air of excitement had been growing for days, and on the morning of June 2, 1979, it finally erupted in a wave of optimism and enthusiasm that hadn't been seen for many years in this Communist stronghold. From dawn, people had journeyed to their capital's magnificent Victory Square, named in remembrance of Poland's part in winning the Second World War. It had been a bitter victory, costing the lives of more than 16 percent of the Polish population—by far the highest proportional loss of life suffered by any country. The subsequent years of Communist oppression had done little to heal the nation's heart and lift its head.

But on that bright summer morning, in spite of so much suffering, the sense of fresh hope was palpable in Victory Square. It seemed that every kind of person of every age had taken to the streets, walking slowly and with a joyous defiance. As usual, most of their clothing was dark and drab, but there were also surprising flashes of color from flowers, rosaries wrapped around hands and pictures of an aging man dressed in white: He was on placards everywhere, many with "Papa" written across them.

Today the Pope, *their* Pope—Karol Wojtyla, His Holiness Pope John Paul II—was coming to Warsaw. Coming to Victory Square. Coming home to his people.

The immensity of this momentous occasion might be lost on readers today, but you must remember that John Paul II was the first-ever Polish pope, visiting Poland, a country under Communist rule and dominated by the Soviet Union. This was a pope visiting a country dominated by the theology of Karl Marx, who believed religion to be "the opiate of the masses."[5]

This was the summer of 1979. In another world, the American Music Awards were declaring the soundtracks of *Grease* and *Saturday Night Fever* as albums of the year, but disco had not yet reached the struggling Polish people, still in the Cold War's grip. The fall of Communism was 10 years away. Under President Breshnev, Soviet power was immense. Emanating from Moscow, it stretched far beyond Russia's borders into countries like East Germany, Bulgaria and Poland. The Iron Curtain lay heavily over Europe, and for the people of Warsaw, there were few rays of hope that could penetrate the gloom.

Against this dark backdrop of a divided Europe, white smoke had risen from the chimney of the Basilica in Rome and the bells had rung out for a new and unexpected pope—not an Italian as predicted, but a Polish hero: Karol Wojtyla. That day, against all the odds, seven million of Wojtyla's countrymen walked a little taller and prayed a little more earnestly.

And now he was home.

In the end, nearly a million people gathered for mass and to hear John Paul II speak. His message was a simple one: "Be not afraid." He spoke of hope, of the love of God and of his certainty in God's plans. "God will answer your prayers." Defiantly, he declared that "it is not possible to understand the history of the Polish nation without Christ." His message was inspiring, the atmosphere electric. Here "the opiate of the masses" was proving far more than just a drug—it was kindling real hope, bringing clear vision of what might be. A ray of sunlight had pierced the dark and dreary curtain of Soviet oppression.

One of those deeply affected was Lech Walesa, a middle-aged family man, a shipbuilder from Gdansk, a committed Christian. Who knows exactly how it happened, but we know that Walesa found himself challenged and inspired by the message and the occasion. What if Poles made a stand? What if this broken, imprisoned people broke out and demanded change? "Be not afraid." The words echoed through his head over the next few days.

Soon afterward, changes began. Small meetings became larger and larger as Walesa gathered shipbuilders together to form a union: Solidarity, the people standing together. By 1981, Communist leaders were so enraged by the now-widespread unrest in Gdansk and across Poland that tanks were sent to quell rebellion. Strict order was restored and martial law enforced. But the first cracks had begun to appear in the Curtain of Iron. A journey had begun that would end with the people's defeat of the mighty empire of Communism.

An Evolution of Thought

The word "revolution" has become a Christian cliché. We talk about "a revolution of thought" or "revolutionary worship" and insist that "our world needs a revolution for Jesus." I get the idea of what's being said, really I do. But I also get depressed that a word that has been so world changing has become so trivialized. To paraphrase U2, the idea of revolution has been stolen, "so we're stealing it back."[6]

"Revolution" is a word with a lot of misconceptions. The first is its meaning. The dictionary defines a revolution as "a great upheaval; a complete change, e.g. in outlook, social habits or circumstances: a radical change in government; to cause radical change."[7] To many, revolution equals rebellion and implies military conflict; to others, it means anarchy and law-breaking. To people of my age, it speaks of jaded communism or youth-group hype.

Yet revolution can mean much more. Martin Luther King's peaceful protests during the Civil Rights Movement in America and those in the Ukraine in 2004 that took Victor Yushenko to power in democratic elections prove that revolution is not always by the gun. My own conversion from depressed Goth to passionate Christian was another peaceful revolution in that it was, without doubt, "a great upheaval resulting in a complete change in outlook, social habits and circumstances." Revolutions often begin under the surface—initiating huge cultural and spiritual changes without anyone really knowing they're taking place. The Renaissance, the Reformation, the Internet—each revolutionary, yet all without a banner or a gun.

The second misconception is how we perceive revolutionaries. Often, the historic record highlights the people who are at the forefront of revolutionary movements. Yet are revolutions about individuals and their shining moments?

What if revolution is more about *evolution*: a gradual process of incremental change, shaped by circumstance and events, flowing through the consciousness of a generation—long before it is articulated in a movement? What if most revolutions begin quietly—in a classroom, a prayer room, a stable—decades before the social upheaval takes place?

At some point, the gradual changes in social DNA reach a tipping point, and revolution breaks upon the consciousness of a nation. Years of oppression in Poland worked their effects on the cellular level, first transforming a few in secret discussions in coffee shops and living rooms, and then reaching a point of no return. New thoughts and ideas emerged, and plans were laid and implemented. Lech Walesa was the hero of the movement, but the evolution began long before the revolution.

My First Revolution

When I was 17, God brought about a revolution in my life. I became a Christian—I committed my life to Jesus. I hadn't grown up in church, and I certainly didn't see it coming. I was attending church at the time because of a girl, but then the cross and the unconditional love of Jesus hit me like a train. More specifically, what hit me was a sermon about Jesus' crucifixion and an explanation of why it had all happened that way. I had always considered Jesus' death a setback for God, not the moment of victory—and I certainly had not considered that it had anything to do with me at all.

> But God demonstrates his own love for us in this: While we were still sinners, Christ died for us (Rom. 5:8).

The realization that Jesus had died for me—despite knowing who I was and all that I had done—hit me profoundly. I was shocked. For me? What about all my emotional baggage? What about the faults I was all too aware of? No one had ever dared to express love for me like this!

I went back again and again to that same church. (The girl had gone, but my attention had been turned.) The more I heard, the more I liked what I heard. The activist in me began to connect with the God of the poor, the Friend of sinners, the God-man living a counter-cultural life. I remember thinking how easily Jesus would fit into the punk scene. He slowly began to make sense of things that had been brewing—evolving—in my heart and mind for years. I believe this spiritual evolution began years before, when I developed a lasting love for counter-cultural music and acquired a social conscience.

In 1979, as Pope John Paul was changing the life of Lech Walesa and the nation of Poland, I was a 10-year-old, discovering music. I loved ska, a weird mix of punk and reggae that was emerging in the UK. I also found the music of The Clash, one of the key bands of Punk. "Hate and War, the only things we've got today, an' if I close my eyes they will not go away."[8]

By 1981, as Solidarity was holding its protests in Poland, Margaret Thatcher was Prime Minister and the UK seemed to me to be in a bad way: inner-city riots, rising unemployment, the collapse of industry. It was a polarized time for the UK. Many people found Thatcher a heroine, a model of strong leadership. I didn't. Even as a 12-year-old, my political juices flowed out of an unclear (but passionate) opposition to what she and her government stood for. Strongest was my feeling that the brand of individualism and capitalism they stood for provided for and defended those with the most, rather than considering the needs of the least.

But music spoke my language. Punk preached of revolution—sometimes in a nihilistic way, offering no solution—but occasionally offering different ideas, championing change and social justice. My politics matriculated in the classroom of The Clash and then took study leave with U2, a band inspired by the Ramones, another landmark punk band. As I grew up, my beliefs were shaped by the music and the message. By the time I was 17, I had flirted with Communism, been signed up to the Labour Party, committed to the Campaign for Nuclear Disarmament and been a regular subscriber to Amnesty International.[9]

Then, I heard of a Jesus who not only knew me and loved me, but also championed the needs of the poor—and I experienced my revolution. I read the Sermon on the Mount, Jesus' manifesto of Kingdom revolution. If this was the heart of the gospel—the defenseless, weak and broken lifted high—if this was the way of Jesus, I wanted in.

The River Is Flowing

Let justice roll on like a river, righteousness like a never-failing stream!
AMOS 5:24

Rivers fascinate me. Starting at some secret spring, the river begins its journey from the mountains to the sea. The force of gravity gives the water a momentum that builds and builds. Snow melts, rain falls and one stream merges with others. The meandering flow grows and gathers speed. Obstacles only add to its creative power. The water detours and zigzags around vast rocks, which one day will relent to the power of erosion or the silent explosion of ice in tiny cracks. Slowly but surely, the water wends its way always and forever downward. The quiet spring becomes a pool, the pool becomes a stream, the stream becomes a river, the river becomes a torrent, and the torrent flows inevitably toward the sea. From humble beginnings, nothing can stand in its way.

Considering what community and discipleship looked liked in 1930s Germany and then envisioning what the Church could become, Dietrich Bonhoeffer came to a startling conclusion, expressed in a letter written to his brother in 1935:

> The restoration of the church will surely come from a sort of new monasticism which has in common with the old only the uncompromising attitude of a life lived according to the Sermon on the Mount in the following of Christ. I believe it is now time to call people together to do this.[10]

Bonhoeffer wrote these words in London, where he lived and ministered from 1933 to 1935. He had come to the conclusion that God was calling him back to Germany to organize resistance against Hitler, and Bonhoeffer's strategy was to establish a small monastic community of brothers at Finkenwalde where pastors could be trained and the Sermon on the Mount outworked.

Bonhoeffer's world was blighted by a growing evil. In 1933, the Nazis insisted that all Protestant churches should come under the control of the Third Reich. Those brave pastors who refused to submit were forced to go underground. In this stark context, Bonhoeffer recognized in Christ's Sermon on the Mount a subversive and revolutionary manifesto for a counter-cultural resistance that could be cultivated into a new form of monasticism.

What do we believe about what we believe? Are the words of the Gospels, the words of Jesus, simply good teachings—an older version of a life-coaching manual? Are they something that sounds inspiring or uplifting? Or do we believe that the world will change if we dare to live them out radically?

At its essence, faith is an inevitable, powerful, creative and revolutionary force. Starting from a tiny mustard seed planted in the hearts of pilgrims like you and me, the gospel takes root. As we join with others, it forges into a stream, moving its way through the world that God passionately loves. Obstacles don't cause a problem—they only add to its life-giving power, which is the flow of the Spirit of Jesus gathering pace and intensity. And so it grows and grows: from stream to river to torrent, changing everything in its path.

The gospel that Jesus preached that day on the Mount is quite simply a revolution. Can you imagine what it was like to hear His words for the first time? "Love your enemies and pray for those who persecute you" (Matt. 5:44). Think about that! Or the Beatitudes (see Matt. 5:1-12), which were Jesus' amazing spin on the words of the Torah—the Jewish Law—that His coming fulfilled (see Luke 4:14-30).

Most days I have to admit my faith doesn't feel revolutionary. Most days it's a struggle. But when the Gospels are taken seriously, I'm convinced that nothing can be the same again—when put into practice, lives, communities, nations and the world will be changed. Gravity pulls the river down. The water cannot be held back or boxed in—it *must* flow. So, too, the gospel cannot be held back or boxed in. It's not a "safe" faith. No, Jesus came to champion the real meaning of the Word of God, to fulfill it, to start a process of subversion, of revolution, of mutiny against the doctrine of the worldly and to raise the flag of the kingdom of God. A Kingdom that is here, a Kingdom that is coming, a Kingdom that knows no end . . . a Kingdom that means that life can never be the same.

A New Monasticism

This book is about new experiments in monasticism. Right now, in certain circles, "monasticism" is a trendy thing to talk about. It's suddenly cool to learn from the monks of old, to recite their prayers, to walk their paths of pilgrimage. In a postmodern world—where deconstruction is the special of the day—ancient spirituality is alive and well and making a comeback. But to apply the principles and practices, we have to start with the roots, surely?

The roots of monasticism lie in the subversion and revolution of the life and words of Jesus. The monastic life was about, as Bonhoeffer reminded us, "an uncompromising allegiance to a life lived according to the Sermon on the Mount." Seventy years ago, he considered his surrounding culture and contrasted it with the revolutionary life according to the Sermon on the Mount, declaring that "it is high time men and women banded together to do this." What about now? What does the gospel have to say to the hundreds of thousands who go under the surgeon's knife because of unhappiness with their looks? What does it say to millions of children who starve while a minority have their fill at the table? What does it say to the nuclear powers, to the media icons, to the millionaire sports stars or to suicidal teenagers? Our world, like Bonhoeffer's, needs radical disciples of Jesus. Our world needs to be turned on its head.

The good news is that the river of change—though still small—is flowing.

Pilgrim Punks, Desert Revolutionaries and New Monks

Monasticism can mean many things to many people. It can mean orders like the Franciscans, Dominicans or the Benedictines. It can mean men with funny haircuts in brown tunics chanting prayers. Some believe that quiet, steady monasticism is irrelevant in our loud, fast, changeable world.

For me, monasticism is one part of a broader awakening in my life and in the lives of some of my friends. It is a new (old) doorway that God has opened—one that connects with the past but gives guidance for the future.

Nearly every major monastic movement began as a violent reaction to compromised religion. Monasticism, at its best, has always been a cry for change—in our own hearts, in an over-accommodating Church and in society at large. This is the form of radical faith that first drew me to Jesus—not the Constantinian, top-down, religion associated with high status and political power, but the faith of the underdog. Angry faith. Twenty-four-hour-a-day, radical, subversive, all-or-nothing allegiance to Jesus Christ, friend of the poor.

It sounds a bit like Punk. Writing an obituary for Joe Strummer (former lead singer of The Clash), journalist Paul Bond highlighted the political and change-making approach of the band:

> The Clash was different. Strummer and his writing part-
> ner Mick Jones wrote music as a call to arms—an appeal
> to stand up and be counted in the struggle against
> oppression. In his first interview with the *New Musical
> Express* Strummer stated, "I think people ought to know
> that we're anti-fascist, anti-violence, anti-racist and we're
> pro-creative."[11]

Monastic revolutions are sometimes aimed at the Church. These monastics wonder why God's people are not living out the gospel and so they aim their counter-cultural lives toward society, modeling godly living and witnessing to those losing touch with Him.

Soon after the Roman Emperor, Constantine, converted to Christianity (and with him, the whole of the Empire), the Church had a tendency to blend with society. Belief and belonging began to be watered down into an all-encompassing religion of the state. At that time, some sought to separate themselves from this luke-warm "cultural Christianity" to live a more spiritual life.

The Desert Fathers founded Christian monasticism when they fled the compromises of the Constantine-established church in the third and fourth centuries. Christians like Saint Anthony fled to the desert, looking to model a different, radical style of disciple-ship, full of sacrifice and continual prayer.

Saint Patrick, a Celtic missionary, was first captured and taken to Ireland as a slave, and then returned years later as a mis-sionary bishop. Ireland was a land that was pagan—druidism and mythology were deeply woven into society. Patrick practiced a lifestyle of prayer, discipleship and sacrifice, influenced by the Desert Fathers of Egypt and Syria. He sought to bring fresh Jesus-life to dead or ungodly practices and festivals, thoroughly committed to bringing light to a dark world. Saint Aidan had a similar approach:

> The Celtic heroes/heroines and their monastic followers sought out the people where they were, in contrast to the early Roman mission which tended to act as a chaplaincy to those who came to them. Saint Aidan and others who followed him took time to be with individuals, drew out their concerns, and shared themselves, the gospel, and their worldly goods with them.[12]

Saint Benedict (490-543), founder of the Benedictines, began his journey when he went to the leader of his monastery, threw down the Bible in front of him and asked, "When are we going to start living this out?" (That's a paraphrase!) Challenged to live radical, devoted lives, Benedict's followers started a movement that still exists today and, in fact, had a major effect on my hometown of Reading, England.

The Cluniacs (tenth and eleventh centuries) sought to center themselves on prayer, even more than the monastics who had gone before. The Carthusians (eleventh and twelfth centuries) aspired to the solitary life and fasted almost perpetually. The Cistercians (seventeenth century) tried to obey Benedict's original Rule more rigorously.

Saint Francis of Assisi (twelfth century), one of the most famous monks, formed his Franciscan movement out of an increasing frustration with organized religion. His band of followers was regarded as so committed to Jesus that Francis's teaching was considered unrealistic by most people. It was too extreme. Even so, both ordinary people and popes loved those teachings for their simple vision to follow Christ and to save the Church.

We may feel as uncomfortable with some of these extremes as we do with the laxity and compromise that threaten to undermine the gospel, but we must acknowledge that monasticism was (as it is now) a decision to follow Jesus in the most sacrificial and sold-out way imaginable. Could it be possible to apply this life-changing and revolutionary living in contemporary culture? Who are the new monks, the new punks, the new revolutionaries?

The doorway that God opened in my life is still open. It's taken me into the world of vows, of communities, of contemplation and of mission. In only five years, it's led me and others from opening 24-7 prayer rooms to planting Boiler Rooms (communities based around prayer and a monastic way of life). It's been nothing short of a revolution.

My Second Revolution

My second revolution began evolving about six years ago when I came across a prayer movement called 24-7. It wasn't a blinding flash of light or a great sermon that led me to 24-7 Prayer—just a flyer on my chair at a youth leaders conference. It was January 2000 and I was attending a gathering with my youth work team from Greyfriars Church in Reading.

Reading is a town of about 200,000, roughly 25 miles to the west of London. It's a typical English town and Greyfriars was a typical Church of England church, on the evangelical side of things. Our youth work . . . well, that was typical, too. We weren't growing much and we weren't seeing our work impact young people in our town much. We wanted more—we wanted to see God come and change things.

The conference was aimed at equipping youth leaders, and our team had all taken time off work to attend. We were expectant that God would show us some new kind of strategy or idea. Then we read the flyer.

"Prayer?"

Is that it, God? Is that what You wanted to say to us?

I have to admit I was a little disappointed. "Here is My great strategy: You should pray more."

As we chatted, however, we realized that although we had worked hard and tried lots of great ideas, we hadn't spent much time praying. We certainly hadn't spent time praying simply because we wanted to hang out with Jesus.

"Prayer it is, then."

Within a month, we had organized a weekend of 24-7 prayer. A room was set aside and decorated. We sorted out a prayer rotation list, dividing the day into hours and signing people up for different time slots. Then, on a Friday night at the end of February, we opened.

My first slot was 3 A.M. on Saturday. I remember going to sleep that night, slightly worried that I might not wake up and slightly upset that I had to. When my alarm went off at 2:45 A.M., I jumped in the car and set off. Arriving at the door of the church, I was a bit concerned: The church looked dark and no one was answering the bell. I took out my key, opened up and wandered down to the prayer room. I could feel my heart sinking at the thought of finding the room empty or of finding someone asleep.

That was when Nathaniel put his head round the door, smiled and called to me to come in. "You won't believe what's been going on."

Little did I know that night would change the direction of my life completely.

For Further Thought

Spend some time reflecting on your life and consider where revolutions have taken place in your life. What were the pivotal, evolutionary moments in your past? What is the journey God is taking you on?

Spend some time reflecting on the Sermon on the Mount, found in the Gospel of Matthew 5–7. Which of the Beatitudes describes you best, and which one challenges you most? How could a fresh allegiance to these words change your life, your city and your nation? Try to work out what would have been fresh and different about these words at the time Jesus spoke them. How are they fresh and different today?

Liturgy

Leader: The Spirit of God the Master is upon us because He has anointed us. He has sent us to preach good news to the poor.

All: Here I am, Lord, send me.

Leader: He has sent us to heal the brokenhearted.

All: Here I am, Lord, send me.

Leader: He has sent us to announce freedom for all captives.

All: Here I am, Lord, send me.

Leader: He has sent us to pardon all prisoners.

All: Here I am, Lord, send me.

Leader: God is announcing the year of His grace.

All: Here I am, Lord, send me.

(Liturgy based on Isaiah 61.)

CHAPTER 2

Beginnings in Thin Places

When Jacob awoke from his sleep, he thought,
"Surely the LORD is in this place, and I was not aware of it."

GENESIS 28:16

A holy place evokes an atmosphere of devotion. It invites prayer.

RAY SIMPSON[1]

When punk started it was so innocent and not aware
of being looked at or being a phenomenon . . .
you can't consciously create something that's important.
It's a combination of chemistry, conditions,
the environment, everything.

SIOUXSIE SIOUX, LEAD SINGER OF SIOUXSIE
AND THE BANSHEES[2]

"Help! Please someone help us!"

The shout broke me out of my daydream. Across the square, only 100 yards away, I saw a man hunched over the apparently lifeless body of a woman.

"Help please, someone help! She's not breathing!"

My friend Pete "Wardy" Ward and I had driven 200 miles to the sprawling industrial city of Manchester, having felt God prompt us to visit the city to pray. We traveled around and prayed at key sites. Wardy had also felt even before we came that we needed to go to the

Piccadilly area in the city center. He didn't know why, but we went anyway. As we wandered around and prayed, not much happened. As we prepared to leave for our journey home, Wardy went to use the restroom, and I heard the cry for help.

Even writing years later, the scene is still clear to me: I remember the blue color of the young woman's face. Her friend was kneeling over her collapsed body, terrified and talking in panicked sentences. He was in despair and seemed to be suggesting that she had taken drugs. As he spoke to me, I could pick up the smell of vodka.

As I called an ambulance, Wardy emerged from the restroom. Someone asked him, "Do you know first aid?"

"No," he said, "but I can pray."

And with that, he placed a hand on the prone girl and began to pray. Almost immediately, she coughed and all the color came back into her face. I was on the phone with Emergency Services and nearly fell over in shock when life rushed back in front of my eyes. For the next 20 minutes, as we waited for the ambulance to arrive, I continued speaking to the lady on the emergency line and Wardy continued to pray. Three more times, the woman went purple—and three more times as Wardy prayed, she coughed and began to breathe again.

This extraordinary process continued until the ambulance arrived. Once it did, we slipped away into the crowd, amazed: Had God called us all the way to Manchester to pray for a young woman, a druggie, to keep her alive for 20 minutes? It sure seemed that way! After all, isn't that the heart of the Good Shepherd, who leaves 99 sheep in safety to rescue just one? It seemed obvious to us that our pilgrimage to Manchester—on a whim and a prayer— had been for the sake of a young woman that most of Manchester didn't care about. It seemed that on that day, God was in the business of giving breath to the breathless.

As we journeyed home, I felt compelled to carry on praying for the woman. I prayed as cars whooshed past on the motorway, and I found myself remembering the vision of Ezekiel and the Valley of Dry Bones (see Ezek. 37). I had seen God give breath to a despised and forgotten woman on the streets of Manchester, and I wondered, *Could He also give breath to a dying and spiritually breathless generation?*

"Come on, God," I prayed. "Breathe life into these bones."

So I prophesied as he commanded me, and breath entered them; they came to life and stood up on their feet—a vast army (Ezek. 37:10).

Three A.M. in the Prayer Room

My breathing lessons had started a few months earlier, in our first little prayer room in Reading. Speaking honestly and with the benefit of hindsight, I realize that at that point in my life, I was overworking and hopelessly under-spiritual. That wasn't my intention—in fact, I was very earnest in what I was doing and in what I believed. But it was all busyness, frantic activity. I hadn't learned how to *be* with God, how to breath in His new life.

When I entered our simple prayer room early that first morning, there was undoubtedly a tangible sense of God's presence, a heaviness. I caught my breath. God was with us. The Creator was hanging out in Room Two of Greyfriars Church Center at three in the morning! I was stunned.

I remember Nathaniel's grin as he explained what had been going on so far: Our young people had been really going for it in prayer. The walls were already covered with their heart cries, Bible verses and pictures. Everyone had remarked how natural it felt to pray.

As I prayed with Nathaniel and Dan (who was also still there even though his slot ended two hours before), I mused about what was going on. I recognized that I had never experienced God's presence so heavily. I had seen some pretty amazing stuff on my 12-year road as a Christian. I had experienced God meeting with me personally. I had been in meetings where God had done amazing things. But here, now, was a space where God's presence seemed to be residing. My theology didn't lead me to believe in special places or buildings. So what was going on?

I began to dream. What might people who didn't know God make of this place? How might such experiences draw followers to Jesus? He was present and on the move in our prayer room, of that I was certain. As I prayed, I remembered something I had read a while ago about the Celtic Christians. The Celts had talked about "thin places," places where the divide between Earth and heaven was thinner, places where it was easier to meet with God. Had I stumbled into a "thin place"? Had our night-and-day prayer shifts with crayons and coffee cups somehow brought heaven a little closer to Earth? It was only seven hours into our first 24-7, and already I was in brain-melt.

Our first weekend of 24-7 prayer will live long in my memory. The room was packed with people wanting to pray—*all the time*. We had young people and students coming from all over town. As we prayed together, I discovered that God had already been calling many others to pray. I found a girl named Ruth who had already begun organizing a round-the-clock prayer rotation. I found students who felt called to pray for the university. I found out that many of our own young people, rather than having an aversion to prayer, had a passion for it.

As that first weekend ended, we immediately planned an entire week of 24-7, and things just took off. We moved into a bigger room at Greyfriars Church and people kept coming. Prayers were answered and young people drew closer to God—it was an amazing time. As we prayed, the idea of the presence of God in a room kept nagging me.

Smelly Rooms, Prayer Pictures and Bad Ankles

One distinctive of our first few weeks in prayer was the smell.

No, it wasn't the unwashed smell that can emerge in a busy room—it was the smell of incense. The prayer room reeked of the stuff. On Day Two of our first full prayer week, I spent at least an hour checking all the candles in the room, looking for a rational explanation for the heady aroma pervading the atmosphere. But I hadn't bought any scented candles! Day after day, the scent of incense returned, deep and heavy. What's more, the aroma returned every time we prayed through the weeks of that year. Unable to locate any source for the scent, we simply concluded that our prayers smelled. The book of Revelation's description of the prayers of the saints rising to heaven like incense was a physical reality in our room (see Rev. 5:8). We laughed when Chris, one of the teenagers in our group, drew a cartoon of God's nose on the wall one day, depicting our prayers like incense rising up to His nostrils.

As we prayed and prayed, this strong awareness of God's presence, the physicality of prayer conveyed in the smell of incense, the writing on the walls and the surprising stories of answered prayer attracted many visitors to our prayer room. We had scrapbooks full of emotional prayers, photographs of beautiful artwork, and stories of miracles large and small. Girls from one local school came in almost daily to pray. I remember grinning as I studied a large picture they had drawn, asking God for lives to be changed, for people to be saved, for healings and for a change in the atmosphere in specific areas of their school. Several months later, when we launched another season of prayer, that picture came out again and a simple phrase was written across it: *All answered.*

> I tell you the truth, my Father will give you whatever you ask in my name . . . ask and you will receive, and your joy will be complete (John 16:23-24).

I had heard a few stories on 24-7's website of people becoming Christians in prayer rooms, but I was amazed when this began to happen in our room, too. I remember praying one morning that salvation would come to the room that day. By evening a young girl came in asking, "How do I become a Christian?"

I need to be clear that running a 24-7 prayer room for young people was not always easy. Many times we were exhausted or close to despair, wondering how we could possibly fill another day with prayer. Malc, Ian, Richard and Penny sometimes prayed for three or four hours at a time on successive evenings in order to fill those punishing nighttime sessions. But as we persevered in prayer, things kept building. Prayer weeks were scheduled in. The venues moved, and God kept visiting with us.

One Sunday in May, as we were holding a 24-7 at the launch of a week of social action outreach, Dan came into the room to cover the afternoon shift. Dan was in his early 20s and had just run the London Marathon in three hours and 23 minutes. His time was doubly impressive because he had badly twisted his ankle three miles into the race when he stepped on a water bottle. Twenty-three miles farther, his ankle was mangled and swollen. He went to one of the London hospitals, was bandaged up, given some crutches and told to rest. It was unlikely his ankle would ever regain its previous strength.

Now two weeks later, this lovely man was in our prayer room, spending time with God while the rest of us fixed up gardens or cleaned streets. Three hours later, Dan left the room without his crutches. He was able to walk again easily and painlessly, and soon his ankle was completely healed.

How could this be? No one had laid hands on Dan. No one had prayed for his ankle. Even Dan hadn't been praying for his ankle. It was almost as if he had forgotten he needed crutches, and then realized what God had done: His badly damaged ankle had been healed by the presence of Jesus. I guess cynical people will propose other explanations. All I know is that Dan went into the prayer room on crutches and he left without them.

Since becoming a Christian, I'd been taught that the kingdom of God was marked by salvation, healing and the occasional miracle, but all that theory had suddenly become thrillingly immediate. Could the simple presence of God bring about healings like this? Could people be drawn to a thin place to find faith? Could our prayers on the streets really save lives? I needed to find out more.

Holy Places, Thin Places

The Holy Place, a place of meeting with God, is a major theme running through the Bible. It begins in Genesis in the Garden of Eden when God walked with Adam and Eve. The patriarchs, such as

Abraham, set up altars to mark places of divine meetings. Jacob dreamed at the place he later named Bethel (in Hebrew "the house of God") and he woke to declare, "Surely the LORD is in this place and I was not aware of it" (Gen. 28:16). He called that piece of desert "the gate of heaven" and commemorated his encounter with God by building an altar.

In the desert, God called to Moses from a burning bush, a physical symbol of the presence of "I AM" (see Exod. 3:1-6). As Moses led the Israelites out of Egypt, the people were instructed to set up a "tent of meeting"—the Tabernacle—where God came to reside, His presence like a cloud. For the Israelites, this wasn't like a group hug or having a "pet god": It was a personal, brooding, awesome Presence that descended deeply on people as they worshiped. As Jack Hayford has said, "The Tabernacle is not a great hall for the assembling multitudes, but a place of personal encounter, where worshippers bring their covenant offerings."[3]

When the Israelites made it to the Promised Land, the Tabernacle became the Temple, a permanent place of prayer and worship. God called for the Temple to be "a house of prayer for all nations" (Isa. 56:7; Matt. 21:13).

In the explosive beginning to his Gospel, John wrote that "the Word became flesh and dwelt among us" (John 1:14, *ESV*). Eugene Peterson brought us the same verse in a different way: "The Word became flesh and blood, and moved into the neighborhood" (*THE MESSAGE*).

The holy places of the Celts were sometimes called "thin places" because they believed that the seen elements of Earth and the unseen dimensions of heaven were more closely connected in such locations. Thin places could be any place of prayer, from a hermit's hut to a rugged cliff or beautiful seascape. The designation of certain places as sacred was not rooted in a pantheistic impulse to worship the location itself, but rather in a desire for a personal encounter with God in particular environments. As Susan Hines-Brigger notes, "The hills, the sky, the sea, the forests were not God, but their spiritual qualities revealed God and were connected to God."[4]

Now many of us might balk at the suggestion that place matters at all. Isn't God omnipresent? Doesn't "sacred space" sound a
bit New Age? We must remember that throughout Church history, the idea of the sacred or holy place is recurring—not "new" at
all. In many Christian traditions, buildings can be consecrated.
In the Anglican Church, a bishop stands outside a new church
building and hammers on the door three times after praying these
powerful words:

> Almighty God, we thank you for making us in your image,
> and to share in the ordering of your world. Receive the work
> of our hands in this place, now to be set apart for your wor-
> ship, the building up of the living, and the remembrance of
> the departed, to the praise and glory of your name; through
> Jesus Christ our Lord. Amen.[5]

Places can also be special for their familiarity, connecting with
us because of their beauty, their peace or the memories we've created there. Ultimately, the thin place for all of us is the heart, and
sometimes being in a place of sacred beauty can soften our hearts
to encounter God. Marcus Borg writes that "a thin place is anywhere our hearts are opened."[6]

Within the Hebrew Temple in Jerusalem was a giant curtain
that separated the people from the Holy of Holies, where the presence of God lingered. When Christ breathed His last on the cross,
the curtain was ripped in two from top to bottom (see Matt. 27:51-
52). Then and there, the divide was broken—God could "tabernacle" with His people, and the place He would dwell would be
our hearts.

At His ascension, calling His disciples to take the gospel to the
ends of the earth, Jesus promised, "I'll be with you as you do this,
day after day after day, right up to the end of the age" (Matt. 28:20,
THE MESSAGE). In fulfillment of that promise, the Holy Spirit
came on the day of Pentecost to Jesus' followers, who were gathered in a particular place (see Acts 2). We have no reason to believe

that a disciple who had chosen to be elsewhere that day would have been baptized with the Spirit—*the place mattered.* Jesus Himself had told them as much when He instructed them to wait in Jerusalem (see Acts 1:4-5).

Paul declared that our bodies are temples of the Holy Spirit (see 1 Cor. 6:19). Right now, Jesus knocks at your heart's door, longing to come in and dwell. And His dwelling is the key. Holy places are not about buildings or structures—they are about relationship. They are about a God who, from the beginning of time, has longed to be with His people. Is it so hard to contemplate that the God who became a man "and moved into the neighborhood" should still want to work in our lives and our world? Is the thin place such a difficult idea to take in?

Incarnation

In my background as a youth worker, I had heard a lot about "incarnational ministry."[7] The idea goes something like this: Jesus chose to come and be among His people to care for them and to save them, and He did so by becoming a man. It follows that ministry done in Jesus' name shouldn't be from a distance, but should be at the heart of culture, in communities where people live, in the places where they hang out. We should live life with people. The wonderful Eden Project in Manchester is a great example of the incarnational approach: Team members have moved into the toughest places in town, because how could they work with young people there without experiencing something of what their lives are like?[8]

As I reflected on what was going on in the prayer rooms, I began to wonder again about John 1. A new question emerged in my mind: What if God wasn't just asking our "ministry style" to be incarnational? What if He was asking us to move *our prayers* into the neighborhood, to "pray open" a thin place for people to encounter His presence? As I tried to make sense of all that was going on, I knew that our places of prayer would need to keep connecting with the world outside the church walls.

God Reads My E-mail

It was becoming clear that our prayer room experiences were not unique. The 24-7 idea of night-and-day prayer was multiplying around the world. The word "movement" gets overused, but 24-7 truly was a movement, and it was becoming a major part of my work, my faith and my life. God was calling us to pray, and by being obedient to that call, we were seeing wonderful growth and blessing. God was doing something, and I was determined to hang on to His cloak to see where He was going.

In a moment of enthusiasm, I sent an e-mail to one of the people at the heart of the escalating 24-7 movement, telling her about our latest prayer week in Reading. Without really thinking about it too much, I ended the e-mail with this line: "This is what I want to do with the rest of my life."

God must have also been online that day, snooping in my mail. He has kept me to that throwaway promise ever since.

A Stupid Idea

After a few prayer weeks, people began to ask, "Why don't we have a venue like this all the time?" In a way, it made perfect sense: We had enough people to pray and the churches were supportive. Yet I have to admit that I resisted. I actually told some people it was a stupid idea. The idea of 24-7 prayer *all the time*—working long hours, focusing all my energies—was it worth it? I resisted for a quite a while.

Secretly, though, I couldn't deny something was happening. I had begun researching Reading's history and discovered its prayerful past, including a Benedictine abbey that had been the center of the town for 400 years before being destroyed by Henry VIII. In conversations around town, prophetic words about continuous prayer in Reading kept popping up—a man with a proven prophetic ministry even prophesied the beginning of "a new monastic order" in Reading. There was a feeling of momentum in these days, even though we didn't know where it was leading.

The Puzzle Takes Shape

Then one Saturday in January, we trooped off to Chichester (where the first prayer room was born in September 1999) to hang out with others who had been doing 24-7 prayer rooms and to hear from God. The first speaker was Pete Greig, the rather reluctant leader of 24-7 with whom I've written this book.

As he spoke, he asked a simple question: "What next?" Where, he wondered, was God leading us? He shared an idea about "third millennium monasteries" where people would pray 24-7 and where the poor would be served, the gospel shared and arts and hospitality would be practiced. He talked about the ancient Celtic Christians who had evangelized Northern Europe with such communities and wondered if we should try it again in our postmodern age. He imagined people traveling from around the world to come, stay and pray. He envisaged 50 of these communities worldwide, all praying 24-7-365. As Pete shared his heart, I got goose bumps.

The people who had gone with me were pretty enthusiastic, too. Was this what God was saying? The monastery idea? I remembered what the prophetic guy had said about a new monastic order. I thought about the foundations of our city—like so many across Europe—as a community of prayer.

I met with Pete (rather nervously) a few days later to talk about this crazy idea of establishing a modern-day monastery in Reading. We met, chatted and came up with the name "Boiler Rooms" in about 30 seconds—it seemed to describe the hidden power we saw these communities generating. At the end of the meeting, I went and sat in the car and just stared into space for ages. What was going on?

As I sat, jigsaw pieces began to fall into place. The idea of thin places—maybe a Boiler Room would be a place for God's presence to reside? Reading was an abbey town—perhaps it was in our historic DNA to be a place of prayer, justice, mission, the arts, hospitality? Could a "third millennium monastery" be a renewal of what was there long ago?

Then I began to think about my life, my journey. I knew that
God had been affecting a change in my life—the era of constant
activity with no prayer was over. I knew that God wanted me on
my knees. Yes, it was great to watch a prayer movement developing, and yes, the ministries I was involved in were changing—but
deep down, I knew that God was reordering my life.

I was a little scared. My life seemed to be careening out of control. I felt like Sandra Bullock trying to take corners at 50 M.P.H. in
that out-of-control bus in the movie *Speed*. These sharp bends
were approaching and I felt totally unprepared to get round them.

I put the key in the ignition and set off for home.

First Steps

So off we went.

Seven of us gathered in Malc and Penny's garden one night to
start plotting a Boiler Room in Reading. Things quickly began
coming together. How could such a weird idea seem so wonderful,
energizing and inevitable? Money was coming in, plans were coming together and people were getting excited about the idea across
the city—Christians and non-Christians alike were enthusiastic
about the plans. Prayer weeks were becoming prayer months. We
prayed for the whole of April 2001.

Our problem was location: Where should the Boiler Room be?
We had no place to house the new Boiler Room community. We
spent weeks scanning the streets and the papers. Empty buildings,
church halls, rental spaces, offices—we looked at everything. In my
mind I knew the sort of place we needed, but it seemed simply not
to exist.

Then one July night (in a fair amount of desperation), we met
once more to pray at McIroy Park, a hill above Reading that had
become a special place to pray—we could see the whole city below.
We gathered there hoping to see some sign, some cloud formation
or giant finger that would lead us. Nothing . . . so we sat down
to chat. Malc shared that a prayer group in the north of Reading

had been praying for us and one lady there had felt God speak about a venue:

"The answer," she said, "is in the abbey. It's staring you in the face."

Maybe we should go to the old abbey ruins to pray? To be honest, I was up for anything at this point but felt a certain amount of despair. Was a scavenger-hunt evening ahead of us, with no clear answers in sight?

We drove down to the abbey ruins and started praying. A few features of the original layout survived Henry VIII's anti-Catholic campaigns: A *hospitium* is used as a daycare and as part of the museum. A brook that once brought water to the monks still runs through the town, and there are a few ruined walls of the main chapel, the treasury and the dining hall. That's where we went to pray: an ancient, ruined holy place among shining office blocks in the heart of Reading's financial district.

As we prayed in the ruins, I glanced over a wall and noticed a large pub with grates over the windows. Walking out of the ruins, we found ourselves standing in the only other remaining part of the original abbey: the south gate, where the last abbot was beheaded. As we stood there, the boarded-up windows of the cavernous Forbury Vaults Pub filled our view. How had we not seen it before? The old lady had been right: The answer was in the abbey. It was staring us in the face.

The Vaults was a huge pub that had been empty for a very long time. The building included a bar area, conservatory, two levels of meeting rooms and two adjacent apartments, one on either side. When we first saw it, an eviction notice for squatters was taped to a lamppost in front of the main doors. With mounting excitement, we copied down the owner's address as Malc prayed and anointed the building with oil. We felt certain that we had just found our home in a condemned old pub.

The next day, I wrote to the owners, explaining our vision for a 24-hour prayer room and pointing out that it would mean 24-hour security for them! A few weeks later, we got the call: The building was ours, rent-free for at least three months—maybe more—until the time came for it to be demolished.

God had given us a building. But there was more.

I was away when the team first got to go in and look around. On my return, Wardy and Malc excitedly showed me the rooms and the potential. Then they told me where we were: "The pub was built on the site of the abbey's millhouse—*we're actually within the abbey's original grounds.*"

With coy grins, Malc and Wardy led me outside to another office building on the corner, also empty. There in front of me was a giant archway. This was the wheelhouse of the mill! The arch itself was not complete, but it was beautiful, even with weeds growing out of the bricks. We stood and looked through to a small stream just beyond.

"And this," said Malc, "this is the Holy Brook, the waterway built by the monks to provide water for the abbey."

God had provided us a building—a thin place—on a significant slice of Reading's spiritual real estate: a Benedictine monastery where people had prayed for centuries before.

I needed to sit down.

For Further Thought

Consider going on a pilgrimage to a thin place that is important to you. It could be a manmade place—a church where you were baptized, for example, or a place where God called you in a specific way. Maybe it is a natural place—a forest, a mountaintop, a beach. If it's possible, you could pilgrimage to a recognized thin place from Celtic or other ancient Christian traditions. Set aside some time to meet with God.

Ask yourself how your prayer life could become more incarnational. Are there ways that the prayers you pray could be "earthed" more in your neighborhood or workplace? Consider tithing your prayer times: What about spending every tenth hour you set aside for prayer to serve the poor, volunteer at a homeless project or visit an elderly neighbor? In this way, you may become God's answer to someone else's prayers.

Liturgy

I delight greatly in the LORD; my soul rejoices in my God.
ISAIAH 61:10

Leader: God's plan of redemption is at work in our world. He brings bouquets of roses instead of ashes.

Silence for all to offer their own prayers for redemption.

Leader: He sends messages of joy instead of news of doom.

Silence for all to offer their own prayers for the broken.

Leader: He seeks a praising heart instead of a languid spirit.

Silence for all to offer their own prayers for the local and global Church.

Leader: God, rebuild the ancient ruins. Renew the ancient paths.

All: Bring renewal to the broken. Bring refreshing to the desert. Bring redemption to the lost.

Leader: Son of Man, can these bones live?

All: Lord, You alone know.

(Liturgy based on Isaiah 61 and Ezekiel 37.)

$\mathfrak{H}$istory Speaks

LORD, I have heard of your fame; I stand in awe of your deeds,
O LORD.
Renew them in our day, in our time make them known;
in wrath remember mercy.
HABAKKUK 3:2

Yet all experience is an arch where thro' gleams that unraveled world,
whose margin fades forever and forever when I move.
ALFRED LORD TENNYSON[1]

The long and winding road, that leads to your door . . .
THE BEATLES, "THE LONG AND WINDING ROAD"[2]

The beams, archways and pillars of the abbey must have created a powerful and imposing setting for the praying community of monks, and the residents of the village of 30 or so thatched cottages must have watched in wonder as this massive imposing abbey, nearly 30 acres in size, was constructed, bringing with it great prestige and wealth. It took decades to complete the building, and it's easy to imagine the excitement on the day when royalty and religious leaders finally gathered in Reading for the abbey's consecration, 43 years after its foundation was laid on April 19, 1164.

The consecration service mixed the luxurious robes and crowns of rulers and bishops with the beautiful choral songs of the poverty-sworn monks. As the service was drawing to a close and the point of dedication approached, Thomas Becket, Archbishop of Canterbury, stood to pray, his voice echoing around the swooping gothic arches of the pristine church. The Archbishop (who would famously be martyred just six years later on the steps of Canterbury Cathedral) chose to consecrate the building, the abbey and the town "to the worship of God for ever and ever."[3]

Holy Ground

Maybe you've been prophesied over from 800 years back in history by a martyred saint, but if not, I have to tell you it's quite a disconcerting experience!

On the day of the Boiler Room's inauguration, October 20, 2001, I sat in the parking lot of Prospect School, waiting for my son Jonathan to finish his music lesson. I was trying to plan the launch for that evening and was seeking God for what He wanted to do. I felt tired from all the preparation we had done—and my car certainly didn't feel like a thin place—but as I read Becket's words again (words that I knew and had read before), I was stopped in my tracks. The challenge of continuous, unbroken worship and prayer in the Archbishop's words hit me again: *He's speaking to us.*

At 9 P.M. that night, I led the 400 or so people who had gathered in a countdown to our launch. At "lift-off," we yelled the familiar 24-7 war cry, "Come on!" and then we prayed: "Once again, Lord, may this be a place where You are worshiped forever and ever." Too many events are described as "historic" but this truly was. We knew that we had a part to play in the ongoing history of our city.

God says through the prophet Isaiah, "My word that goes out from my mouth . . . will not return to me empty, but will accomplish what I desire and achieve the purpose for which I sent it" (Isa. 55:11). The psalmist says, "Your word, O Lord, is eternal" (Ps. 119:89). When God speaks, His word does not dissipate, but it continues to be fulfilled in every generation. As we launched the Boiler Room in Reading, there was a sense that Becket's prediction was still resonating—so much so that when we declared the abbey a place of 24-7 prayer (literally, "worship forever"), there was an instant, instinctive "Amen!" from the people. It was thrilling to realize that—in giving ourselves to prayer—*we* were becoming an answer to the prayers of our predecessors: those of Thomas Becket and of thousands of monks who had laid down their lives to pray, not to mention many modern saints who had prayed in longing for God to do something in Reading.

The First Days

Those first days were a mix of excitement and terror at what we saw unfolding in front of us. Our little prayer room quickly became an oasis for people to come and meet God. I was struck by the breadth of prayer: loud and silent, creative and simple, groups and individuals. I was also struck by the way people were drawn in. On our launch night, a Buddhist family came to hang out and one of our team had the privilege of telling them about praying to Jesus. We often welcomed business people in suits, Goths all in black and teenagers in school uniforms. We were even visited by the local traffic warden, who came in, muttered a silent prayer and knelt before the cross before going out and ticketing the cars parked outside! Local young people were beginning to come in and explore this strange town center venue: "The Christians in the pub" had become a hot topic, and many wanted to know what was going on.

The ripples from the Reading Boiler Room were also making their way to other cities across the UK and beyond. Boiler Rooms were launched in Manchester (in the northwest of England) led by Oria Dale, a wild Canadian pilgrim with a heart for practical prayer, and in Staines (West London, near Heathrow Airport) led by Tim Rose, an experienced youth worker with a passion to weave prayer together with outreach. Both Oria and Tim became firm friends who joined us on this journey of discovery and sacrifice.

The first days were hard. I can't tell you how terrifying it was to have so many people gather at the start and then watch as one by one everyone went home, leaving a few of us alone to pray until the next person wandered in. I remember the feeling of fear: What had we gotten ourselves into? Gradually, however, a rhythm of prayer and of life began to emerge. Our compass points for exploring this new territory were ancient Celtic monasticism and the ruined old Benedictine abbey on our doorstep. We began to plan, to live, to explore and to study.

Stand at the crossroads and look; ask for the ancient paths, ask where the good way is, and walk in it, and you will find rest for your souls (Jer. 6:16).

Saints Speaking

A little reading opened my eyes to the rich spiritual history into which we had stumbled. With amazement, I discovered that Celtic monasteries like Bangor Abbey (558-810) in Ireland had been practicing 24-7 prayer more than a thousand years ago—not for an occasional week, but continually *for more than 200 years* while working out their prayers in a deeply integrated, life-affirming spirituality! I fell in love with the Franciscans' radical heart for the poor and for mission, as well as the delightful practicality and hospitality of the Benedictine Rule, which swings from the spiritually sublime to the hilariously mundane. (One piece of guidance instructs the monks to "remove their knives" when going to bed, "lest they accidentally cut themselves in their sleep.")[4]

The church where I was working at the time was called Greyfriars, which, I discovered, was a reference to the grey robes of Franciscan missionaries who had come to Reading in the 1200s. The Franciscans initially settled on some marshland to the north of the town before being allowed to build a church in 1280 on the exact site where Greyfriars now stands. Closures, periods of emptiness, a short tenure as a jail (Oscar Wilde wrote his celebrated *Ballad of Reading Gaol* while imprisoned in our church!) and its reopening in the late 1800s have given the building a colorful history. The whole city was, it seemed to me as I learned more, haunted with memories of its prayerful past: streets, buildings, churches, a river and even the beer in some of the local pubs betrayed the influence of Reading's spiritual heritage.

Admittedly, the abbey had suffered periods of excess and compromise under the authority of a few abbots who exploited their position of power in the town. There were plenty of disputes over the course of the abbey's life, but my eyes were opened to how much of its story was good and godly.

One striking detail was that at the time of Henry VIII's disillusion of all British monasteries in 1536, Reading was one of only three abbeys in England for which no charge could be brought nor corruption found. The King's agents claimed to have traveled the country and found manifest sin, vicious, carnal and abominable living among the little and small abbeys. (The scathing report, conducted by just four men in six months and covering hundreds of nunneries and monasteries, was superficial at best, and almost certainly politically motivated. The three largest monasteries—including Reading—whose abbots sat in Parliament and whose approval was required in order to pass Henry's Suppression Act, were found faultless and even praised in the report, making its veracity a bit suspect.) Reading Abbey had become hugely significant during its 400 years, hosting bishop's consecrations, royal weddings and even sessions of Parliament during the era of the plague.[5]

When confronted with the order to hand his monastery over to the Crown and to break connection with Rome, the last abbott, Hugh Farringdon, refused. He was imprisoned in the Tower of London, tried, convicted and then hung, drawn and quartered for his refusal to recant. His execution took place under the south gate of the abbey, immediately opposite the modern Boiler Room.

As we dug deeper, we were encouraged to discover the rhythm of work, rest and prayer that the abbey employed. At Reading, Manchester and Staines, our desire was to pray in a way that would make a tangible difference in the world. With Pete's help, inspired by Scripture and the ancient Celtic monasteries, we compiled a list of the following six essential Boiler Room practices:

1. Prayer
2. Pilgrimage and hospitality
3. Learning
4. Creativity
5. Mission
6. Justice

We were startled to discover that the abbey, in whose shadow we were living, had practiced the same radical disciplines 800 years earlier! Far from pioneering an obscure path, we realized that we were joining a well-worn trail winding back 2,000 years. Even the name "Boiler Room," which had been plucked out of the air, turned out later to have been the name that Charles Spurgeon used to describe the prayer rooms associated with his evangelistic preaching!

What has been will be again, what has been done will be done again; there is nothing new under the sun (Eccles. 1:9).

We will look in detail at each of the six practices in the second section of this book, but in the remainder of this chapter, I would like to detail some of the surprising links we uncovered between the practices in history and the practices in the Boiler Rooms' present and future.

The Practice of Prayer

"I have posted watchmen on your walls, O Jerusalem; they will never be silent day or night. You who call on the Lord, give yourselves no rest, and give him no rest till he establishes Jerusalem and makes her the praise of the earth" (Isa. 62:6-7).

We were called to pray. Our Boiler Room had been born out of many seasons of night-and-day prayer, and our desire (at least initially) was to fill every minute of every day with prayer. However, we quickly settled into a far more sustainable rhythm of disciplined daily prayer cycles, filling roughly 120 to 140 out of the 168 hours in a week.

Over the past six years, prayer has slowly but surely become a deep passion in my life. I'm eternally grateful to 24-7 for helping me fall in love with prayer. Prayer is where I spend time with my Father. Prayer is the place where reflection and learning become a reality. Prayer is my harbor in storms; prayer is my first place to share good news. I truly love to pray. And prayer has also become the mainstay of the communities we have seen birthed. Prayer has made sense of our belonging, our mission, our needs and the needs of world. Prayer has become our primary place of campaigning and our primary place of repentance. John Wesley once famously declared, "God does nothing but in answer to prayer."[6] Does that mean that God needs our prayers to act? I'm not sure. I am convinced, however, that our constant activity is fruitless without first making that humble act of kneeling to pray. I am convinced that prayer is not only our greatest privilege, but also our greatest source of power. Our prayers are still "powerful and effective" (Jas. 5:16).

Tim Rose told me a story of effective prayer in Staines, where a woman had literally hobbled into their prayer room. She explained that her injury came from a skiing accident that had left her with three tendons severed in her leg. She was in terrible pain. Upon making it in, the lady who brought her, along with a member of the Boiler Room team, prayed for her and asked God to heal her. She was due to have surgery the following Tuesday, but when she reached the hospital that day, she had an X-ray that showed the tendons had sewn themselves back together and no surgery was required.

Toward the end of our second year at the pub in Reading, we took a "prayer audit" of our Boiler Room. We found that in a regular week, our rhythm of prayer included the following:

- Monday lunchtime corporate prayer for the Reading team
- Services of Evening Prayer and a Friday night Compline[7]
- One night of prayer by students from Reading University
- One alternative worship evening
- Regular prayer for people from local offices and businesses

- Two school Christian unions coming into pray each week
- More than 30 people in the same prayer slots each week
- Between 120 and 200 people coming to pray each week. This included up to 12 groups (such as youth groups, Christian unions or intercession groups).

One of the many visitors was a girl named Jen, from Sheffield. "Being here," she said, "has opened up a new world and lifestyle of prayer to me, a new fascination and interest in the Bible and a new dimension and stage in my relationship journey with God."

As other Boiler Rooms developed, intentional rhythms of daily and monthly prayer interspersed with regular retreats also emerged. Some people might view our commitment to prayer as a bit extreme, but the Benedictine abbey that shaped our town (like thousands of other monasteries across the world) was committed to an even more rigorous rhythm of prayer. Daily, the monks would congregate seven times for prayer, beginning early in the morning with Matins and ending with Compline before bed.

From our own base of prayer, I knew we had to engage with the community and world around us. If all we did was pray—if we spent all our time in our nice prayer rooms—then we would become little more than a "holy huddle." The prayers had to be worked out.

The Practices of Pilgrimage and Hospitality
"Share with God's people who are in need. Practice hospitality" (Rom. 12:13). Here was our next connection point with Reading Abbey: Hospitality was a strong strand of Benedictine life. The Rule of Saint Benedict makes elaborate provision for hospitality, insisting that visiting strangers or pilgrims "who come to the monastery, be entertained like Christ Himself, because He will say, 'I was a stranger and you took me in.'"[8]

When guests arrive at a Benedictine house of prayer (and, according to the Rule of Saint Benedict, "a monastery is never without them"[9]), the monks are required to wash the visitor's feet, and then the abbot prays and reads the Bible with him or her. A monk is assigned to look after the guest's accommodations.

In order to curtail grumbling at the extra work, this monk is given the right to recruit helpers.

The day before Saint Martin of Tours (d. 397) was confirmed, he met a beggar who was freezing without a coat. Filled with compassion, he cut his coat in two and gave half to the beggar. That night Martin had a dream in which he saw Jesus wrapped in the beggar's half of the coat.

One ancient Celtic poem by an unknown author describes hospitality like this:

> O King of the stars!
> Whether my house be dark or bright,
> Never shall it be closed to anyone,
> Lest Christ close His House against me.
> If there be a guest in your house
> And you conceal aught from him
> 'Tis not the guest that will be without it,
> But Jesus Mary's Son.

Reading Abbey's fame meant that it was a place where Benedict's Rule for hospitality and refuge were applied often. They cared for travelers and pilgrims, and those in need in the local area could find a place of refuge within its walls. Amazingly, when our Boiler Room opened, we found this same spirit at work. Alongside the practical love and care we could give to the local young people who hung out nearby, we found ourselves inundated by modern-day pilgrims who'd heard about us by word-of-mouth and traveled from all over the globe to spend time with Jesus. In our first 18 months, we welcomed hundreds of visitors from all over the UK, 5 Australians, 10 Spaniards, 3 Mexicans, a group of Danish youth workers, 4 Swedes, 2 Swiss, 1 German, 1 South African, 2 Indonesians and 1 Taiwanese, along with maybe 20 visitors from the United States.

Pete had expected this to happen, but I had not been so sure. Tentatively we wrote on our brochure that "we would like to rekindle the pilgrimage that occurred as part of the everyday life of the abbey." Once again, history seemed to be an instrument God was using.

The Practice of Learning

In 1955 to 1956, Benedictine monk Jean LeClercq delivered a series of lectures to his brothers at the Institute of Monastic Studies at Saint Anselmo in Rome, after which his lectures were written down and translated.[10] Central to his teaching was the difference between the monastic heritage of learning and the "scholarly approach" of academia. While scholars look to debate and critique, monks rely on meditation on the Bible, the writings of the Desert Fathers and classic literature. Their aim, rather than building knowledge, is to seek God. Their aim is devotion.

The Benedictine monks at Reading Abbey would have seen study as a major part of their days, and their priority would have been the study of the Word of God. However, study and learning would have stretched to many other areas of life: the arts, working the land, the cultures of the world through the pilgrims who came to visit. Learning did not take place only within the world of books, but came through contemplation, listening to others and prayer.

As we began to consider the place of learning in 24-7 Boiler Rooms, we felt led not to the classroom, but to the prayer room—to the disciple gazing in wonder at the Lord, reverencing and worshiping Him. Isn't it fascinating how often God speaks to us when we worship? When we change the subject of our attentions from ourselves to Christ, we put ourselves in the true place of learning.

Because learning is a long-term process, we began to take in longer-term visitors in Manchester and Staines. We called them "Wild Geese" (a reminder of the Celtic Christian symbol for the Holy Spirit), people committed to following the Spirit and to seeing where He led them. These pilgrims stayed for three to six months, sometimes even a year. They came to pray, to serve and to learn. "Wild Goose" was the forerunner to the Transit Course (more about that later), which now runs in a number of our Boiler Rooms.

Having been captured by the heart of God in multiple prayer rooms, I knew there had to be so much more than I'd already seen of Him. I knew more than anything that the intimacy of the prayer room would lead me to involvement

in a most broken and hurting world. Joining the life and
work of a Boiler Room through a Wild Goose year gave me
an opportunity to explore how that link between intimacy and
involvement could look in real life—how I could be the answer to
some of those prayers prayed for a broken generation.
MATILDA, WILD GOOSE PILGRIM IN STAINES

The Practice of Creativity
This practice seemed obvious to us because of the creative nature of
our prayer rooms in the past. Instinctively, people prayed through
pictures or with poetry, music and dance. Our prayer rooms always
seemed to be covered with graffiti and filled with sounds of song
and drum. How can you limit prayer to mere words?

Creativity characterized the old monasteries, too. They produced exquisite illuminations such as the famous *Book of Kells*,
ethereal architecture, skilled gardening and incomparable choral
music. In the ruined cloisters of Reading Abbey, a plaque explains
that a song called "Summer Is A'cumen [a-coming] In,"[11] written
by the monks at the abbey, is the oldest piece of sheet music in
the world. Accounts show that the abbey was a thriving arts center, particularly expressing their worship and devotion in song
and poetry.

Since the beginning of Christian worship, artistic expression
has been a part of how we glorify God. Whether in Michelangelo's
ceiling in the Sistine Chapel, a U2 show—where it sometimes
seems that "God has entered the room"[12]—or the crayon drawing
of a six-year-old, art shows that words alone cannot adequately
express the glory of God and convey our worship to Him.

Our Reading prayer room produced so much poetry that
Lani McGuire (a visitor from Melbourne) and Heather Seaton (a
youth worker and artist from Reading) compiled and illustrated
an entire book of moving and occasionally amusing pieces. The
Manchester Boiler Room spent six months in a temporary warehouse home in the center of the city, and although the outside of
the building looked drab and industrial, the creativity of the team
brought the inside to life. From atmosphere lighting and drapes,

to beautiful canvases, moving poetry and heartfelt prayers written on the walls, this Boiler Room shouted creativity and reflected a little of the radiant glory of God. The creativity reflected the
people who were part of that community, too. Skaters, the homeless, students, families, church leaders and refugees—all were part
of this complex, diverse, beautiful prayer community.

In this creative atmosphere, it was apparent to most that this
place, these prayers and this community were not to be held in or
closeted away. God was sending us out.

The Practice of Mission and Justice

I have chosen to introduce mission and justice together because
they both exemplify a core idea drawn from monastic tradition.

Inspired by the stories of the ancient Celtic communities,
I began to dream about the missional power of prayer. In my spirit's eye, I could see young people praying and weeping in the Boiler
Room for friends who did not yet know Jesus, and then God giving them an opportunity when they left to show love or kindness
to those friends. I could see God calling people during their hours
of prayer to cross cultures as missionaries or to cross the street to
show His love to a neighbor. I could see a homeless man being fed
by someone on the way home from a prayer hour. Prayer, mission
to the lost and mercy to the poor—I felt more excited than ever by
the life of endless possibilities that God seemed to be promising us
as we gave ourselves to Him in prayer.

In the Benedictine Rule, care for those in need is a major theme.
Provision for the elderly and sick is primary: They are to be "treat-
ed with kindly consideration and allowed to eat before regular
hours."[13] Perhaps most striking is the commitment to a simple,
sacrificial and generous life at the outset of a brother's time at the
abbey. "If he has any possessions, he should either give them to the
poor beforehand, or make a formal donation to the monastery,
without keeping back a single thing for himself, well aware that
from that day he will not even have his own body at his disposal."[14]

Saint Francis of Assisi embodied mission-minded, compassionate spirituality. Fresh from his conversion experience, he founded a

group of brothers committed to a Rule of poverty, chastity, humility, obedience to God, prayer, work, harmony and preaching. In pre-
senting him to the pope, Cardinal Giovanni di Sao Paulo declared
that Francis "was convinced the Lord wishes to renew the faith of
the Holy Church, all over the world through him."[15]

Francis befriended lepers, gave to the poor, cared for widows
and showed love to anyone in need. His Rule required lifestyles of
unselfish activity, which had a radical effect on the Church and on
issues of social justice throughout Europe. But compassion for
the poor was only one strand of this outward life: He was just as
committed to mission and to preaching, springing from a well of
inward devotion.

With such a cloud of witnesses cheering us on, we committed
ourselves to pray, but also to reach out—to love, to touch, to engage,
to get our hands dirty as we shared Jesus with others. We soon discovered that God was way ahead of us.

Imagine this: It's 1:30 P.M. on a Saturday and things are quietly humming along at the Boiler Room. We had been open maybe
a couple of weeks. A few people are praying, a few people are chatting. Malc and Penny are looking after the building.

Half an hour later, 100 young people are there, 30 of them outside drinking. A stereo outside is blasting Marilyn Manson while
kids skateboard in the parking lot. There are tons of young people
crammed inside, just chilling out. God had brought together the
Boiler Room and the young people who hung out in nearby
Forbury Gardens Park. Apparently, a local policeman had suggested they should hang out in our building rather than in the park—
makes sense, I guess.[16]

It would be wrong to present this as merely chance. Malc
and Penny Peirce had been working with these kids for years.
When we opened, I remember our hopes that one or two of these
young people might connect with our work—but none of us
thought it would be like this! Young people with all sorts of
needs were drawn to our place of prayer on a daily basis. Nearly
every Saturday for the next two years, the Boiler Room was a
place of refuge for these young people, a safe base for hanging

out and a place of practical friendship.

Many of the young people were in great need. Most Saturdays we spent looking after teenagers—some as young as 11—who were too drunk to stand. There were conversations about struggles with self-image, and practical help with school exclusion issues, homelessness, drug abuse, crime. All this suddenly became the business of the Boiler Room.

Was this prayer? Was this mercy? Was this mission? We began to learn it was all three. It was the Celtic thin place. It was the Franciscan compassion. It was the Moravian sense of mission.

For Further Thought

Discover whether there is a monastery or a historic mission anywhere near you and organize a visit or retreat.

Liturgy

Teacher, which is the greatest commandment in the Law?
Jesus replied: "Love the Lord your God with all your heart
and with all your soul and with all your mind."
This is the first and greatest commandment. And the second is like it:
"Love your neighbor as yourself."
MATTHEW 22:36-39

Leader: Lord Jesus, You lived Your life on Earth doing only what the Father commanded You. Let us be true to You, Lord Jesus, as You were true to Your Father.

All: Father help us, may we be true to Christ.

Leader: You ate with the tax collectors and sinners. You were compassionate to the mistreated and the alienated. Jesus, may we have Your compassion toward others.

All: Father help us, may we be kind to others.

Leader: You showed mankind the Father. You demonstrated the love of God to the world. You call us to be Your witnesses.

All: Father help us, may we take the gospel to the nations.

(Liturgy based around the Rule of the Honorable Order of the Mustard Seed, *founded by Zinzendorf and the Moravians.)*[17]

Chapter 4

From Buildings to Communities

For we were all baptized by one Spirit into one body—
whether Jews or Greeks, slave or free—
and we were all given the one Spirit to drink.
1 Corinthians 12:13

God isn't just an advocate of community—
He is community.
It's part of His nature.
Danny Brierley[1]

We'll walk hand in hand
we'll walk hand in hand
we'll walk hand in hand someday
"We Shall Overcome," Baptist hymn
from the early 1900s,
recorded later by Pete Seeger

The phone call came completely out of the blue. We had been praying in the Forbury Vaults Pub for nearly two years when we received a call from the owners, telling us that they wanted us out of the building in a month. Our house of prayer was to be knocked down. We were about to become homeless.

The Reading Boiler Room had been on an amazing journey. Countless hours had been filled with prayer, hundreds of young people had made the Boiler Room theirs—for many of them, it was their first contact with Christians and with prayer. What's more, we had received funding from the local government, including a £20,000 (nearly $40,000) grant to work with young people at risk of committing crime. Us! A prayer house! The Boiler Room had hosted prayer meetings, youth workers' gatherings and visits from mission teams from around the world—and now new Boiler Rooms were launching!

And yet . . . there were the beginnings of some unease among us. What did the future hold? What was God calling us to?

One of our challenges was the sense of community that was emerging in the Boiler Room. I remember watching with amusement as a 15-year-old homeless boy drank coffee with a regular visitor whose godmother was the Queen. A number of businessmen spent time working alongside young people clearing rubbish from the local park. Swedes, Mexicans, Americans and Australians found a spiritual home in our dilapidated pub alongside drug addicts and alcoholics.

One Saturday afternoon, a young girl asked us when we were going to "do church" for the people who came along. Although she wasn't a Christian, she forced us to face a question we'd been avoiding for fear of all the politics surrounding the word "church." We didn't look like a normal expression of church, and most of us belonged to congregations elsewhere—but we were doing most of the activities described in the book of Acts: meeting together daily, breaking bread, caring for the poor, preaching the gospel and praying continually.

Reading—Place of Sanctuary (May '02)

The following extract from my journal gives a snapshot of what was going on:

Over the weekend we had a couple of night visitors—a guy on a bad trip and a girl who'd been dumped in town by her boyfriend at 3 A.M. both arrived at our door. Each was tough in different ways, but being open 24-7-365 means that people know we're here. During the weekend we had our usual run of mopping up puke and looking after people when we could. I guess the test of our prayers is when we have to live them out. That's true during the day, too. We certainly needed a safe place on Saturday afternoon/evening.

About 5:30 P.M., a small but very violent group of football supporters headed into the park nearby where many of the young people we know were hanging out. They started chucking glasses, bricks and tons of other stuff at the stunned kids. Until police on horseback arrived right outside our building, people needed somewhere safe to be.

Just before 6 P.M., we opened our doors and tried to help get kids off the streets, sometimes taking them home or to a hospital. About 40 teenagers stayed till around 10 P.M. A small but very hardworking team made it happen, with lots of amazing help from the older members of the Forbury crowd. It was kind of cool to have Goths in black coats outside the building guarding it, others getting people organized, telling them to quiet down and respect the place, and more still making coffee, cleaning up and making the place their own.

Out of a bad situation with lots of tears and worry, we managed to all be okay and in God's house, the Boiler Room. Many people found a place of safety. Many wanted to pray, lots wanted to talk. One guy remarked the following day that he hadn't ever thought about God until the Boiler Room opened—now he did a lot. And what was weird was that during the day, we had been asking God to build on what He was doing, to take things to another level in our relationship with kids and prayer. On an evening when I was pretty scared, God moved and showed Himself.

In October 2003, we met as a team to consider what might be next for the community and to make sense of the owners' decision to ask us to leave. Surely with such amazing stories, God would want us to carry on. Yet how?

The first of our concerns was money: We had none. Our basic costs far outstripped our regular income, which came mainly from small gifts from individuals. Money had been short for a while—once we even considered turning the electricity off to save money on lighting! Now we needed to consider whether we could afford to keep going at all.

The second was a prophetic word, brought by a member of the team. Andy Wilson felt that God had spoken to him about our future, that it was "time to remove the capstone." The word connected with us—the abbey mill arch in the parking lot had a huge capstone, the stone at the top of an arch that takes the weight and stress of the whole arch. But *remove* it? It would make the arch collapse! Someone else drew us to 1 Peter 2:7, which says that Christ is our capstone. Surely we shouldn't be removing Him! What was God saying?

The phone call helped us understand this confusing word from God. Having originally offered us a three-month stay, the owners of the Forbury Vaults had let us stay nearly two years. Now, at our moment of confusion about the prophetic word, they phoned to give us one month's notice—they intended to demolish the building. Had the *building* become our capstone? Had our venue become more important than our Christ?

We had always said that the Boiler Room was a community, not a building. Now we had the chance to prove it.

On October 23, 2003, we held our second birthday event. We celebrated stories of God's goodness and worshiped and prayed together. It was our usual gathering of punks, monks, skaters and other interested people. At the end of the evening, we made the announcement: It was time to leave.

Little did we guess that God was *really* removing the "building capstone" for the Reading Boiler Room. For the next 15 months, we went underground, until another word of guidance (this time from a prayer leader in northern England) led us to another semi-derelict venue, this time in Caversham in the north of Reading.

That 15-month period was hard, sometimes demoralizing. We rented a student house for a while, shared an office in a church and ran prayer rooms wherever we could get the space. Penny, Malc and the team spent cold months in the Forbury Gardens Park, hanging outside now with the young people. Then the park was closed for refurbishment, and many of the young people scattered to the river, the railway station, wherever they could.

As we journeyed and struggled, we began to face issues within our team, some of them painful and difficult. God put us in the fire. He was refining us and the call on our lives, and the crucible He used was *community*.

Boiler Rooms as Communities

Just as a family is still a family even if it's made homeless, so too we were still a Boiler Room. A house helps a family to function and relate, but it does not make a family a family.

As we regrouped and recognized that our identity was relational and not dependent on a building, more and more people began asking whether Boiler Rooms were in fact churches. In Reading we had non-Christians wanting us to be their church. In Ibiza we had people coming to Christ through our mission teams without an ongoing church community. In America we had a large church wanting to plant a Boiler Room as a congregation, and the Salvation Army was already using Boiler Rooms as part of their church-planting strategy.

But was this right? Might it be divisive? What about situations where Boiler Rooms were supported by existing churches? Strong voices expressed strong opinions on both sides of the argument, and so, in 2004, we gathered 50 24-7 leaders in the Pyrenean mountains of Spain to discuss this thorny issue. We had commissioned papers from three well-known Christian leaders.

Central to our discussion was the question of what Boiler Rooms looked like in pioneering circumstances. In these scenarios—where there is no other relevant Christian witness that can disciple the converts—we agreed that Boiler Rooms could (and indeed should) be church plants. But what about situations like Reading? The answer very much depends on your ecclesiology. In the last 50 years, theologians like Lesslie Newbigin have helped refocus the Church on our primary call to incarnate the gospel in missional community, and we have no hesitation in describing all Boiler Rooms as missional communities. As such, they may be considered "churches" in the sense of *ekklesia* (*ek*: "out of" and *klesis*: "calling"), which is the predominant New Testament word for "church," and simply describes a purposeful assembly of Christians.

Church history, however, has complicated and occasionally confused this simple definition. 24-7 celebrates the rich ecclesiological insights of sacramental, liturgical and non-conformist traditions and works closely with various denominations. In light of this reality, we have to recognize that the word "church" is not one that can be used casually and should not be applied carelessly. To describe a Boiler Room as a church could be misleading or confusing in some situations.

This is part of the reason that today we continue to use the term "Boiler Room" for all of our communities. Part of the attraction is that the name can describe an ecumenical Christian community working with various churches to bring renewal and to catalyze mission (for example, the Salvation Army Boiler Room in Wandsworth, South London) or to describe a church plant in an unevangelized community (for example, the European party island of Ibiza).

We had undergone quite a radical shift. What had started as a prayer room had morphed into a monastery, and now we found that a Boiler Room's core was an understanding of community. Which meant that we had some learning to do.

What Is Community?

"Community" is a buzzword. We can live *with* a community or *in* a community. We can go online and join a Web community made up of shoppers, activists or astronauts. We can interact within a community or with other communities. We hope to be included in a community, yet as Groucho Marx expressed, we have our doubts: "I would never belong to a group that would accept someone like me as a member."[2]

It's easy to find resources and teaching about community from a Christian perspective. (It's quite a cool thing to talk about right now.) But what is the Christian distinctive when it comes to community? If a Christian community is to be different, surely it has to begin with Christ Himself: "Christian community means community through and in Jesus Christ."[3]

Most communities gather around someone or something. Some people follow a charismatic leader; others come together in common passion for a cause. For the Christian, Jesus Christ is the reason we can express and experience community. "In Christ we who are many form one body" (Rom. 12:5). Paul expresses that Christ "is our peace" (Eph. 2:14), the peace between ourselves and others, the ability to live in harmony. Our first aim must be for *Christ-centered* community.

Most communities draw values or direction from their source. When I was younger, I often longed to join the anti-nuclear protest camps at military bases in the UK. I saw the communal living and togetherness that was expressed as a radical expression of that cause: people prepared to give up home comforts and securities for something they believed.

Our common community values can be drawn from our triune God: Father, Son and Holy Spirit. Community begins *with* God; it is a reflection *of* God. He exists in perfect relationship.

It makes sense that when God created Adam, He saw the man's need for relationship and community, and so created Eve. There was Adam, made in the image of God, reflecting all that was good and wonderful about the Creator, yet where was relationship within the world God had made? The Creator Himself worked in this three-in-one communal state, yet His creation had not the same depth. God was quick to remedy Adam's solitude, and we, Adam's children, have longed for community ever since.

Any idea of Christian community must start with Christ and with the communal God we worship.

Community in the Bible

The nation of Israel began with a family unit, which became the backbone of the nation's early society. The family began with Abraham and his son Isaac and grandson Jacob. Jacob (later called Israel) had 12 sons, whose families became the 12 tribes of Israel. This family bond shaped the idea of nationhood. Whether held as slaves, wandering in the desert, fighting for their "land of milk and honey," learning to be a kingdom or suffering in exile far from home, God's chosen people saw themselves as one nation, under Him. The Old Testament is a record of their struggle to maintain community with God, each other and the people around them.

In the Gospels, we see Jesus inviting people into a similar kind of family unit with the 12 disciples and His other followers. It's worth noting that the first Christian community was begun by Jesus Himself! The Early Church, as described in Acts 2:42-47, reflected this family ethos and gives us our model for Christian community:

- *They expressed a rhythm of life.* "They devoted themselves to apostles' teaching and to the fellowship, to the breaking of bread and to prayer."

- *They worshipped together and saw what God was doing.* "Everyone was filled with awe."

- *The Holy Spirit was at work among them.* "Many wonders and miraculous signs were done by the apostles."

- *They were united.* "All the believers were together and had everything in common."

- *They were generous and did not hold on to their own goods at the expense of others.* "Selling their possessions and goods, they gave to anyone as he had need."

- *They were committed to a rhythm of corporate meeting and worship.* "Every day they continued to meet together in the temple courts. They broke bread in their homes and ate together with glad and sincere hearts."

- *They impacted the city around them.* "Enjoying the favor of all the people. And the Lord added to their number daily those who were being saved."

The Early Church gives an immensely powerful picture of how Christian community can operate. I love how organic and simple it is, how it encourages a continual flow of new believers and the sharing of lives and resources. If our communities looked like this, we would be in a good place.

Gathering with Jesus

I'd like to suggest that the most basic model of Christ-centered community can be found in Matthew 18:20. As Jesus and His disciples discussed how to relate to each other and the effect of their agreement in prayer, He made an amazing promise: "For where two or three come together in my name, there I am with them."

Truly incredible! Before we get into big groups or into discussions of whether or not what we do is church, before we organize a budget or find a building for ourselves, I'd like to suggest three fundamentals for Christian community:

1. Christ-Centered Community Should Be Intentional

The two or three gathered together "in my name" must be intentional, with mutual purpose in their activities. Let's face it: We are good at meetings in the Church. We do them well; we do them often. It's tempting to see this meeting obsession and to react against it—to focus on relationships in meetings that aren't meetings. I know friends who "do church" in the café, friends who believe that it's a sense of connection that's important, not what they do or where they do it.

Church and community can have many different forms, just as God has created a world of many different facets and cultures. But community cannot be Christ-centered without being intentional, without a coming together "in His name." Without "His name," we lack purpose, we lack meaning, we lack authority—we become just another gathering.

It could be argued that Jesus always had an agenda in the friendships He built. He was relational, yes, but His relationships were intentional. In our early days in Boiler Rooms, we found that in our desire to make things accessible, we made things optional: "You don't have to do things this way." Our heart was to include anyone who wanted to be involved, but in doing so, we began to lose our intentionality, our reason for doing things. We began to lose what God had called us to. In trying to be "all things," we were in danger of becoming nothing.

Jean Vanier, founder of the L'Arche communities, argued that "the difference between community and a group of friends is that in a community we verbalize our mutual belonging and bonding."[4] A Christian community should have an agreement about why they meet. Maybe there is an agreed-upon set of values or purpose, maybe a rule or agreement of how the community should live—this is the conclusion we came to in 24-7. From this conclusion came our Boiler Room Rules. (These will be explored in the next chapter.)

If we are intentional, prayer and worship will ground the community. The spine of the Benedictine community is their rhythm of prayer, sometimes seven times daily. In the midst of their work, study and service, they regularly stop to pray, to center themselves on Christ, to acknowledge that He is the reason for their community—their intention, aim and vision.

2. Christ-Centered Community Should Be Spiritual
Jesus promised that where people gathered in His name, "I am there." Christ's presence makes community a spiritual place, where we practice the presence of God in all things. In John 14:18, Jesus promises, "I will not leave you as orphans; I will come to you." Jesus

practices His presence among us by His Holy Spirit.

When we opened our first Boiler Room, people remarked about how they could sense the presence of God. This should not have surprised us. The Spirit of God is what marks out the monastery from a self-help center or a clinic. The presence of God is central to what goes on—the atmosphere, the approach to life. The practice of daily prayer reminds us of the need to stop, to remember Christ and to worship Him.

There is both a devotional and also a missional aspect to this. There is the connection of man with Christ and the intention to build our communities around that. There is also the implication of that, because Christ longs to bring His creation back to Him, to see the lost saved, the dying brought to life.

We should never forget that a Christ-centered community is a spiritual and a Spirit-filled place. We should expect Christ to invade our activities, to surprise us with His presence, to answer our prayers and to challenge our comfortable living.

3. Christ-Centered Community Should Be a Safe Place

The third thing that we can learn by Jesus' promise is the simplest, yet perhaps the most profound. When we combine shared human relationships (the two or three) with the presence of Christ ("I am with them") we should expect the best of this combination of love. We should expect this environment to be both welcoming and challenging, both free and accountable. This combination of people gathering and of Christ's presence should be a safe place—a Christ-centered community must be a place of safety for the individual and for the group.

"Accept one another, then, just as Christ accepted you, in order to bring praise to God" (Rom. 15:17). What does this mean for us in practice?

- *Christ-centered communities should welcome others.* New people should be able to join. Different people should be welcomed, regardless of culture, origin or ethos.

- *Christ-centered communities should be places of belonging.* If we define our gathering by Christ's presence, the unwelcome should feel welcomed and the unloved should feel loved.

When I first met the people at the core of 24-7 Prayer, it was the safety and love that impacted me the most. Gathered around a beachside fire with people from different nations whom I barely knew, God spoke to me through the honesty, vulnerability and personal commitment that each showed the others. I knew this was a safe place for me and for my family. I was drawn in by the love of God, expressed through loving friends. This depth of relationship at the core of the movement is the most cherished and valuable thing to me—more than our work or our roles, we are friends for life. We gather around Jesus to express Christ-centered community.

Christian communities can reflect Christ, who has promised to be at the center of them. They can reflect His acceptance, which paid no attention to prejudice (see Gal. 3:28). They can reflect His selfless love, which took Him eventually to the cross (see Phil. 2:1-11). They can reflect the unity of the triune God and the unity Jesus prayed for His followers (see John 17). They can reflect His serving nature, which He demonstrated by washing the feet of His disciples:

> "Do you understand what I have done for you?" he asked them. "You call me 'Teacher' and 'Lord,' and rightly so, for that is what I am. Now that I, your Lord and Teacher, have washed your feet, you also should wash one another's feet. I have set you an example that you should do as I have done for you" (John 13:12-15).

Community Is Christ—Not a Model

In *Life Together*, Bonhoeffer concluded that "he who loves community destroys community." As we embark on a journey of discovering community, there are many pitfalls. If community itself becomes our aim, we become elitist, assuming that we are more learned or more authentic than others. If pursuing community itself becomes our aim, we lose the sense of welcome, because receiving the stranger might unsettle our balance. If pursuing community itself becomes our aim, we may seek to raise ourselves and "our project" up at the expense of others. None of this reflects Christ.

The reason for community is to help us follow Christ and to help us help others live Christlike lives. The reason for our communities must be missional, to see the gospel taken to the nations, to the lost. The reason for our communities must be the ongoing ministry of our Christ in His world. These communities can look very different—like the Carmelite communities of silent prayer, the Taize ecumenical center of retreat and renewal, the Missionaries of Charity in Calcutta founded by Mother Teresa and Father Andrew, or like Sojourners in Washington, D.C. Whatever they look like, these communities must be for Christ, must be about Christ and must be centered on Christ—or we run the risk of destroying the very community we seek.

For Further Thought

Take some time to visit a variety of expressions of community. Use the Internet to find out about communities near you and visit them. Maybe you could focus on a community based around prayer, one based around activity and maybe one based around a Rule or values. Journal your thoughts and consider how the three are different and how they are similar. All of 24-7's Boiler Rooms are open to visitors and you can find details at www.boiler-rooms.com.

Liturgy

Begin with silence and reflect on those with whom you live in community.

All: God we pray for our community, our *cymbrogi* [Celtic], our "companions of the heart." We ask You to be the center of who we are. Be the God who guides our steps. May we be a Christlike community—humble, loving and available to Your leading.

Leader: Lord, we pray for our community. We pray that You would build us as You built the Early Church. After Pentecost, the Church of Christ formed, and they committed themselves to the teaching of the apostles.

All: Lord, anchor us to Your Word. May we hear Your voice.

Leader: They ate together, sharing life and rejoicing at what God was doing in their midst.

All: Lord, fill us with joy. May we see Your glory.

Leader: All the believers lived in wonderful harmony, holding everything in common. They sold whatever they owned and pooled their resources so that each person's need was met.

All: Lord, give us Your generosity. May we share our lives.

Leader: They followed the daily discipline of worship in the Temple.

All: Lord, teach us to worship. May we walk humbly with You.

Leader: People liked what they saw. Every day their number grew as God added those who were being saved.

All: Lord, help us to be a light to others. May we see salvation in our midst. Lord Jesus Christ, Holy Spirit, our life-giver, God our loving Father, Three-in-One Savior, God in relationship: Would You bless and keep us as a community? Help us, guide us, lead us, Lord. Amen.

Rhythms:
The Ancient Art
of Breathing

The Boiler Room Rule

CHAPTER 5

The Ancient Art of Breathing

Pete Greig

It is not possible for us to say, I will pray, or I will not pray,
as if it were a question of pleasing ourselves;
to be a Christian and to pray mean the same thing,
and not a thing which can be left to our own wayward impulses.
It is, rather, a necessity, as breathing is necessary to life.

KARL BARTH[1]

"Have you been welcomed to New Zealand yet?"

The beautiful young woman, who introduced herself as Kaye, had waited patiently to talk to me at the end of a meeting in Wellington, New Zealand, where I had just finished speaking to a large crowd.

"Yes, of course," I grinned, feeling suddenly very English and a bit stupid for reasons I could not yet fathom. "We've been made very welcome. Everything's great. Great people. Great hotel—trouser press, peanuts in the minibar. Everything."

"But have you," Kaye repeated, "been *welcomed*?"

There was a stillness about her and a determination. I was flustered.

"Erm, yes," I said again, trying to work out what she was getting at and whether perhaps she might be crazy. "Yesterday we went up in the cable car and tomorrow we're hoping to . . ."

Kaye stopped me with a smile and rephrased her question: "Pete, do you know what a *hongi* is?"

Only a vague idea. "Not really."

"A *hongi*," she said, "is the traditional Maori greeting with which we welcome people to our country. By sharing the *hongi* you are no longer considered *manuhuri,* a visitor. You become *tangata whenua,* one of the people of this land. From then on, you are obligated to share in all the duties of the land. In years gone by that meant tending crops or even taking up arms with us in times of war."

"Wow!"

"Yes, it's a big deal," she laughed.

"In that case," I said, understanding her question at last, "No, I haven't been welcomed to New Zealand yet, and I would be honored if you would do so."

Solemnly, my Maori friend stood and we faced each other. She explained that we would touch noses "to exchange the *ha,* which is the breath of life," and we would touch foreheads "to share our dreams and aspirations with each other." She took my right hand in hers, placed her left hand on my shoulder and invited me to do the same. Chairs were clattering and people chattering noisily as they exited the auditorium, but we stood there squarely, arms linked, face to face.

I remembered seeing the *hongi* on television, but now that it was about to happen to me, I suppressed an urge to giggle like an eight-year-old embarrassed by shows of intimacy. Slowly Kaye bowed her head and I did the same until both our foreheads and noses were touching. And in this unusual posture, we paused for a few moments, sharing our dreams and exchanging the breath of life, before parting with broad grins. The desire to giggle had gone. I no longer needed to blather politely about trouser presses, either. In that moment of stillness, I sensed that something significant had taken place. I felt welcomed.

The Rhythms of Life

The Lord God formed the man . . . from the dust of the
ground and breathed into his nostrils the breath of life,
and the man became a living being.
GENESIS 2:7

The Maori *hongi* is rooted in a creation myth with striking similarities to the Hebrew creation story in the Bible, even though it originates with an equally ancient people from the other side of the world. Rich with symbolism, it is a profound metaphor for many of the interactions described in this book relating to prayer, community and missional hospitality. As we turn from looking at the "roots" of the Boiler Room movement in Section 1 (the story of our origin) to explaining our "Rhythms" of life in Section 2 (how we do it), the *hongi* has much to say . . .

The *Hongi* of New Life

This journey of salvation began, for each one of us, with a *hongi*! God welcomes us into His kingdom, not with a cold theological handshake, but with an intimate invitation to draw near so that He might breathe His life into our nostrils (see Gen. 2:7). In response to that invitation, we receive into our mortal bodies the new life of the Holy Spirit and begin to share His dreams and aspirations (see 1 Cor. 2:16). Through God's *hongi*, we are accepted as citizens of heaven, with all the privileges and duties incumbent upon members of a holy nation (see 1 Pet. 2:10).

The *Hongi* of Prayer

Just as the *hongi* is reciprocal, so too is prayer. When we come close to the Father, we don't just receive His life and walk away gratefully. We also give back to God by sharing with Him our breath and by allowing our dreams and aspirations to mingle with His.

We generally find it much easier to receive from God than to give to Him in prayer. In New Zealand, as I prepared to receive that *hongi*, I confess that I had an insecure and childish reflex. Realizing that an attractive woman who I barely knew was actually about to touch my nose with hers and to solemnly breathe my breath, I worried that my breath smelled bad or that I might give her my cold or that the exchange might somehow seem sexual.

And so, during the *hongi*, I actually held my breath. How like my prayer life that moment of resistance happened to be! So often I fail to reciprocate in prayer because I am too ashamed of my own pollution and too aware of my own inadequacies to breathe easily in God's presence. I am happy to receive His breath but I cannot believe that He would want to receive mine. And so my prayer life is reduced to a one-way shopping list of wants and needs, demands and invoices, and I fail to truly return God's welcome. For fear of being known, I take but I do not give—I allow myself to be blessed, but I do not bless Jesus the way Mary did, who simply gave Him her undivided attention. This unconditional attentiveness and willingness to relax in His presence is, He told Martha, the best kind of welcome we can give Him (see John 10:42).

The *Hongi* of Community

As well as learning to breathe in and out with God in reciprocal prayer, we are also called to breathe with others in close community. It is impossible to divorce the two, "for anyone who does not love his brother, whom he has seen, cannot love God, whom he has not seen" (1 John 4:20).

We have seen that Boiler Rooms exist at the crossroads between the vertical axis of prayer and the horizontal axis of community. Our communities are not just a demographic coincidence, friendly fellow members of a special-interest group. No, we commit to one another intimately and vulnerably, giving our lives and aspirations to be lost and found in something bigger and more complex than our own egos. To breathe together intimately, we must coexist in vulnerable proximity, exhaling and inhaling God's vibrant aliveness, but also (and less dreamily) sharing our bad breath and common colds! Community is not community if we regard it merely as a laboratory for our own ideas or as a service provider for all our emotional needs. (Those with gifts of leadership, in particular, need to beware this approach.) The picture of the *hongi* reminds us that community is reciprocal: We breathe together and we dream together, not imposing our ambitions on others, but allowing them to be blended, enhanced and sometimes painfully subverted. As a result, communities are inevitably messier and may appear to achieve less than teams focused on a streamlined, single vision.

The *Hongi* of Hospitality

The *hongi* provides an insight into the depths of our interaction with God in prayer and with one another in community, and it challenges our outward interactions with those who don't yet belong to our community. Jesus sends us out to extend to strangers the kind of intimate, unconditional welcome that He has already given us, saying to all who will receive it, "You belong here! You are no longer a visitor to this place but *tangata whenua*. You are home." Christian communities are an embrace waiting to happen. We are called to practice prodigal hospitality to our neighbors— regardless of their appearance, usefulness, sexual orientation or level of need. In fact, recalling the startling way in which God has welcomed us in our sin, we should (though we often don't) have a particular affection for those who are more obviously broken.

Breathing In

Bono once asked the extraordinary South African Archbishop Desmond Tutu if he ever got any time for prayer and meditation. "What are you talking about?" shrieked Tutu with a broad grin. "Do you think we'd be able to do this stuff if we didn't?"[2]

As we seek to establish a life-dynamic that balances prayer and action, receiving and giving, being and doing, we must remember that the priority is always the inward breath. Adam was mere dust until God first breathed into his nostrils. Likewise, a newborn baby cannot cry until she has taken her first great gulp of air, a breath that unfurls her lungs like a sail and begins a process that will last as long as her life. The midwife knows that nothing else is more urgent than that first breath—everything else in life will flow from there. In just the same way, as we seek to develop a rhythm of life, we cannot breathe out God's life and God's dreams through the kinds of hospitality, mission and justice described in this book, until we have first breathed them in by being with Him.

The monastic impulse is to withdraw from the myriad distractions of ordinary life in order to be alone with God. In fact the actual word "monk" derives from the Greek *monachos*, meaning "a

solitary person." We are called to be *fruitful* (see John 15), but only
by being rooted in Jesus. We are commanded to *go and preach the
gospel* (see Matt. 28), but first we must come to Jesus' side. As the
story of Mary and Martha reminds us, our mission is first and
foremost to be *with* Jesus—to minister to Him—and secondarily to
do things *for* Him. In fact, more accurately (as Mother Teresa taught
us), our mission is *only* and entirely to minister to Jesus, which we
do primarily through prayer and worship, and secondarily by finding the face of Jesus in the faces of the poor and the lost. This has
profound implications: It means, for example, that we don't just pray
in order to "get people saved." We also "get people saved" so that they
can pray—which is the greatest privilege of human existence.

The author David Adam, reflecting on the priorities of the
Celtic Saint Ninian, observes, "It is popular to say that the Church
exists for mission; this is only a half-truth, for the Church exists to
worship God and to give glory to him. The hyperactive Church is
in danger of offering itself and a way of being busy without reference to God: even some study groups are in danger of talking
more about God than they ever talk to him."[3]

It's not just the Church that can be "hyperactive." We live in
a frenetic culture that seems at times to be seeking to rebuild the
Tower of Babel in its craving to consume and conquer:

> They said, "Come, let us build ourselves a city, with a tower
> that reaches to the heavens, so that we may make a name
> for ourselves and not be scattered over the face of the whole
> earth" (Gen. 11:4).

Like those ill-fated builders, we desire to be connected. We are
driven to make a name for ourselves; we reach for the skies with
new technology. In our pride we aspire to be like God. We covet His
omniscience, compulsively consuming ideas on an unprecedented
level as bewildered citizens of the Information Age. We covet
God's *omnipotence,* exercising ever greater power over nature and an
exhausting compulsion to compete and control. We covet God's
omnipresence, making ourselves available to whomever, wherever,

whenever via mobile phones, satellite tracking and Internet hotspots. And so, by building our towers toward the heavens, the curse of Babel falls upon us.

Societies are fragmenting into tribal factions at the very time when our technologies purport to connect us together more than ever before. Humans clearly aren't designed to be in any more than one place at a time! No wonder we find ourselves exhausted by e-mail and other technologies we expected to liberate us. And as for our quest for omniscience, the Information Age is arguably more chaotic and confusing, with higher suicide rates, than any previous age in human history. In such a frenetic context, the call to withdraw from busyness, to switch off our mobile phone, to ration our use of the Internet and e-mail, to swap doing for being, is a radically prophetic one. As John O'Donohue says in his book of Celtic wisdom, "There is an incredibly subtle and powerfully calculating industry of modern dislocation, where that which is deep and lives in the silence within us is completely ignored . . . The inner world of the soul is suffering a great eviction by the landlord forces of advertising and external social reality."[4]

Speaking Without Speaking

Three monks used to go to visit the renowned Desert Father Saint Anthony every year. Two of them would talk a great deal, firing their questions at the wise old man, but the third monk never said anything. Eventually, Anthony turned to this silent brother and asked why he traveled such a long way to visit him every year and yet never wanted to ask any questions. "It is enough to see you, Father," replied the monk.

Oxford theologian Benedicta Ward says, "By the time people feel that just seeing us is ministry, words like this will no longer be necessary."[5]

The gospel spreads from person to person like a contagious, life-giving virus. Too often my attempts at evangelism resemble a person trying desperately to pass on to others an illness that I'm not carrying. I may know all about the gospel-virus and how it works.

I may be able to explain its merits eloquently and with unparalleled passion. But the simple fact of the matter is that if I'm not carrying it, the virus will not spread. It is only when I spend time breathing in the presence of Jesus that I catch His contagion and I become infectious with the gospel in the sort of way that Saint Anthony was.

I once stayed in the house of a man named Donald who, as a teenager, was powerfully used by God during the great Hebridean Awakening of 1949 to 1953. It was a remarkable time—entire communities on these remote Scottish islands came to know Jesus. God's presence was so heavy across the whole region that on one night, about 75 percent of those who responded to God did so before they even reached the church! Donald, with whom I had the privilege of staying, was perhaps the most effective intercessor of that revival. The 14-year-old child's prayers would often welcome the Holy Spirit and usher in the accompanying conviction of sin in a way that no one else could. During this season, Donald's greatest priority was prayer, and consequently he carried the presence of God so powerfully that, on one occasion, a man gave his life to Jesus simply after shaking hands with Donald without a single word being spoken. Donald was carrying the gospel virus and sometimes he didn't even have to speak for the contagion to spread.

The world does not need more words. It doesn't need a busier church, nor does it need—God help us—a better-branded gospel. What the world needs are people like Saint Anthony and Donald who have spent so much time in the presence of God that their very life has become a form of blessing.

This profound inner transformation does not happen only by some mysterious process of divine osmosis in prayer—although that is part of it. We are also changed to become more like Jesus through the gritty reality of honest relationships, faithful suffering, embarrassing levels of accountability and the daily discipline of praying, even when we don't feel like it and when we don't seem to get anything out of it for weeks on end.

Christopher Jamison, Abbot of Worth Abbey (seen on the popular BBC reality show *The Monastery*), is often asked why he first became a monk. He admits, "I have offered various answers for various contexts. But the answer I really want to give is: I don't know. I do not know why I became a monk because the reason I joined is not the reason I stayed. I joined thinking I could save the world by being a monk; I stayed because the monastery became the place where I discovered my own need to be saved. Before I could offer sanctuary, I had to find it."[6]

As we receive from God in prayer, we are changed. Slowly, more slowly than we expect, we become the message we are called to preach. Like Abbot Christopher Jamison, we have to find sanctuary for ourselves before we can offer it to anyone else. Like Anthony of the Desert and Donald of the Hebrides, our very presence may eventually minister to people, without words. Like Peter and John, even our harshest critics may one day acknowledge that we have been with Jesus (see Acts 4:13).

Breathing Out

Life begins by breathing in, but unless we breathe out, we die! The primary call, as we have seen, is to withdraw in prayer, but we are also commanded to go out from that place of intimacy in order to advance the kingdom of heaven. In recognizing this outward thrust, we are stepping outside the solitary meaning of classic monasticism. Boiler Rooms are not purely monastic. They combine the inward impulse toward prayer and intimacy with a strong outward "apostolic" thrust to preach the gospel, make disciples and bind up the brokenhearted. The word "apostle" comes from the Greek *apostolos,* which describes a messenger, "one sent forth with orders." We therefore sometimes refer to the Boiler Room approach as "aposto-monastic," in that we seek to combine the inward call to intimacy in prayer with the outward commission to involvement in practice.

Monasticism at its best has always combined these two dynamics. For instance, one historian recognizes in the Celtic saints "a surprising combination of apostolic and anchoretical [hermit-like] ideals."[7] Celtic saints would often have a cave, an island or an isolated hut in the woods where they retreated regularly to be alone with God before launching back out as those sent forth to preach, plant monasteries, cast out demons or perhaps even to advise kings and queens. Saint Ninian's cave at Glasserton, where he appears to have hidden away to pray, and his "White House" monastery "point to a rhythm of life that moved between activity and outreach and then a return to stillness and solitude: a balance between serving people and worshiping God."[8]

Breathing In and Breathing Out

He will keep your soul.
The Lord will guard your going out and your coming
infrom this time forth and forever
Psalm 121:7-8, *NASB*

There is a terrible medical condition called Ondine's Curse in which the central nervous system does not regulate breathing. The condition is named after a Greek myth about a water nymph called Ondine who fell in love with a knight and was thereafter cursed to stay awake in order to breathe. The condition affects only about 400 people worldwide, and they are kept alive by using ventilators. For them the most natural, subconscious act of breathing is laborious work, requiring deliberate thought and conscious control. Sadly, the mortality rate among sufferers is high.

In this second section of *Punk Monk*, we will look for sustainable rhythms of life that can, like the central nervous system, regulate breathing—helping us to balance the apostolic and monastic dimensions of our call as naturally and easily as possible. If we only ever inhale, we hyperventilate and quickly go crazy. If we only ever exhale, we faint. The challenge is, of course, to regulate our breathing naturally and evenly.

Bono says that he agreed to champion the Jubilee Campaign because he'd at last found in it a strategic outworking for his unbridled idealism. "Nothing is worse," he says, "than a bleeding heart without a plan." Too many of us are at postgraduate level in conversational Christianity and theoretical theology, with no heart-intention of actually doing the stuff we discuss. We talk endlessly about justice, mission, prayer, eschatology or shapes of church, but we simply don't know where to start when it comes to actually *doing* anything to make a difference. An effective idealist is someone who dares to turn ideas into lists—he may have an impossible dream, but he also has a next step that is entirely possible. Jesus was led by the Spirit and yet He had a definite plan. He was flexible (think of the way He responded to the woman with the bleeding problem when He was on an emergency run to the house of a dying child), yet He always had a clear agenda underlying everything He did and said.

As Boiler Rooms grew in number and in maturity, we realized that it was important to bring some clear and practical guidelines to explain what we were doing, and to resource the people who shared our dream of seeing Millennium Three monasteries established all over the world that could pray persistently while reaching out effectively to the poor and the lost. Like Bono, we needed a strategic plan to harness our big ideas into something practical, sustainable and replicable.

As Andy explains, the development of the Boiler Room Rule (see appendix 1) has been a lengthy and complicated process, but it has brought thrilling clarity to the vision and, far from intimidating people, it has inspired and excited many to sow their lives into a communal lifestyle of disciplined prayer, creativity, mission, hospitality, justice and learning. As Celtic scholar Ian Bradley notes:

> Could it be that in the postmodern, pick-and-choose spiritual supermarket we now inhabit, people are actually craving commitment, discipline and obedience? . . . Maybe in our dumbed-down and easy going culture, Christians should be both proclaiming and living out the essentially counter-culture message of commitment and discipline which is so clearly found in the Celtic and Anglo-Saxon monastarium.[9]

Chapter 6

The Boiler Room Rule

*Therefore, I urge you, brothers, in view of God's mercy,
to offer your bodies as living sacrifices, holy and pleasing to God—
this is your spiritual act of worship.*

Romans 12:1

*We will work simply and quietly.
Even if we never see wonders with our own eyes
or hear them with our ears,
we are planting the kingdom of heaven into the nations
and will look for the fruit which grows from it.*

Count Nicklaus Ludwig von Zinzendorf
Founder of the Honorable Order
of the Mustard Seed[1]

*Breathe, keep breathing
I can't do this alone*

Radiohead, "Exit Music (for a Film)"[2]

Phil Togwell, 24-7's UK leader, and I went to meet with a successful Christian businessman, Paul, who had asked to see us. As we sat there eating toasted sandwiches and drinking tea, Paul got into the reason why he wanted to meet us: He was fascinated by the idea of Boiler Rooms and believed that we needed one in Central London. His vision wasn't for one tucked away somewhere in the

UK's capital—he was thinking about a Boiler Room right in the heart of "The City," the original square mile of the City of London that is now a center for European and global business. "We need prayer to be at the heart of this place," he told us, chewing on his sandwich. It made a lot of sense.

The conversation went up a notch when Paul told us about the buildings his company owned and the empty basements we could use for a Boiler Room. He was offering us some of the most expensive office space anywhere in the world, rent free! Which would we like? With mounting excitement, I went through the list of his properties and noticed one on Tabernacle Street.

I grabbed Phil's *A to Z* street directory and when I finally found its location, I began to look at the surrounding neighborhood. I was stunned: Worship Street crossed Tabernacle at the end of the block. The John Wesley museum was nearby. *What was this place?*

Soon we were on our way across London to have a look, and as we walked from Worship onto Tabernacle, we saw a pub called The Prophet.

"Okay, God . . . we hear You," we laughed.

Paul led us to a 1970s office block and down to a large forgotten basement, saying that he'd also be willing to shoulder all the costs of renovation. It was perfect. We prayed and sensed God's call for us to be there. I have to admit that it felt a little weird. It seemed to break all the rules. At that moment, we had no one to lead the Boiler Room, no team to run it, no sense of what God wanted there, not much at all. But soon we realized that God had hijacked us.

It's That History Thing Again

A few weeks later, Phil and I made some discoveries about this new building. As I was out walking the area, I found a sign: "Forty yards to the west of this plaque was the site of The Foundry, John Wesley's First Chapel."

I glanced to my left and then paced out 40 yards and could hardly believe it when my steps landed me immediately at the door of our new building.

Not for the first time, I felt a little overwhelmed. I was standing on the spot where 250 years ago, John Wesley had founded Methodism and launched the ministry that was to transform Britain. Roy Hattersley, an MP who wrote a biography of Wesley, put it like this: "He had been sent into the world to preach redemption. *Sola fide*, by faith alone. He created a new church through which that all-consuming belief could be preached to his universal parish. And in doing so, he became one of the architects of the modern world."[3]

History was biting at our heels once more. We had accidentally stumbled into one of the most extraordinary locations in modern Christian history. A few days later, the distinguished Minister of Wesley's Chapel (which is seen as the Mother Church of world Methodism and is located on the next street), Lord Leslie Griffiths, confirmed that our new building was indeed situated on the exact site of the birthplace of Methodism. The City Boiler Room found a leader in Jude Smith and launched in June 2005, on the site of Wesley's ministry. It was his base for 40 years.

The Foundry's story resonated with everything we felt called to do. Lord Griffiths wrote in article in 2005 in which he stated that he believed that "all the significant things that happened to shape the Methodist Church we all love took place during the 40 years Wesley was headquartered at the Foundry."[4] The Foundry was originally a munitions factory. An explosion had led to its closure. Wesley rented it from the government, and like many of our Boiler Rooms, the building was in bad shape. The roof leaked so much that while the great Wesley preached, buckets had to be positioned to catch the rain.

Wesley's ministry was invariably short of cash—so much so that he often resorted to begging. He knocked on door after door, asking for financial help for the work he did with the poor. Suddenly our endless financial appeals and monthly worries over money for the Boiler Rooms didn't seem so bad.

The Foundry had been a place of prayer and purpose. Wesley would reportedly spend two hours in prayer a day before his rigorous schedule of preaching. "God does nothing," he said, "but in answer to prayer."[5]

The Foundry was also home to some incredible outreach:

- A school was established for children from the poor neighborhoods around the building. The school taught them and also provided equipment, clothing and food.

- The school's headmaster began, almost by accident, to meet with prisoners from the nearby Newgate Prison, and a prison ministry was formed. The Foundry workers often accompanied men to their executions, to comfort and support them.

- Wesley established a fund that allowed him to provide medical care to the poor of the area.

- He established a revolving loan fund, where families in dire financial need could be helped. Some fledgling businesses were also helped by Wesley's fund.

- The Foundry also had an almshouse for the poor that offered a place for widows and children to stay. Wesley insisted that visiting preachers should always sit with the occupants of the almshouse for meals.

As I learned more about Wesley's Foundry, I found myself praying that this dynamic spirituality and entrepreneurial approach to mission would spring up in our Boiler Rooms. Wesley had built to last and had impacted nations through his passion and commitment to God's call. We, too, needed to build for the long term. Pete Greig often talks about the need for our generation to play a long game. "Too many people," he says, "are missing their destiny a year at a time because they're too scared to think in decades!" It was time to grow up fast. We knew that God was with us and that we needed to take Boiler Rooms seriously by daring to dream big.

Bringing Some Clarity

In September 2004, the 24-7 community gathered in Barcelona with some difficult questions to discuss. Among them was the question of what these Boiler Rooms actually were, and how the various communities should relate together.

Initially we had simply watched in amazement as people all over the world caught the vision for communities of prayer, mission, creativity, hospitality and justice. But it had become clear that unless we brought clarity, the term "Boiler Room" (and, more important, the vision behind it) would soon mean little or nothing at all, and the incredible potential of the "rooms" would be rendered neutral.

We drew up a simple document to define the vision for Boiler Rooms and offer guidance for how communities could live out the six practices day to day. A little later we showed this document to a wise old monk at Turvey Abbey. He laughed. "This is marvelous," he enthused. "You've drawn up a monastic rule."

Rule of Life

In his book *Finding Sanctuary*,[6] Abbot Christopher Jamison tells the story of Pachomius, one of the early Desert Fathers, who was arguably the founder of the Monastic Rule. This is how it happened:

Various young men would come out into the Egyptian desert to seek teaching and instruction from the renowned Pachomius. The hermit often asked them to stay, hoping they would learn from his example. He devoted himself to serving them, working tirelessly and praying devoutly for their growth.

But nothing happened. In fact, the young men began to enjoy having Pachomius serve them! "They even started to abuse him," Jamison writes, "and exploit his apparent timidity." Still Pachomius remained patient, trusting and hoping that somehow his humility might make an impact on them.

It came to a point, however, when enough was enough—Pachomius determined on a different approach. He sat the young men down and outlined the way of life he expected them to lead from that moment on. "He laid down clearly how a monk should live," Jamison concludes. "In this way he created the first monastic rule for community."

Pachomius called his community *koinonia*, a Greek word from the New Testament used to refer to the Early Christian community. By the time of the old hermit's death, *koinonias* had been established across Egypt.

Every major monastic movement decided at some point that it needed a rule of life by which to work, serve and live. The Augustinian Rule brought order to a fragmented movement. The Benedictine Rule balanced prayer, study, work, food and rest to create an orderly way of life for their monasteries. Francis's Rule was both inward and outward, balancing poverty, chastity, humility and obedience to God in prayer, work, harmony and preaching.

In 1940, Brother Roger started a community called Taize in the Burgundy region of France. Central to the community is passion for the Church and for reconciliation between denominations and individual Christians. The community is ecumenical, with approximately 100 men living there from both Protestant and Catholic traditions. Many recognize Taize for its unique style of music, using repeated phrases with simple melodies to compose a powerful and contemplative style of worship song. The community welcomes thousands of pilgrims each year from around the world. In the summer months, the monks provide hospitality to as many as 6,000 visitors. Taize has also become an increasingly significant gathering place for young people, with its week-long International Youth Meeting gathering thousands from the worldwide Christian family.

The Rule of Taize has five components:

1. Daily Bible reading and intercessory prayer
2. Giving of a 10 percent tithe
3. A balanced use of time for work, leisure, family, skill development, worship, rest and sleep
4. Action for justice and peace

5. Participation in a local cell group and in larger plenary
   gatherings

Our Boiler Room Rule seemed too important to rush, so we
spent a week to come up with the beginnings of a rule, which we
then spent a year revising, challenging and discussing before it was
finally adopted at our Round Table in September 2005. The Boiler
Room Rule shapes the second section of this book (and can be
found in full in the appendix).

The Heartbeat of the Boiler Room

We needed to establish a way to support and sustain the Boiler
Room communities without controlling or crushing them. Just as a
doctor has basic checks to establish the life and health of a human
being, we set about finding the heartbeat, the life-blood and pulse
and, ultimately, the breath of these new monastic communities.

Signs of Life: The Heartbeat
We had learned that Christ-centered community was the heartbeat of Boiler Rooms, pumping life around the body. This commitment to Jesus-style community led us to a simple definition of
what Boiler Rooms are:

> A 24-7 Boiler Room is a simple, Christ-centered commu-
> nity that practices a daily rhythm of prayer, study and cel-
> ebration while caring actively for the poor and the lost.

Signs of Life: The Life-Blood and Pulse
We knew that God had called us to bring prayer and practice
together in the life of our communities. Leviticus 17:11 says, "the
life of a creature is in the blood," and we all know there is no
pulse without blood! The life-blood of a Boiler Room is prayer,
and we can tell because a pulse of loving practice beats strong
and steady.

A 24-7 Boiler Room exists to love God in prayer and to love its neighbors in practice. These purposes are contextualized in community and expressed in a defined location.

How would these purposes be outworked? The 24-7 Prayer movement was inspired by the Moravian community at Hernhut, which prayed for more than a century starting in 1739. The leader of this group, Count Zinzendorf, and many of his influential friends lived by a powerful Rule of Life that vowed to be true to Christ, to be kind to others and to take the gospel to the nations.[7]

In essence, Zinzendorf's vow takes us right back to the heart of what it means to follow Jesus in obedience to His Great Commandments (to love God with all your heart and to love your neighbor as yourself), and His Great Commission (to go into all the world). These three aspects of discipleship may be expressed in a triangle:

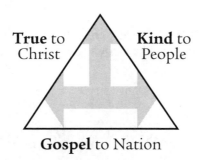

True to Christ   **Kind** to People

Gospel to Nation

Signs of Life: The Breath

The triangle is helpful, but what does it mean more practically to be true to Christ, kind to people and to take the gospel to the nations? How should we live out these three commitments in community? How could we live them as naturally as breathing? With great excitement, we realized that our six Boiler Room

Practices flow from the three principles, bringing lofty ambition down to earth in practical action.

1. What does it mean to be true to Christ?

   • We live prayerfully.
   • We celebrate creativity to His glory.

2. What does it mean to be kind to people?

   • We practice hospitality.
   • We express God's mercy and justice.

3. What does it mean to take the gospel to the nations?

   • We commit ourselves to lifelong learning that we might shape culture and make disciples by being discipled.
   • We engage in mission and evangelism.

These practices can be expressed in another shape—this time a hexagon, pointing out like arrows from the triangle of our three core principles.

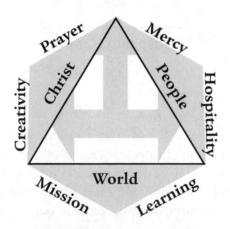

The three principles are expressed through six practices, providing a rhythm for communal living—our breath—to ensure that we balance our commitment to the poor with prayer, our creative expression with hospitality, and so on. Without such a rhythm, we will tend toward our preferences to become one-dimensional and biased, caricatured by our own peccadilloes.

The Customary

Even with these foundations for Boiler Rooms, people kept asking really specific questions:

- What does it mean to live a life of prayer in practice?
- How do I practice creativity when I can't draw?
- How can I care for the poor when no poor people live in my neighborhood? (I could only stare, stunned, at the young man who asked this question.)

In response to these types of questions, we wrote some guidelines (called a "customary") to accompany the Boiler Room Rule. The ancient monasteries would often add a customary to their rule as an explanation of how their values were to be worked out in practice. At our 24-7 Round Table in Hernhutt in September 2005, where the Moravian monastic community had prayed 24-7 and Zinzendorf had outworked his vows, we adopted the Boiler Room Rule.

The Rule didn't emerge lightly. It was the product of five years of hard work, hammered out on the anvil of real life and relationships and forged in prayer. Perhaps in another five years it will have changed or grown, as we continue to dialogue and explore— the Rule is fixed yet flexible and always to be applied with grace.

We discourage any group from rushing into the Boiler Room lifestyle because it's important to prepare ourselves before we enter into any new pattern of living. Before we get into the details of the Boiler Room Practices, I want to consider one more question: How do we shape our lives to enable this Rule to be expressed?

Making Space

Brother Tom stood up to read at the start of the Compline service. "Our reading tonight comes from a lecture given by a Dominican abbot to the World Congress of Benedictine Abbots, in Rome in September 2000." This wasn't the most gripping introduction in world history, but then he said something that floored me: "The glory of God always shows itself in an empty space."[8]

A bunch of us had gathered at Turvey Abbey to catch up and to pray, and that night we had decided to join the monks and nuns for Compline. I had entered the chapel stressed and worried—we had so much to achieve in those two days, and we were way behind on our agenda.

But Brother Tom was talking about space rather than business. The reading was a discussion about why monasteries are attractive, and the speaker gave three reasons. "First of all, because your lives are of no particular purpose. Second, because they lead nowhere. And finally, because they are lives of humility."[9]

This was new stuff. Weren't our lives as Christians meant to be "purpose-driven"? Wasn't the aim of my life to go somewhere?

The Dominican abbot's argument was simple: What makes monastic life useful to God is the space it gives Him. Rather than filling our lives with ambitions, places to go and goals to achieve, a monk's or nun's life has meaning "because of an absence of progression, which points to God as the end and goal of our lives."[10] No job or promotion or task takes the place of the Kingdom.

If we are to look at living by a rule of life, we must consider the context of this living. A rule can't simply be transferred into someone's existing pattern of life—if truly embraced, the rule restructures everything.

I have noticed three areas in which the Boiler Room has challenged and—I hope—changed me.

The First Challenge: Separation

At first look, it might seem like the Bible is contradictory about engagement with our world. John's Gospel declares that "God so loved the world" (3:16) while John writes in his letters, "Don't love the world's ways. Don't love the world's goods" (1 John 2:15, *THE MESSAGE*). We are called to be separated (see 2 Cor. 6:17) but then to go into the world (see Matt. 28:18-20). Is Scripture really at odds with itself? John Stott suggests an alternate view: The Bible demonstrates our need for a double conversion, first out of the world and into Christ, then back into the world with Christ.[11]

John Skinner, the founder of the Northumbria Community, describes a monk as "one who separates from everybody in order to be united with everyone." Monasticism is sometimes misrepresented as a complete removal from the world. Skinner's assertion is that monasticism instead is about a separation *from that which divides us*—separation from wealth, from status, from exclusive relationships, sometimes even from speech.

Saint Francis urged his brothers to rid themselves of land or possessions, seeing that it only divided. "Possessions are often the cause of disputes and sometimes violence. If we owned them we would be obliged to carry arms to defend them—and to do that would hinder us in loving God and our neighbor."[12] Are there things that you hold on to and cherish that divide you from others? What "rights and precious little wrongs"[13] do we allow to get in the way of our love for God and those around us?

Since my teenage years, I have struggled with fears and insecurities about being forgotten, overlooked or rejected. I struggle with the desire to be accepted, and that sometimes separates me from others and God when I need to be invisible—or maybe when I need to speak a difficult truth. I regularly battle with a fear of being bypassed. A "Pick me!" approach to my life has carried on from games in the school playground to the temptation to be on a platform or to take the best jobs or opportunities for myself. This may bring some short-term reward to my pride, but it is often at the expense of those around me. Stepping back and allowing others to take the limelight is difficult for my ego, but in separating myself from recognition, I can more easily gain unity with my brother, and in that way serve God.

It is an interesting experiment to consider how some of the monastic vows connect with our lives. Is a new vow of silence, for example, one that disconnects our Internet or mobile phone? Is it one that turns off our TV or removes us from the crowd? Can we embrace a vow of poverty by choosing to not earn a bigger wage or not seek that new promotion? Could we choose to wait sometimes, to be happy with little?

Perhaps most challenging is a vow of celibacy. Being married with five children perhaps undermines my credibility to say anything on this issue, yet surely celibacy is about sexual fidelity as well as abstinence. How do I apply this in both thought and deed? For those of you not yet married, there are times to lay down the desire to be with others, just as there are times to take that up again. I know some who have chosen to go a season without a boyfriend or girlfriend. I know some who feel that singleness is part of their journey and have chosen to embrace it, sometimes with joy, sometimes with tears.

To return to John Skinner's advice: Let us separate ourselves "in order to be united to everyone."

The Second Challenge: Availability

In the summer of 2005, 24-7 sent mobile mission teams across Europe. Moving from place to place, they sought to pray, love and share Christ wherever they went. Part of their briefing requested that they travel light.

> Go! I am sending you out like lambs among wolves. Do not take a purse or bag or sandals; and do not greet anyone on the road. When you enter a house, first say, "Peace to this house." If a man of peace is there, your peace will rest on him; if not, it will return to you. Stay in that house, eating and drinking whatever they give you, for the worker deserves his wages (Luke 10:3-7).

Many Christians are embracing the call to live their whole lives traveling light, living simply so that they are available to God to be used in whatever way He chooses. Brother Tom's reading suggested that monastic life "has no purpose" and is "going nowhere." At first this sounds like an insult, but it is meant to be a compliment. In committing to a daily routine of prayer, work, study and rest, the communities make space, and into that space they have invited Christ.

For some of us, the call might be to be "de-centered," to remove our agendas, ambitions and even good causes and simply surrender the center ground to Christ. As we lay down the baggage of our ministries, insecurities and purposes, we can travel light and be readily led by Christ.

To be available does not necessarily mean not to marry, have kids or a job. It simply means the readiness and the ability to put Christ above all these other priorities. Where He leads we will follow.

An Early Church bishop named Irenaeus believed that a true search for God could only come with the concept of *apavia*, a Latin word that means "roadlessness." Irenaeus called for "a state of complete trust in the direction of God rather than human decision."

In my own life, I must admit how often I'm more available to Christian ministry than to Christ Himself. I'm *theoretically* available to Jesus, but in reality the cares of this world constrict and constrain my ability to obey. I have felt God encourage me to start small in this area—for example, to resist opening my laptop on a train journey, but instead sit there, pray and see if God speaks. Or perhaps I need to be available to talk and interact with those around me. The challenge that God has most clearly put before me is to put people and their needs far above my inbox and my paperwork. I need to be available so that He is able to put me to good works.

"The meaning of a monastic life is that it goes to the Kingdom. Our story is the story of humanity on its way to the Kingdom."[14]

The Third Challenge: Humility

Humility is the ability to see ourselves as God does. It is not trying to *be* God, as Adam and Eve did in the Fall, but refusing to deny the good people we are, and by so doing, deny God's creativity and glory revealed in our lives. How do we get this right?

Clothe yourselves with humility.

1 PETER 5:5

I love the example of Saint Francis, who accepted leadership of his orders but "was determined it should not displace his humility."[15] His custom at the start of each season was to appoint a personal guardian, usually the most junior friar, and to meticulously defer to him. Imagine that! Imagine the impact if every senior pastor deferred to the church's newest member, if every CEO sought advice on a weekly basis from his most junior employee, or if we all listened more intently to the words of children and insights of the poor.

Humility is maybe the most difficult of these three challenges because it is so alien to our human nature. Cardinal Hume, the former leader of the English Catholic Church said, "It is a very beautiful thing to see, but the attempt to become humble is painful indeed."[16] However arduous, humility is the doorway to both the separation and availability we explored above. As we embrace humility, we realize we have nothing to prove, no need for big ambitions or positions. As we embrace humility, we surrender the center ground to God and give Him the empty space to fill with His glory.

To embrace a rule means that we must be humble in our view of ourselves, not thinking we have "arrived," but also not torturing ourselves when we miss the mark.

Standing at the Crossroads

In Robert Zemeckis's wonderful film *Castaway*, Tom Hanks plays a Fed-Ex executive, Chuck Noland, marooned on a desert island for four years. When he returns, he finds that his funeral has taken place, his wife has remarried and his world has shifted forever. In the final scene, Chuck stands at a rural crossroads, map in hand, with the whole of North America in front of him. He can go anywhere. In that moment of choice, he hesitates—overwhelmed, yet excited by the freedom of a boundless world in front on him.

As we enter into these next chapters, I admit to feeling a little nervous, but excited, too. We're about to explore the Six Practices of a Boiler Room, and my anxiety stems from knowing that the ground here is so huge, the task so enormous, that everything may seem daunting and uncharted. Yet I'm glad, because others have been here before, and in these ancient paths we can find wisdom and guidance for life.

> *Stand at the crossroads and look; ask for the ancient paths,*
> *ask where the good way is, and walk in it,*
> *and you will find rest for your souls.*
> JEREMIAH 6:16

For Further Thought

Plan and take a short fast, a time of separation. Traditionally, a fast can be from food, but you might consider other aspects of separation. What about a week without TV or e-mail, a day without your phone, a silent retreat, maybe a month totally without gadgets? Take some time, just you and God.

Liturgy

Leader: Lord, today we enter the next steps in our journey of life.

All: Walk with us, O God.

Leader: We are standing at the crossroads and looking for a path.

All: Guide us, O God.

Leader: We ask for the ancient paths; our desire is to seek where the good way is.

All: Speak to us, O God.

Leader: An obedient discipline will hear Your direction and then walk in it, as You lead us to the ancient and right paths.

All: Give us courage, O God.

Leader: The Lord promises us, walk in this good way you will find rest for your souls.

All: Give us rest and peace, O God.

(Liturgy based on Jeremiah 6:16.)

CHAPTER 7

The Practice of Prayer

Lord, teach us to pray, just as John taught his disciples.
LUKE 11:1

Real prayer is life creating and life changing.
RICHARD FOSTER[1]

She's starting to live her life from the inside out.
THE FLAMING LIPS, "THE SOUND OF FAILURE"[2]

"What reaction do you have when I mention the word 'prayer'?"
I was met by a sea of blank teenaged faces.

I guess I shouldn't have been surprised. It was the first time I had gone to another church to share about what God had been doing in the Reading Boiler Room. I arrived full of enthusiasm, equipped with good stories and jokes, a computer presentation and even some art from our prayer room. I introduced myself quickly and then went for that killer opening question.

Suddenly a hand went up. "Boring," she said.

"Irrelevant and meaningless," said another.

"Cold prayer meetings at church," chipped in a third.

The list went on. As I drove home I thought, *What have we done to prayer?* How could the practice of prayer, this place of divine connection between man and God, have become so boring? What I struggled with the most was that I knew this was true of my own church—and I had been responsible for leading some of those boring prayer times.

Celtic Punks

"Boring" was a word you could definitely not use to describe the Celts. For starters, their appearance: The Early Celtic Church records[3] that the priests and missionaries had a distinctive haircut—not the normal monk's tonsure (bald patch), but shoulder-length hair shaved at the forehead. If this sounds a little like the "mullet," popular during the 1980s . . . you're not far off.

Now you may be thinking, *What's so amazing about that?* You've seen many mullets at your local church meetings! But J. M. Clark writes that from medieval records, it's clear that the monks also "tattooed certain parts of the body, especially the eyelids."[4] Can you imagine? The burly punk-like traveling missionaries arrived in villages across Northern Europe dressed in simple tunics, long hair flowing from a large circular bald patch on the tops of their heads, eyelids, face and body covered in usual markings, preaching about Jesus with a passion and fire that captured people's hearts wherever they went.

The Celts weren't boring. And they took all their passion, creativity and wildness right into the heart of their walk with God—in prayer. The prayers themselves were vibrant—sometimes liturgical, sometimes spontaneous—they breathed life. Many Celtic prayers reveal a poetic nature and a love for story and history, with special emphasis on the created world and on communion with God and with men and women. Centuries later, these words still evoke passion and devotion in believers worldwide.

Their prayers were often set in community. At Bangor Abbey (558-810) a community grew that became one of the most influential places of prayer in Ireland. Although it's difficult to confirm, it is thought that Bangor Abbey prayed 24-7 for much of its 250-year life, until the Vikings destroyed it.

They often withdrew to pray. Saint Cuthbert (634-687) often withdrew to spend entire nights in prayer before his teaching, healing and evangelistic journeys. "When he was based at Lindisfarne he waded out to what is still called Cuthbert's Isle to commune with God in the harmony of sea and sky."[5]

Their prayers were woven into the reality and beauty of life. In their monasteries, a daily rhythm of work and prayer (similar to those initiated in the monasteries of the East) developed and remained a distinctive of the Celtic Church. Ray Simpson writes that they "never lost touch with the rhythms of the 'still center' of Iona." He continues, "The days were filled with prayer, study and manual labour."[6]

Their prayers had direction. The Celts' commitment to prayer didn't end in a hermit's cave, as so many other monastic traditions did. The Celts withdrew with the purpose of preparing to "go," and go they did—out into the nations. Not surprisingly, this devotion to prayer was accompanied by the miraculous, and there are many stories about the signs and wonders witnessed by those early Celtic believers. In *Ecclesiastical History of the English People*, the famous historian Bede recounted incredible stories of the miraculous:

> Among innumerable other miraculous cures wrought by the Cross . . . certain youth had his lame arm healed . . . How a traveler's horse was restored and a young girl cured of the palsy . . . of the signs that were shown from heaven when the mother of that congregation departed . . . How Ethelwald calmed a tempest when the brethren were in danger at sea.[7]

Boring? Irrelevant? To the Celts, prayer was the dynamic lifeblood of their communities.

A Prayerful Community

A Boiler Room Is:
True to Christ by Being a Prayerful Community
Practicing a Daily Rhythm of All Kinds of Prayers
on All Occasions

Discovering prayer is the strongest flavor in the Boiler Room story. In Reading, the journey began with a realization that we were not very good at prayer, and from there, our first prayer room began to change us and to impact others.

I remember one long nightshift in particular. It was about 4:15 A.M., and my mind was in a state of flux. I had seen and heard so many terrible stories over the previous few days from young people facing horrific personal challenges, things I wouldn't want my kids to ever face—things that young people shouldn't have to deal with. As I began to pray, I wondered what it was that we were doing. It was like there was little me sticking my hand up to try to do something to bring change. Were these prayers really worth it? It felt like an auction and I had turned up with no money.

There's a legend sometimes told about Abraham Lincoln that came back to me that night. As he passed a slave auction one day, he saw a beautiful girl being bid on by a huge crowd of men. "What am I bid?" the slave auctioneer yelled, egging on the filthy, lustful crowd. Lincoln was horrified at the scene and terrified of the consequences for the girl, so he entered the auction, bid and eventually won. The girl was brought to him. "You are free to go," he told her.

"I can go anywhere?" she asked, rather stunned at the offer. "Then I'd rather stay with you."[8]

I began to write:

> I find myself in a giant hall. Surrounding me are thousands of young people—battered, bruised and broken. Then suddenly a voice says, "What am I bid?" A young girl stands before the crowd of lecherous, sneering men. "What am I bid for this piece of flesh?"
>
> The men start to cheer and shout figures.
>
> "Ten."
>
> "Twenty."
>
> "Fifty."
>
> "One hundred."
>
> *What can I do, God?*
>
> I start to bid. I have to save her. The cost becomes huge and I begin to waiver. Can I afford this? What price will I pay?
>
> The dream stops.
>
> I'm alone again but the faces are real enough. Alice being sold into prostitution. Jack with a revolver in his

mouth. Kat covered in cuts and bruises. John falling into crime. Laura alone and desperate. Steve, heroin needle in his bulging vein.

"What am I bid?"

The voice shatters the silence. The auction is on. The bidding has begun. It will continue day and night until the end. Most of the bidders desire only use and abuse. Satan drives them on. For him, young lives are for destruction. Chaos is his aim.

God is there, but He has chosen *us* to go into the auction. His desire: that we bid for everyone. Are we willing? The cost will be huge. We may have to give our lives.

The currency is prayer
The price is massive
But the prize is glorious
What am I bid?

That night and through the penning of that poem, I felt God impressing on me the urgency of what we were getting ourselves involved in. I felt convicted that I had often played with prayer, giving God my good ideas to bless rather than coming to Him to find out *His* ideas. I had met many lonely and struggling young people that week and had attempted to give my best answers, but in that moment, I began to grasp a little of how God felt about those individuals, and a little about how He wanted me to respond.

It began on my knees.

What Is Prayer?

We can pray in many different ways according to context, mood and personality. As Paul reminds us, we can and should come to God "on all occasions with all kinds of prayers and requests" (Eph. 6:18).

1. Prayer Is Personal

At its simplest, prayer is about you and your Father in heaven. The writers of the Westminster Catechism declared, "man's chief end is to glorify God and enjoy Him forever."[9] Prayer is a means to that end. Jesus prayed often (see Luke 5:16) and withdrew to be alone to pray (see Luke 4:42). His intimate relationship with His Father led the disciples to request, "Lord, teach us to pray" (Luke 11:1). Richard Foster believes that prayer is the key to entering the heart of God,[10] and Pastor Bill Hybels has written that "the most intimate communion with God only comes through prayer."[11]

2. Prayer Is Participatory
It is also good to pray with other people. Jesus declared that when two or three gather in His name, He is there with them (see Matt. 18:20). Praying together builds community and builds the Church—corporate prayer formed the backbone of the Early Church (see Acts 2:42). When we pray together we can catch each other's dreams; we can say "Amen" (So be it!) to the hopes and prayers of each other.

3. Prayer Is Powerful
"The prayer of a righteous man is powerful and effective" (Jas. 5:16). Jesus prayed before all the key moments in His life: before His baptism (see Luke 3:21), at the start of His ministry (see Luke 4), before choosing the disciples (see Luke 6:12). Even in the hardest moments, like those before His death, prayer was His lifeline to the Father (see Matt. 26:36-46). "Real help comes from GOD. Your blessing clothes your people!" (Ps. 3:8, *THE MESSAGE*).

4. Prayer Is Practical
As we have mentioned before (and as we will do again), prayer and practice go together. There is also a connection between our prayers and the way God chooses to answer them. Sometimes when we pray, He calls us to be the answer.

> *I pray for a release from the bonds of addiction for me and my boyfriend. I am 20 years old and have been using heroin since I was 15. I feel I have many battles to fight, and I have a long hard journey ahead of me. I pray for the strength to see it through, and come out the other side. Lord, You know my needs and wishes, my rights*

and wrongs, my strengths and weaknesses. I pray for You to
lift my anger and sadness and my cravings for the drugs
that harm me. Make me a better person.
ANONYMOUS PRAYER FROM THE READING BOILER ROOM

When we began the first Boiler Room, we knew that God was taking us on a journey of depth. We had been taking a journey into continuous prayer, hours and hours of individuals or groups praying day and night—but this process was not about the *quantity* of prayer, but the *quality*. It was about deepening our own walk with Jesus and providing space for others to know Him in a deeper way.

As we pray, we allow God to take us on a journey of experience that can lead to prayers being answered. But more important, we are led to new understanding of how God works and how we should respond. P. T. Forsythe suggested that "prayer is to religion what original research is to science."[12] Through mistakes, setbacks and new experiences, we began to explore some consistent patterns in the prayer that was going on.

- Boiler Rooms explored *continuous prayer,* or the *laus perennis.*
- Boiler Rooms developed *rhythms of prayer*—different times, different styles, different paces of prayer.
- Boiler Rooms modeled *prayer in action.* Often we have found that God begins to answer prayers through us or challenges how we can act in response to what we pray.

Consistent Patterns of Boiler Room Prayer

Continuous Prayer
When the Reading Boiler Room began, our intention was to have prayer 24-7, 365 days a year. Our aim was to build a schedule of regular prayer times for individuals or groups that would be booked in at the same time every week. Around these regular times, we would build a continuous cycle of prayer.

After a short time of investigation, we began to find that the idea of 24-7 prayer was not a new thing. We discovered the idea of the *laus perennis*, which in Latin refers to the ministry of continual praise and prayer. Pete Greig recalls:

> With mounting excitement we discovered that, through-out history, God has raised up communities like ours, committed to the *laus perennis*, especially at times of spiritual and social crisis. These prayer movements have sometimes been the very calling card of revival and transformation.[13]

We have mentioned before about the desire of God to meet with us. His desire was embodied the moment that "the Word became flesh and blood, and moved into the neighborhood" (John 1:14, *THE MESSAGE*). In chapter 2, we considered how this desire showed itself in God's relationship with Adam and Eve, with the Patriarchs and in the Tabernacle and Temple. In Deuteronomy 4:7, the Israelites boast of their God saying, "What other nation is so great as to have their gods near them the way the Lord our God is near us whenever we pray to him?"

As Jesus died on the cross, the curtain to the Holy of Holies was ripped in two and the way was made clear between God and us. Our sin removed, humankind could be in relationship with God. The new temple became the human heart, and God's desire was for *tamid* with us, for constant relationship. "Do you not know," wrote Paul, "that your body is a temple of the Holy Spirit?" (1 Cor. 6:19).

This is the inspiration for the *laus perennis*. The practice of constant prayer is both a symbol of our renewed relationship with God and fuel for that relationship. For the relationship to stay fresh and alive and growing, we need the conscious, disciplined activity of seeking the presence of God. A season of constant prayer provides both a place and a practice.

> The prayer room is a picture of something going on all the time in the heart of every believer. It helps us maintain the flame of worship upon the altar of our lives. We leave the

prayer room encouraged and enabled to keep on praying consciously and subconsciously through the trials of the day ahead.[14]

The *laus perennis* is about constant prayer on a number of levels. It is about personal prayer, Paul's call to "pray continually" (see 1 Thess. 5:17). It is about intercessory prayer, about "watchmen on your walls" called to "never be silent day or night" (Isa. 62:6). It is about answering the call of Jesus to "watch and pray" (Matt. 26:40-41). It is about imitating Christ, who often withdrew to pray for the whole night (see Luke 6:12). Continuous prayer is about a personal practice of the presence of God.

In continuous prayer, we also celebrate the perpetual prayers of the nations, chasing the sun around the globe, and we celebrate the perpetual prayers of the saints, ringing down through the ages in one, unbroken song. Here's a rough guide to how the *laus perennis* has been expressed throughout Church history:

The Early Church put constant prayer as the centerpiece of its communities for the first three centuries. Saint Cyprian (d. 258) challenged his fellow African Christians to "be as vigilant at night as in the light of day." The writings of Athanasius of Alexandria (296-373) tell us that such seasons of night-and-day prayer were common throughout the first three centuries of the Christian era.

The Desert Fathers emerged in the fourth century in response to the secularization of Christianity by the Emperor Constantine. They retreated to the wilderness and committed themselves to unceasing prayer and disciplined lives. They sent out missionaries who impacted (among others) the Celts, like those of Bangor Abbey (558-810) in Ireland.

The Acoemetae (fifth to ninth centuries) were renowned for generations for their great learning and also for their commitment to perpetual prayer. The splendor of their religious services contributed to shaping the liturgy.

Many monastic movements expressed this discipline of prayer in regular times of prayer each day. As mentioned in earlier chapters, the Benedictines celebrate seven times of prayer each day.

Signing up for the monastic life meant saying goodbye
forever to a full night's sleep . . . Many monastic buildings had a staircase that went straight down from the dor-
mitory into the chapel to ease the pain of going from
sleep to their work of praying in the cold and dark of a
winter's night.[15]

Major church movements such as Methodism and the Salvation Army
were punctuated by continuous prayer. John Wesley famously
recorded his prayer time at 3 A.M. on New Years Day 1739, when the
Spirit of God descended in an incredible way. While all of England
was partying—a nation drunk on gin—Wesley was in prayer.
Perhaps William Booth was inspired by Wesley's experience when
he called the Salvation Army to night prayer in London in 1865.

Jonathan Edwards committed Americans to a seven-year season of
prayer in 1744. His call to pray "speedily" and "constantly" in a "dark
day" resulted in an incredible spiritual awakening in the Colonies.

Pentecostalism was birthed at Azuza Street, Los Angeles, in 1903
with a three-year, 24-7 prayer season. Richard Foster wrote that
"meeting day and night for three years, Azuza Street was an all-
inclusive fellowship."[16]

Today, on Pastor Cho's Prayer Mountain in Seoul, South Korea,
and at the International House of Prayer in Kansas City, the spirit of
laus perennis goes on.

Life in a Boiler Room begins to bring into focus the need to keep
praying. Through healing and sickness, through new life and death,
through setbacks and encouragements, God calls us to "always pray
and not give up" (Luke 18:1).

Rhythms of Prayer

My first time in America, I visited my friends Casey and Amy
Johnson. On a spare day, Amy stuck me in the car with their son,
Cainan, and drove me to Cambria, a region of California by the
Pacific Coast. It was breathtakingly beautiful.

We were going to see an amazing annual event: elephant seals
calving. Every spring, these remarkable mammals arrive on the

beach to feed, rest and birth their young. These seals were *huge*—
the males would crush you if you went near them. And here I was,
on the other side of the world from my home, watching babies,
mums and grumpy dads having fights with each other. I was
struck by the sense of it: They're at this beach for only a while, and
they're here with a purpose—because they know it's a place of supply. It struck me that sometimes we're in seasons of movement
and supply, and sometimes in seasons of journey, loneliness, birth,
death, rest. It's the way the world He made works.

To pray day after day will naturally take you through different
emotional seasons. There are times of joy and times of mourning,
times filled with hope and times when it is hard to have faith.
There are times of noise and times of silence. To keep the discipline and perseverance required to pray continually means that
you begin to experience different styles and types of prayer: New
models, ancient disciplines, silence, liturgy, open prayer, prophetic prayer. Our prayer flows in rhythms.

In Reading, we discovered that we could not—and did not need
to—maintain praying every minute of every day. We began to develop
a weekly schedule of prayer: Times of corporate prayer, times of personal prayer, times when we knew prayer would take place each day.

Here is a typical rhythm of prayer in a Boiler Room:

- Daily times of prayer, where everyone is welcome. These
  are sometimes open prayer, sometimes liturgical.
- Weekly rhythm of prayer slots, in which individuals or
  groups come at the same time each week to pray
- Monthly rhythm of 24-7 weeks (for example, the first week
  of each month begins 24-7 prayer from Sunday to Sunday)

Learning about seasons and rhythms was vital to our understanding about praying within a Boiler Room or a community.

The rhythm of daily prayer. Very early on, we noticed how easy it
was, even in a house of prayer, to end up not praying together. As
a team, we had to ensure that we prayed together at least once a

week. To this we added times of liturgical prayer, times of individual prayer and times when different themes or issues were prayed about. In West London, the team operated a schedule of daily prayer in which everybody stopped at midday to gather and pray. Without this rhythm, our busyness can steal the very reason that we have come together.

A rhythm of styles. With 2,000 years of Christian prayer, we have a treasury of models and styles of prayer at our disposal. However, we often choose to ignore these disciplines, particularly the older ones, preferring to stick to musical worship or the traditional prayer meeting. In the last five years, groups around the world have been exploring ancient spiritual disciplines. In the City Boiler Room you can join in with *Lectio Divina* or sacred reading. In Brighton, arts and poetry have formed a key part of their rhythm of prayer. In West London, the team has begun to write liturgy, based on passages from the Bible that have been important to them.

A rhythm of life. The Celts believed that the Bible showed a God who "expressed rhythm in the universe."[17] Creation's story was one of days (seasons of creation), including one of rest. Just as we are called to recognize this day of rest in the concept of "Sabbath," so too we can reflect these godly seasons in the way we live and work. A look at the life of Jesus in Luke's Gospel shows that He lived in a seasonal way:

- Times of being visible (see Luke 3:22) and times of being hidden (His first 30 years)
- Times of work and times of rest (see Luke 6)
- Times of feasting and times of fasting (see Luke 5:33-39)
- Times of testing (see Luke 4:1-13) and times of affirmation (see Luke 3:22)
- Times of gathering (see Luke 5) and times of withdrawing (see Luke 4:42)
- Times of joy (see Luke 10:21) and times of lament (see Luke 22:39-46)
- Times of life and times of death (see Luke 23 and 24)

In our prayer lives, we need to be committed to rhythms and seasons. When was the last time you withdrew to pray? Sometimes a Boiler Room will enter a season of focused prayer or activity, maybe around a mission or around an important event. But there is also the need for withdrawal, for closing of doors and for individual or group reflection to consider what God might be saying and where He is leading. Sometimes in our activity we can forget to withdraw. Our lives should reflect work, but also rest. Fasting and feasting are both legitimate seasons in the life of a Boiler Room.

Prayer in Action

Mother Teresa believed that her prayer life did not end when she left her room and entered her day. Caring for the poor was as much a prayer as the words she uttered in secret beforehand. It is time to "incarnate" our prayers.

Faith and action go together. James was bold enough to suggest that others could show their "faith without deeds" but he would "show you my faith by what I do" (Jas. 2:18). When Jesus described people's relationship with Him as a vine and branches (see John 15), He connected two simple refrains: He called His disciples to "remain in me" (v. 4) and to "bear fruit" (v. 16). We cannot express our faith in words or in spirituality without the actions to back this up. This includes our prayers.

In Kansas City, the team's prayers for the poor led them to begin to serve the city's neediest children. In Calgary, as the team prayed for a venue, they found a building at the heart of the city's greatest need—in the red-light district.

One of my favorite things about being involved in 24-7 Prayer is getting to know the Salvation Army. Years of prayer have now taken place in several nations among S.A. Corps. The team in the Salvation Army's 614 group in Vancouver prayed continuously for two years in the Empress Hotel in that city. It was not surprising to us when Salvation Army Boiler Rooms began—we now have two in Wandsworth and Liverpool.

The Wandsworth Salvation Army Boiler Room exemplifies this idea of incarnated prayers. As a church, the Wandsworth Corps adopted the practices and principles of a Boiler Room. Their rhythm of daily prayer is naturally expressed in their care for the poor and needy in the area, which then opens a door for people to join their church. When you go to worship in Wandsworth, you sit with the rich and the poor, the homeless, the mentally ill, the influential, the young and the old. This has been their prayer—now it is their practice, too.

Boiler Rooms also provide a place for "prayer dreams" to come true. In a Boiler Room, a young person comes in to pray. As she does so, maybe God moves her heart to pray for the homeless in her city. As she leaves the prayer room, she finds out about a project serving meals to the city's homeless next Sunday, where she can volunteer to serve tea and baked potatoes and discover the fascinating and engaging lives of people whom society excludes or forgets. Often we are called to be the answer.

Often when we ask God to intervene, He looks at us and formulates His prayer, just as He did with Isaiah. He asks, "Whom shall I send? And who shall go for us?" (Isa. 6:8). Will we answer with the same enthusiasm as Isaiah?

"Here am I. Send me!"

The Heart of Revival

Arthur Wallis wrote that "When God intends great mercy for His people, the first thing He does is to set them a-praying," continuing that "at the heart of every revival is a spirit of prayer."[18] Whether it is an awakening in America, revival in the Hebrides or the transformation of communities as witnessed in George Otis's films, a move of prayer is always a precursor to God's moving. Often the move of God comes at the darkest times. If we want to see the tide turn in our world today, then we need to pray. This is the vision of Boiler Rooms, and it is expressed in three simple ways: transforming prayer, contagious prayer and continuing prayer.

1. Transforming Prayer

We need to pray with a big vision. Each Boiler Room has an aim of transformation, not only in its home city, but also in its home nation. Early on in the life of 24-7, we coined the adage, "Pray like it all depends on God, and live like it all depends on us."

Practically, this can be expressed in a number of ways, for example, a commitment to pray during periods of mission, such as the recent Soul in the City event in London. It can be expressed in intercessory prayer, hosting weeks of prayer, or prayer walls. It can be expressed in providing a place of prayer in difficult times (for example, the Iraq War).

Praying with vision is about prayer at the heart of needy places. When a series of terrorist attacks hit London in the summer of 2005, pray-ers from the City Boiler Room took to the Underground, praying for peace and calm in the places where people were scared, in trains like the ones in which bombs had been detonated.

2. Contagious Prayer

As we pray, others catch the drift. As a team prayed at the Hultsfred Rock Festival in Sweden, others were drawn in. In a church meeting at New Life Church, Stockholm, in May 2005, Patrick told me about a girl who crawled into the prayer tent on her hands and knees. It turned out she was a practicing witch. She was "pretty out of it," Patrick told us, "and she was rather shocked to find herself in a prayer room, but she ended up hanging out with us all week."

As we pray, God will touch those around us. As you pray at your school, street or office, expect God's presence to be at work. Expect those who are seeking God to be drawn in. In a Boiler Room, the prayer room has an open door. We encourage those who have no faith to pray just as much as we do those who are Christians. The key is that we emphasize Christ-centered prayer. He is our plumb line. He is the one to whom we pray.

> *The presence of God and the Holy Spirit*
> *in the Boiler Room is tangible.*
> JO FROM KENT, VISITOR TO THE READING BOILER ROOM

3. Continuing Prayer

One of my favorite guys in Reading was Matthias. Our first contact with Matthias was when he came in to sign himself up for

eight hours of night prayer. We tried to encourage him to do a little less to start with but were shamed to discover that one entire
night of prayer was what God had told him to do each week, and
for a season he did so. Matthias knew that a key to seeing change
was to keep going and to sacrifice.

> *Thank you, Lord. All the sensible prayers I have prayed over the
> last 12 years have come true—all within the last five months.*
> ANONYMOUS PRAYER IN THE READING BOILER ROOM

Through transforming, contagious and continuous prayer, I
believe we can see a change. It's time to recognize that we have a
role to play, that we have a responsibility, that we can be praying
for God's kingdom to come in the world.

Broken

Committing to a prayerful life is not always easy. I felt this chapter would not be complete without honestly discussing the challenges we have faced.

Probably the toughest challenge of all has been the personal
pain of spiritual opposition and—amongst the miracles—the reality of unanswered prayer that we have all had to endure. I could
tell you many stories, but I guess the story I am best placed to tell
is my own. I do so with some hesitancy, mainly because it still
hurts, but also because sometimes there can almost be some sort
of inverted glamour in pain or hardship.

During one of my wife's, Karen's, pregnancies (we have five
kids), she developed gestational diabetes, a form of the illness
that usually clears up after the birth of the child. It can usually be
controlled by diet. Initially, everyone expected Karen's diabetes
to follow that same pattern—but it didn't, and soon Karen was
insulin-dependant and injecting four times a day.

From there, Karen's health has taken many twists and turns.
She is often tired and ill. The frustration it causes her is painful
enough to watch, but the physical effects it has had on her have

sometimes been overwhelming. Of course, Karen has often been prayed for—it's painfully ironic that a family involved in a prayer ministry hasn't had their personal prayers for healing answered. But that is the reality.

In the summer of 2002, we learned that Karen was pregnant with our fifth (and final) child. It was a wonderful surprise and an amazing joy, but it was also a challenge to Karen's health. Pregnancy and diabetes do not go well together, and so it was to prove.

In January 2003, with baby Daniel at 26 weeks, Karen went into premature labor. After a few hours, the labor stopped, but it was obvious that this was going to be tough for Karen and for Daniel. There were many false labors, frantic ambulance rides, many shocks, many days of bad news. There were times when it looked like I might lose them both, but somehow I could still sense the presence of God with us.

Throughout the whole process, we had a powerful sense of being held by the prayers of others. We had supportive phone calls from all over the world. One friend had a dream on that first January night in which she was literally pushing the baby back in. Daniel had to stay in the womb for as long as possible, and we believe God helped him and ultimately saved him, our miracle baby.

On February 18, Daniel Isaac James Freeman was born by Caesarean section. He came through okay—as did his mom!—but we were told to expect some extended time in the special care unit, that he might have diabetes himself.

He spent two hours in special care, was home in a few days and is a strong, healthy and lovely child.

Daniel's birth was a landmark time for me to see how faithful God is. He answered some of our prayers, but many still remain unanswered. Karen is still ill. We have had many difficult days since then. For us and for many others, pain is part of the journey.

Within the 24-7 movement there are many who have similar stories. Pete and Samie Greig have had to endure an incredible struggle as Samie battled with a brain tumor and its consequences, which still affect her today. Pete's chapter entitled "Pain" in *Red Moon Rising* is one of the most inspiring and challenging stories I have ever read.[19] To know Pete and Samie while Karen has endured all she has been through is an incredible gift, because I know I can look at them and see a picture of living for Christ in the midst of terrible pain, and share the struggle with understanding unanswered prayer.[20]

And we are certainly in good company. The suffering of Moses, Joseph, Paul, Peter, Stephen and Jeremiah all show how God uses hard times and brings glory from them. And ultimately, we look to Jesus. Suffering was part of the Messiah's pilgrimage, as the writer of Hebrews points out:

> Let us fix our eyes on Jesus, the author and perfecter of our faith, who for the joy set before him endured the cross, scorning its shame and sat down at the right hand of the throne of God. Consider him who endured such opposition from sinful men, so that you will not grow weary and lose heart (Heb. 12:2).

And what was the joy? Regaining His Godness? His Throne? Being on the Father's right side? According to this passage, His joy is clearly *us*. It's you and me, His people whom He "rejoices over with singing" (Zeph. 3:17). The freedom, release and renewed relationship with you and me—*that* was His joy. In his biblical commentary, Matthew Henry writes:

> He had something in view under all his sufferings, which was pleasant to him; he rejoiced to see that by his sufferings he should make satisfaction to the injured justice of God and give security to his honor and government, that he should make peace between God and man, that he should seal the covenant of grace and be the Mediator of it, that he should open a way of salvation to the chief of sinners, and that he should effectually save all those whom the Father had given him, and himself be the first-

born among many brethren. This was the joy that was set before him.[21]

Suffering is the way that God chose to bring about salvation in the world. I know that in my wife's pain, my family has grown. I know that Jesus has glorified Himself in the midst of suffering. If pain is also part of the price involved in seeing cities changed, in seeing lives rescued and saved, if I have to go through (comparatively minor) pain for the sake of the Kingdom, then that is joy to me. Suffering can be part of my walk as long as Jesus is the Lord of more lives, more cities and more nations.

And of course, that's not all of our joy! Ultimately, we have an even greater joy to come: Eternal Life. Heaven. Being with God. One day Karen will worship Jesus, bowing before Him healed, well, full, restored. One day Jesus will come to bring the ultimate healing, the ultimate joy.

The One on the Throne will pitch his tent there for them: no more hunger, no more thirst, no more scorching heat. The Lamb on the Throne will shepherd them, will lead them to spring waters of Life (Rev. 7:14-17, THE MESSAGE).

For Further Thought

Experiment with a rhythm of prayer for a month. Find some simple daily liturgy; organize some corporate times of prayer. Build in a retreat or a silent time. Keep a journal of how you find it, and explore whether God might want this to become part of your walk with Him.

Liturgy

You are famous, God, for welcoming God-seekers,
for decking us out in delight.
PSALM 5:12, THE MESSAGE

Leader: Jesus, we come before You, humbly, quietly, in obedience, seeking Your peace.

All: In the morning, O Lord, You hear my voice. In the morning, I lay my requests before You and wait in expectation.

Leader: Where morning dawns and evening fades, You call forth songs of joy.

All: God of light and glory, as the dawn brings in a new day, we remember Your mercies are new each morning. We praise You for this new day you have made. Take it, use it, and bring glory to Yourself. Take our lives, take our work and efforts, take our thoughts, take our very breath and use it for Your glory.

A short period of silent prayer is held to consider what today will bring and to offer our day and ourselves up to God.

(Liturgy based loosely on Psalms 5 and 65.)

Chapter 8

The Practice of Creativity

God spoke: "Light!" And light appeared.
GENESIS 1:3, *THE MESSAGE*

*The Christian is the one whose imagination
should fly beyond the stars.*
FRANCIS SCHAEFFER[1]

*I think people ought to know that we're
anti-fascist, anti-violence, anti-racist, and we're pro-creative.*
JOE STRUMMER, THE CLASH[2]

During the summer of 2004, God spoke to me profoundly about mission and creativity through a mission team working in Ayia Napa on the island of Cyprus. Ayia Napa has become one of the summer capitals for vacationing fans of R&B and Hip Hop. Mixing prayer, mission and practical kindness, the team's aim was to show Jesus to those visiting the island.

I had arrived to give some support for a few days, but as I stepped off the plane, I began to wonder what I was doing there. Ayia Napa is filled with the trendy, beautiful, young and mostly wealthy and successful. And then there was me: a skinny 35-year-old bald guy, with no muscles or suntan to show off. I felt nervous and totally out of place, but the trip became a highlight for me. I witnessed a team committed to Jesus and to the island—a team that lived out their faith in a vibrant and intensely creative way.

At the center of the team's activities was prayer. The team had a prayer space in a room at the old monastery in the center of the town. Their stone "cell" housed a cross, a map of Cyprus, turntable decks, prayer requests from people they had met, and the usual mix of art you'd see in any other 24-7 prayer room.

After prayer each night, some of the team went to a club close to the monastery to meet people, chat and pray for them if they could. They also went to dance and worship. The team leader, Bex, explained that the team sought to dance differently—with true freedom and without all the sexual undertones common in the clubs. It was amazing to witness the atmosphere changing, people joining in—just a small group worshiping Jesus in a creative way influenced the whole vibe of the club.

Members of the team also went in pairs around the streets, chatting, caring and offering to pray. It wasn't like cold calling— there were no tracts or pressure. They just said hi and let the conversation go, offering to pray when they could. The effect was incredible.

A woman asked for prayer to be able to have a child—the team prayed then and there on the street. A young guy who had come to Ayia Napa partly to get away from the faith of his Christian foster parents met the team, chatted and asked to meet again. A jewelry trader asked for prayer and expressed how it had touched her—she wanted to meet the team again. A man who had had some bad experiences with Christians expressed his amazement at the accept- ance these Christians showed him, even though he was drunk.

I loved spending time with the Ayia Napa team. It reminded me of why we're doing what we do—why we're praying, why we're seeking after God, why we're sharing Him. In Matthew 9, we read that Jesus looked on the crowd and had compassion because they were helpless and harassed, like sheep without a shepherd. But He lamented, "the harvest is plentiful but the workers are few" (Matt. 9:37). In Ayia Napa, Bex and the team answered that call by offer- ing all of their creative gifts to God. They embraced and empow- ered their dance, their art, their ideas and their kindness to touch an island that was lost. Our creative God created something new in a least-expected place.

A Creative Community

A Boiler Room Is:
True to Christ by Being a Creative Community
Where Artistic Expressions of Prayer and Worship
May Take the Form of Art, Sculpture, New Music, Poetry,
Dance, Fun and a Celebratory Lifestyle

Most people who know me will tell you I can't sing. In the early nineties, as a fresh-faced new Christian, I volunteered to help organize a church event where we were to walk through the main street of our town worshiping together. It was meant to be a celebration. When the music tracks that we were to sing with temporarily broke, I offered enthusiastically to help lead things *a cappella*. Ten seconds later I was hauled off stage and an alternative singer was found.

In truth, I have a voice like a drain—but I have always loved to sing. Singing worship to God is one of the most popular of our creative responses to God. (Maybe that's because we don't have to be Pavarotti to get involved.) But when it comes to other aspects of the creative arts, it gets a bit harder. What if you can't paint or write or dance or sculpt? Is creativity even a valid way to worship God?

Whatever our response to these questions, it's hard to dispute that the arts and creativity are a great gift that God has given humankind. We live in a world where music can lift the soul, where stories can ignite the imagination. Medical studies have shown the benefits of laughter. Painting and photography can deepen our appreciation of light, color and detail. God has inspired artists to give us representations of historical events. He has gifted scientists to discover incredible media that allow us to see our world like never before. We even live in an age where the arts can help those who struggle with learning difficulties, through art and music therapy.

Solomon, believed to be the writer of Ecclesiastes, considered that "there is a time for everything, and a season for every activity under heaven." He concluded that, as well as many other things, there is "a time to weep and a time to laugh, a time to mourn and a time to dance" (Eccles. 3:1,4).

To understand this gift of creativity and to learn how we should apply it wisely, I believe we must start with God Himself.

God the Artist

The God of the Bible is a creative God. Genesis 1 tells us how "God created the heavens and the earth" (v. 1). Our Creator danced through six days of skies and seas, of birds and animals, of plants and trees, and then the creation of man and woman. He looked at all He had made "and it was very good" (v. 31). God had a smile on His face.

The act of creation seemed spontaneous, yet incredibly planned. It was ordered, yet immensely creative. God the Father was at work. The Word, His Son, Jesus, was there (see John 1:2) and the Spirit too was present, "hovering over the waters" (Gen. 1:2). You get the feeling that the urge to create is part of the very nature of God. Creativity is part of the divine DNA.

The Celts embraced this idea in their worship. They celebrated Christ as the center of the universe, as the "keystone of creation."[3] Part of their worship was to enjoy creation, to marvel in it. They saw Christ as the means for redemption of creation—they believed creation would be transformed and redeemed. They embraced the call to be stewards of creation as a natural response to a creative God. Columbanus suggested that "if you want to know the Creator, first understand and know creation."[4]

It's obvious that God did not create purely for function—beauty fills all He does and who He is. When He downloaded His plans for the Temple in Jerusalem, for example, He asked for "precious stones" (2 Chron. 3:6) and for ornate columns that had no structural purpose. "God is interested in beauty,"[5] and His interest is never stagnant. He is constantly creating. David's prayer of repentance in Psalm 51:10 asked God to "create in me a pure heart, O God." A refrain of the psalms and of Jeremiah was the witness of God doing "a new thing" (Jer. 31:22).

God creates through the life He has created. He is the Potter and He shapes us, His clay (see Jer. 18:1-12). He makes the sun rise and set. He is our very breath. The Nicene Creed calls Him "the Lord and the lifegiver." God creates all good gifts we enjoy (see 1 Tim. 4:4). God creates in answer to prayer. Everything, every aspect of life, comes back to Him. "All things were created by him" (Col. 1:16).

God is creative in the way He works, thinks and operates. Jesus confronted problems with creative solutions (see John 8:7). He was arguably the most creative communicator who has ever opened His mouth. His parables painted word pictures that drew people into an understanding of God, an understanding that the Pharisees had removed from the people.

God created. God *is* creating. Finally, God *will* create. "Behold, I will create new heavens and a new earth" (Isa. 65:17). God will be creative in the future, bringing together creation and history to make a dwelling place for Himself and His people. Then truly will the Lord "create a new thing."

Creativity Celebrates God

The creativity of God asks us some big questions regarding humankind's creativity. Pastor and writer Eugene Peterson points out that "'create' is a word that is used in the Bible exclusively with God as the subject."[6] For the other five Boiler Room Practices, we exercise them by imitating Christ and the way He lived, but in the creative realm, it's a little harder. We are not infinite—we can't create something from nothing.

Michael Card suggests that "we are not imitators of God in this dimension" and reminds us of the temptation to pretend at being "little gods."[7] So if imitation of God is not the way to express creativity, what is?

In my opinion, there is no doubt that men and women can create. The difference between God's creativity and mine is that I can only create from what He has made. I love to write poetry, but my words, my ink, my paper were all made by God, at least indirectly. My inspiration might come from creation or my life and emotions, all of which He created. Francis Schaeffer wrote that God "can create out of nothing by His spoken word,"[8] and obviously, people do not have the same ability. But "create" rightly describes both divine and human creativity, because human ingenuity is a reflection of the Creator.

I remain even more convinced of this when I consider that we are made "in the image of God" (Gen. 1:27). Card explains, "We are all fashioned in the image of God, who is an artist."[9] When my daughters spend an afternoon painting beautiful pictures, I'm convinced that they are expressing and witnessing to the Creator God who made us, expressing something of what it is to be a human being in His image.

If Card is right—that the creative impulse in each one of us reflects God's image—we can enjoy art that is not made by Christians. We can enjoy its technical merit, its portrayal of color or rhythm, its concept of the world when it connects or even contrasts with a Christian worldview. Hans Rookmaker, in his famous *Letter to a Christian Artist*, suggests that there are "norms for art that are part of God's creation."[10] As an artist taps into a unique view of color or design or gets a grip on complex forms, he is merely responding to something God has put there, and in that we can find the beauty of God.

While praying in a prayer room in Guildford recently, I began to sing "Grace Under Pressure" by the band Elbow.[11] As I reflected on the song, it drew me to think of friends who were struggling, and called me deeper into prayer. I put the song on the CD player, turned it up loud, and experienced one of the deepest prayer times I'd ever had.

Christians did not write "Grace Under Pressure." (Indeed, it ends with a curse word, something that might lead some to not listen at all.) Yet in that song, I found an expression of God's love for my friends, as well as a meditation on Jesus' life on Earth, in which He expressed immense grace under pressure. Something deeply woven in the song revealed God the Artist to me.

This doesn't mean that all creativity is sacred or that our creativity can't be misused—it can and often is. But I believe that the creative impulse we have in common asks us to look beyond our churches, worship songs and bookshops to find the beauty of God in the creativity that exists in our world.

As we create, we celebrate the goodness and creativity of Artist God. In many churches, a "celebrant" presides over the service of Communion—an interesting term for a service about a man's death! Yet for us it *is* a celebration. The Catholic Church's Eucharist Prayer for the 17th Sunday in Ordinary Time expresses this theme: "Lord, we receive the sacrament which celebrates the memory of the death and resurrection of your Son, Jesus Christ."

Psalm 145:7 calls us to "celebrate your abundant goodness and joyfully sing of your righteousness." God is to be celebrated! As we splash color on a canvas or enjoy the interaction of words and notes as we compose a song . . . as we dance with all our might . . . as we cook a meal or enjoy expressive clothes . . . we celebrate the God who made us and our world. We celebrate the God who is an artist, the beautiful God whom we love.

The job of a celebrant is also to respond—to respond in joy to all God has done to inspire our creativity. When we express a picture of praise, a poem or a song, the origin of our work is not us but what God has done. Responding is the Spirit's work in us.

We have the gospel of a creative God to declare! Our worship, our prayers, our lives should reflect His nature. We can't possibly be drab and dry, stale or bland, as we attempt to reveal the glories of God to our world. A creative God longs to create in our lives, to create even in our responses to Him.

Bezalel

When the Israelites were in the desert, God established the Tabernacle and filled Bezalel with His Spirit to design the prayer room. Bezalel was a skilled craftsman, inspired by God, to make carvings and designs that would help decorate the Tabernacle and point others to God (see Exod. 31:2-5). Bezalel is the first man

recorded in the Bible as being filled with the Spirit. That honor fell
to an artist!

> See, I have chosen Bezalel son of Uri, the son of Hur, of the
> tribe of Judah, and I have filled him with the Spirit of God,
> with skill, ability and knowledge in all kinds of crafts—to
> make artistic designs for work in gold, silver and bronze, to
> cut and set stones, to work in wood, and engage in all
> kinds of craftsmanship (Exod. 31:2-5).

Bezalel and his workmate, Oholiab, were given a tough job: to
come up with all the designs for this intricate, detailed and beautiful place of worship in the Israelites' desert home. There were
tables to fashion, ornate and decorative pieces to make, garments
to be woven, and the altar itself to be completed. This was to be the
place where Moses would meet with God, where "the pillar of
cloud would come down and stay at the entrance, while the LORD
spoke with Moses" (Exod. 33:9).

Was Bezalel's work functional? Some, yes. Was there a practical point to everything God's Spirit inspired him to make? Well,
no—a tent in the desert filled with gold and designed like a palace?
Yet it was here that God wanted to meet with His people, in a place
of beauty.

As we worship and follow God in the tabernacle of our hearts,
in our prayer rooms and in the world He has given us to celebrate,
what is our Bezalel call? What creativity is God calling us to un-
leash in our lives and in our communities? "Biblically speaking,
the making of art is not an option but a command."[12]

Creativity Speaks

Earth from the Air by Yann Arthus Bertrand is (in my opinion) one
of the most beautiful and powerful books ever made. It is also
one of the largest, as likely to break my coffee table as sit on top
of it. It is also a big seller: 1.5 million copies worldwide, translated into 19 languages.

Earth from the Air is a book of amazing aerial photographs of our world, its people, its cities, its beauty. The photographs mix the power and splendor of the natural world with the wonders of people, industry, cities and landmarks that make up our world. Bertrand's aim is for his photography to highlight the issues that face our world: poverty, the environment, trade, globalization. The essays that accompany each chapter are stunning. In his introduction, Herve de la Martiniere explains that "this is the testimony of a citizen of the world at the dawn of the third millennium, who wants to show his vision of the earth, its beauty as well as its failures."[13]

Earth from the Air is a modern example of the power of creativity, but the monastic movements also believed in the communicative powers of the arts. Whether it was paints, friezes, mystery plays or sculpture, the arts were a method of communicating Jesus. The Celts wrote of natural symbols to express God, making nature sacramental. Noel O'Donoghue calls this approach "imaginal," using the knowledge of God the Creator to perceive His presence in His world.[14] A young Orthodox monk, Brother Aidan, concluded that "the imagination is a faculty for seeing, rather than inventing."[15] In the context of our prayers and worship, art and creativity often allow us to discover new aspects of God we haven't seen before, either for ourselves or through someone else's creativity.

This has certainly been my experience as 24-7 prayer rooms have evolved, filling with pictures, prayers and Bible verses written on the walls—the very rooms breathe creativity. And here, ordinary people have often found God:

A young man spends his two hours in the prayer room carefully doing an intricate design based on one Bible verse, inadvertently engaging in Christian meditation.

A teenage girl writes a simple prayer on the wall of a prayer room. Maybe she has been too nervous to speak out the prayer in a prayer meeting, but here, alone in the prayer room, she has the space to speak her heart. As people come through the room and read the prayer, they share its sentiments and echo an "Amen." Sometimes when spoken prayers are too big a step, the creative arts can bridge a gap.

A student paints a glorious picture of Christ. The next day a young man enters the prayer room for the first time, offers a tentative prayer upon seeing the Face. He weeps. The young man's eyes have been opened through the strokes of a paintbrush, just as 300 years ago, Count Zinzendorf committed his life to God after looking at a painting in an art gallery.

The Freedom of Creativity

Thankfully over the past years there has been a realization within some deep-hearted priests that if you banish poetry and the other expressive arts to the dim cloisters of our faith, then what takes place is in effect the banning of God thinking aloud.
STEWART HENDERSON, POET, SONGWRITER AND
BBC BROADCASTER[16]

Linnea Spransy is the resident artist at the Kansas City Boiler Room. She is also responsible for what many would describe as a new form of art.

I first met Linnea in a borrowed Buick at the Kansas City Airport. After a long flight from Canada, I was looking forward to sleep, but when I heard a little about Linnea and her pieces displayed at the new Boiler Room, I asked her to take a detour to show me. I wasn't disappointed.

At 25, Linnea reached a crossroads in her life where she found her artistic gifts growing and her happiness with life diminishing. In this place of struggle, she found Jesus once again and returned to her art education at Yale, resolved not to try and prove herself with her art, but instead to find her identity and confidence in Christ.

At the same time, Linnea had begun to study the natural world and particularly the "almost supernatural" laws that governed it. Within these rules and structures, it appeared to her that there was limitless creation. Linnea sees God working within parameters and rules that He Himself has set.

Linnea's idea was to transfer these principles to art. Working with a huge canvas, Linnea sets rules for a piece and then within those rules, creates. What emerges are patterns of incredible beauty and symmetry.

She presented this art as her final piece to her professors at Yale, in an area called "The Pit," where students are often criticized severely. When the lecturers studied Linnea's work, positive comments began to flow. One remark that stuck with her was from a lecturer who found it hard to criticize her work, since she had discovered a new way of making art. The creativity of God in creation had released Linnea to create some spellbinding artwork.

Creativity is a tool that releases many to be themselves. Michael Card tells of a Romanian songwriter, Nicholae Moldoveanu, who was imprisoned for 12 years hard labor under the oppressive Ceausescu regime in communist Romania. His crime was being a Christian. In prison, he was denied pen and paper in order (so his captors thought) to make writing impossible. Nicholae covered his window with soap film and wrote music with his finger. Once finished, he would commit the piece of music to memory. As a condition of his release from prison, he was told he must stop writing Christian songs. His reply? "Just keep me here and save yourself the trouble. I will never stop worshiping my God with my praise songs."[17] Today, the 360 songs he composed while imprisoned are sung in churches across Romania.

Creativity releases praise, prayers and even people:

- Sometimes a vision of Christ or a prophetic word can't be expressed in words, but a paintbrush can record the vision in someone's mind.
- Sometimes a heart-cry can only be expressed through a song.
- Sometimes a prayer is too hard to utter but can be released in the pages of a journal.

Most of all, creativity releases one particular group of people: artists. We all have the ability to create, but there is no doubt that some have a special gift. For Christian artists, life has sometimes been hard. Questions of appropriate subject matter have limited individuals' creativity for generations. From Rembrandt to Bono, the question of "Christian art" has been a millstone. Often artists are sidelined in the Church: How can I express my gift in my church? Where is the space to express myself? Where can I dance? Where can I paint? How can I use my poetry in worship?

Christians can play a key part in the arts, both in our churches and in culture. They have the opportunity to be salt and light, to bring perspective, to loose Christ into the most "secular" of media. Steve Turner believes a Christian artist is like an irritant: "Just as people think they have removed God from all consideration of a particular question, the Christian annoyingly puts him back on the agenda in some way."[18]

Just as creativity releases us, it's time for us to release the artists.

The Practice of Creativity

Paint grace-graffiti on the fences.
PSALM 17:6, *THE MESSAGE*

Boiler Rooms often end up looking like explosions at a crayon factory—they are all about creativity in communication with God. How can prayer be limited to words? You can also pray nonverbally with music, dance, poetry, painting and sculpture. And because God is the Creator, His presence catalyzes artistry and often lends an anointing to artwork created in His presence.

The practice of creativity within a Boiler Room has at its heart the principles of life, speech and release that we have looked at. Space is given for the practice of creativity in several ways.

First, Boiler Rooms embrace the arts. Boiler Room communities often have space set aside in their venues and money in their budgets for facilitating the arts. Plans and dreams have included recording studios, pottery kilns, prayer gardens, dark rooms, art studios and writing areas—all have found homes in various Boiler Rooms. In Reading, resident artists are given space to work on projects and sometimes to hold exhibitions, and many Boiler Rooms have resident artists on the team.

Second, Boiler Rooms allow the mess. Creativity can be messy, and Boiler Rooms are places where mess is tolerated. This mess is not just the paint on the floor or a need to tidy up after a bunch of teenagers has been let loose with spray cans. The mess can be of thought, too.

Prayers and paintings that question and doubt are allowed just as often as pictures that are theologically correct. People of no faith are welcome to create as much as those who have faith. Boiler Rooms have hosted art days, Goth concerts, dance workshops, film nights. The words of secular prophets like Thom Yorke or Bob Geldof can be found on the stereo or written on the walls just as often as Christian writers or musicians.

Writing about the right environment for creative thought within organizations, Margaret Wheatley believes chaos and order are a formidable mix. Rather than avoiding chaos or change, it should be embraced or held in tension with order, for "without the partnering of these two great forces, no change or progress is possible. Chaos is necessary to new creative ordering."[19]

Third, Boiler Rooms give space to individual creativity. Creativity is not simply a matter for artists. My three-year-old son, as he grapples with crayons and paper, has as much right to be creative as Raphael or Constable. Boiler Rooms accept and affirm all forms of creativity, at all levels.

In the past years, Boiler Rooms have not only showcased artists and their art, but have also hosted art days, DJ workshops, songwriting classes, circus seminars, poetry classes and jewelry-making groups. The heart of this creative space is the prayer room. There, alone, anyone is free to express prayers and worship in a landscape of creative opportunities.

To release creativity is always a challenge. If you desire your faith in a neat and tidy box, you may find it difficult! But the mess and the wonder of the creative arts does have a friend in Jesus.

When Mary chose to worship Jesus in a messy way (see John 12:1-11), with oil, tears and hair, Jesus embraced her worship and affirmed her when others objected. Walking with Christ is not always a neat and tidy business. Remember that C. S. Lewis saw in Jesus Aslan, the not-so-safe lion.[20]

For Further Thought

Spend a week on your own creative retreat. This can be done in your normal pattern of life, but it involves moving wholehearted-ly into being creative. Discipline yourself to be creative in the way you respond to the Bible: Write poems and draw pictures rather than write notes. Take your friends to see a film and go for a cof-fee to discuss it afterward. Take a walk in nature during your week. Resolve to think creatively when problems arise. Cook creatively. Dress creatively. From what you learn on your retreat, begin to build creative disciplines into your life.

Liturgy

Praise the Lord, O my soul. O Lord my God, you are very great;
you are clothed with splendor and majesty.
PSALM 104:1

Leader: Like the blazing sun, rising in the east, Your splendor shines throughout the Earth, Your glory reaches to the heavens.

All: At the beginning of the day, we adore You, God of Creation.

Leader: You spread Your love like a blanket across a sleepy world. You comfort us with Your words of tenderness. You cradle us in Your arms.

All: At the beginning of the day, we adore You, God of creation.

Leader: You hold us within the vastness of Your world. We are lost in the vastness of Your love. We cannot begin to grasp the vastness of Your thoughts.

All: At the beginning of the day, we adore You, God of creation. May we know You, Lord, but not so much that we are no longer surprised by Your grace. Not so much that we are no longer overwhelmed by Your joy. May our walk with You be like a sunrise each morning. May Your love herald a new day in our journey. Amen.

(Liturgy inspired by Psalm 104.)

CHAPTER 9

The Practice of Justice and Mercy

I tell you the truth,
whatever you did for the least of one of these brothers of mine,
you did for me.
MATTHEW 25:40

At the end of the twentieth century, most of us will have to repent,
not of the great evils we have done,
but simply great apathy that has prevented us from doing anything.
MARTIN LUTHER KING, JR.[1]

In the city, souls awaken, bodies shaking
oh pull me up let me see the view.
SIMPLE MINDS, "WALL OF LOVE"[2]

My wife had been in and out of hospital since the start of the year, and my as-yet-unborn son looked as if he might not survive his birth. As I sat in the waiting room after hearing Karen's latest prognosis, I felt utterly desperate. What was God doing?

As I mentioned, the last few months of Karen's pregnancy with Daniel were a traumatic time. One night I remember leaving the hospital feeling so desperate for God to move that I questioned myself: Was this about me? Had I sinned in some terrible way? Did my love for God not have quite the right integrity about it?

As I walked home, I saw a homeless guy asking for spare change. Without thinking, I emptied my pockets. What I gave him must have been nearly $20. *Maybe that will release some new healing for Karen. Maybe being kind to the poor might release a blessing for me.* As I walked further, I began to be convicted. I viewed kindness for the poor as some way of bribing God to hear my cries.

> He has showed you, O man, what is good. And what does the LORD require of you? To act justly and to love mercy and to walk humbly with your God (Mic. 6:8).

It seems that many within the Western Church have been looking for shortcuts over the last 20 years, shortcuts that will unlock blessing—the "five keys" to the nation, the "three steps" to revival, the "new understanding" of ancient blessings. I have even heard the verse above quoted as a key to success: If only we will care for the poor, then God will pour out His blessings. But what if God simply wants us to obey Him, to just love people?

The prophet Micah calls us to walk humbly with God, and we should note that his emphasis is on the *journey* with God, not the arrival. When we walk humbly, we abandon our agendas and stop trying to protect our ministries or enhance our reputations. We aim to put God on the pedestal, not ourselves.

Micah calls us to act justly, but we are told that the poor will always be with us (see Mark 14:7). Our job is never finished. He calls us to love mercy, but we know that we'll never "get done" loving and giving this side of heaven.

So if this is a task with no end, what does that mean? Why does Jesus call us to act justly and love mercy in a world where there will never be enough of those to finish the job? Why? Because this is the nature of God. This is the divine dream: for the mercy of Christ to flow from the cross and to flood our lands, for the justice of God to roll down like a river (see Amos 5:24).

To love the poor is not to gain a spiritual key or arrive at a destination. It can never be a program or a shortcut. *It is to love as God loves.* To act justly and love mercy is to demonstrate the very nature of Jesus Christ, the Christ whose death on the cross brought mercy and justice together in an eternal embrace.

A Just and Merciful Community

A Boiler Room Is:
Kind to People by Being a Just and Merciful Community
Where the Practical Needs of the Local Poor Are Met
and Where Liberation Is Championed

This is the first Boiler Room practice to contain two values: mercy and justice. To be honest, we spent a lot of time wondering which one it should be, and ended up with both.

Our heart was to come up with a practice that expressed the call to express kindness to the poor and to those in need. We also wanted to express the need for Boiler Rooms to be places of campaigning and action, where the cause of the oppressed or downtrodden is championed. There is a combined passion to feed the homeless and to advocate on behalf of the homeless—"mercy and justice" sums up these complementary desires. Just like the Celts, we believe Christ is the Champion of the poor. The Celts believed that "prayer and involvement in human needs were deeply entwined."[3]

Mercy is about undeserved grace. In the Old Testament, the Hebrew word *hesed* is often used, referring to right conduct toward fellow men or loyalty to the Lord, or both. In essence, what God requires from us is to love each other and Him. Sometimes the word *hesed* is actually translated "love" (for example, see Hosea 6:4). The dictionary definition of "mercy" includes "forbearance toward one who is in one's power; a forgiving disposition; compassion for the unfortunate."[4]

The understanding of acting *justly* in Israelite law was to not mistreat the alien, widows and orphans. God declared that if "they cry out to me, I will certainly hear their cry" (see Exod. 22:22-27). In the Bible, *justice* shouldn't be denied (see Exod. 23:6) or perverted (see Lev. 19:15). To deliver justice requires wisdom (see 1 Kings 3:28) and discernment (see 1 Kings 3:11). Justice is a way God acts toward mankind, and the cross is the ultimate demonstration (see Rom. 3:25). Justice is also something demanded of us: "Follow justice and justice alone" (Deut. 16:20).

Interestingly, "mercy" and "justice" are often found together in Scripture. In God's call through Zechariah, mirroring a similar message in Micah, mercy and justice are nonnegotiable to obey God:

> This is what the LORD Almighty says: "Administer true justice; show mercy and compassion to one another. Do not oppress the widow or the fatherless, the alien or the poor. In your hearts do not think evil of each other" (Zech. 7:9-10).

Mercy and justice also combine explosively at the cross, where Jesus died in our place and expressed the love and forgiveness of God. True mercy only exists in tandem with just actions. True justice is only expressed when meted out in a merciful way.

The Character of God

God is merciful and God is just.

God's character oozes mercy. It flows from every part of who He is. He delights to show mercy (see Mic. 7:8). Mercy was, and is, the impetus for His redemptive acts (see Isa. 63:9). James saw that "the Lord is full of compassion and mercy" (Jas. 5:11), while the writer to the Hebrews saw the throne of God as the place where mercy is received (see Heb. 4:16). In the life and death of Jesus, we see mercy at work: in the way He relates to people, in the way He treats His ever-stumbling disciples, and in His ultimate act of love on the cross. "But because of His great love for us, God, who is rich in mercy, made us alive with Christ even when we were dead in transgressions—it is by grace that you have been saved" (Eph. 2:4-5).

Justice also flows from the very center of God's character. God loves justice (see Ps. 11:7; Isa. 61:8) and it is the "foundation of [His] throne" (Ps. 89:14). He "will govern the peoples with justice" (Ps. 9:8). Isaiah describes justice as God's "measuring line" (Isa. 28:17). Justice is God's passion:

In faithfulness he will bring forth justice; he will not falter or be discouraged till he establishes justice on earth. In his law the islands will put their hope (Isa. 42:3-4).

Sometimes justice and mercy challenge us because they seem like magnets repelling each other. We meet people in great need who ask for mercy, yet we ask questions of justice. *Is this fair? Do they deserve different treatment than others?* Many questioned the Boiler Room's involvement with the excluded teenagers of Reading. *Who will pay for that broken window? Did we invite trouble when we made friends with these kids?* we asked when another wallet was stolen. Sometimes situations of injustice shattered us and all we wanted to do was give up. Yet the life and death of Jesus spurred us on. At the cross, mercy and justice came together. There, justice was done for our sin and the mercy of God embraced us "while we were still sinners" (Rom. 5:8).

In the *Lord of the Rings*, the relationship between Gollum and Frodo highlights the conflict of justice and mercy. Gollum was a murderer, and Frodo's best friend, Sam, knew he would kill again, given half a chance. Justice demanded Gollum's death, but mercy enabled Frodo to see from the perspective of his own burden of the Ring. He knew it was the Ring that had warped Gollum, and he knew that he could easily walk down that path, too. He remembered the words of Gandalf:

Deserves death! I daresay he does. Many that live deserve death. And some that die deserve life. Can you give that to them? Then be not too eager to deal out death in the name of justice, fearing for your own safety. Even the wise cannot see all ends.[5]

The mercy and justice that beat at the heart of God must become our heartbeat. He has shown us mercy; therefore we should lay down our own lives (see Rom. 12:1). If justice is the foundation of God's throne, it must be the foundation of our lives too (see Zech. 7:9). Will God be merciful to us if we fail to show mercy to others (see Matt. 5:7, Jas. 2:13)? What justice can we expect if we fail to show justice to others (see Isa. 58)? Mercy and justice flow through the character of God. They should flow through us, too.

Made in His Image

God created man in his own image, in the image of God he created him; male and female he created them.
GENESIS 1:27

Consider that for a moment. The people we sit next to in the train, the people who live next door, they're made in the image of God, and the love He has for them is immense. Each one is of value to God (see Ps. 139). He died for us out of love (see John 3:16). He delights in each of us (see Zeph. 3:17).

Boiler Rooms are regularly visited by the street-sleepers in the area. Perhaps it is the spiritual warmth that brings them in, or maybe it's the chance at a nice cup of tea and a warm building. I'm not sure. Whatever the reason, it's a challenge because it makes us feel uncomfortable. Sometimes they smell. Sometimes they're drunk, or their social skills don't qualify them for the local yacht club. To my shame, I've sometimes walked away from the discomfort. But more and more often, God reminds me that He has made all people in His image, and I choose to stay, uncomfortable as it may be.

This truth means that we must treat all persons with respect and dignity. God does, and so should we. God's image imprinted on each individual is the starting point for a practice of mercy and justice. Jesus declared:

For I was hungry and you gave me something to eat, I was thirsty and you gave me something to drink, I was a stranger and you invited me in, I needed clothes and you clothed me, I was sick and you looked after me, I was in prison and you came to visit me (Matt. 25:35-36).

Investing in the Designed, Not the Deserved

There will always be poor people in the land.
Therefore I command you to be openhanded toward your brothers
and toward the poor and needy in your land.
DEUTERONOMY 15:11

Over the last five years, I have made some good friends in a Dutch community called "Foolish Things." This group of Jesus-followers shows mercy in the red-light district and runs a café opposite Central Station in Amsterdam. The café, which is the relational base for their work as well as a business, is called *Dwaze Zaken,* which means "foolish business."

The cross was "foolish business." It made an offer of mercy to a sinful world before we had made a step. Mercy is "foolish business," because it is about *the designed,* those created in God's image, not about the deserving, those who have their act together.

About a month after we opened the Reading Boiler Room, we allowed the building to be used for a Saturday prayer gathering. Intercessors and church people gathered to pray for the young. They called out to God that the young would feel drawn to church, that the church would reach out to them. At the end of the prayer meeting, many of the people approached me to complain about the Goths and Skaters hanging out in the building. They complained that they couldn't park their cars because young people were skateboarding in the parking lot. They complained about the noise from the young people in the prayer room.

They complained about the kids for whom they were praying.

The teenagers of the Forbury were not deserving in the eyes of those who prayed for them that day, but the mercy and justice of the God who had designed them in His own image was already at work. If we want to follow God's lead, we must remember that *none of us* deserves God's mercy, and *all of us* can receive it.

Friends

Day to day at the Reading Boiler Room, we met incredible and courageous young people who challenged almost everything we thought we knew about mercy and justice. The lessons were learned in the context of relationships with young people, with the homeless, with needy families. In Staines, Wandsworth, Calgary and Kansas, the same context has applied: Real learning takes place in real life. Jesus was a "friend of tax collectors and sinners" (Luke 7:34). The difference between being a friend *of* and being a friend *to* sinners is massive. Jesus mapped out the route to real relationship, and He invites us on the same journey.

One of our friends in Reading was Mike, who struggled to attend school regularly for a number of reasons. We chatted often about how school was going, celebrated when he managed a full week of attendance, and stood with him when things weren't so good.

Liz was 14. Most Saturdays, she tried to forget about her week and got drunk with her mates in the park. Often we took her in so that we could be with her when she was sick, and her friends would come in with her and gather round. I was amazed by the sense of commitment these friends had to each other. The sense of community was strong.

We made friends with Paul, who is currently in prison. He was sometimes violent and other times the kindest man you could meet. He lived rough. Once we found him sleeping in an unused railway car. He struggled with drugs and alcohol, and would steal to finance his drug habit. He was eventually arrested and is at the end of a two-year spell in prison at the time of this writing. Paul writes to us and has joined a Bible study group in prison. He recently wrote that he knows "that God is around for him."

These friends are typical of those we met in our two years in the Forbury Vaults. The mercy of God drew the lost and lonely to our door, and the justice of God brought the excluded and downtrodden to challenge us.

The Church: Reshaping the Existing Order

"The method of the church's impact on society at large should be twofold. First, the church must announce Christian principles and point out where the existing social order is in conflict with them. Second, it must then pass on to Christian citizens, acting in their civic capacities, the task of re-shaping the existing in order in closer conformity to its principles."[6]

William Temple, Archbishop of York, wrote this challenge in the 1940s to a Church that played a major role in society and social change. Sixty years later, economic and social injustice are often hidden and those in need are those outside of the system's reach. Now as much as ever, the Church is called to be an agent of change.

> Say no to wrong. Learn to do good. Work for justice. Help
> the down-and-out. Stand up for the homeless. Go to bat
> for the defenseless (Isa. 1:13-17, *THE MESSAGE*).

This justice mandate must be expressed both locally and globally. God's Spirit might prompt us to show mercy through practical care for prostitutes who walk our streets at night, and may prompt us to oppose the injustices at the root of prostitution. But the reality is that we live in a time of global injustice, where the needy often finance the growth and success of the richer nations. In these times of unprecedented global connections, the Church must show mercy and act justly both at home and abroad.

Standing with the Wronged

To act justly means we should be angered by injustice. To show mercy means to stand with people who are wronged.

Jesus walked out to John in the desert to be baptized. John couldn't believe that the Messiah was coming to *him*! "I need to be baptized by you, and do you come to me?" (Matt. 3:14). But Jesus insisted, "to fulfill all righteousness," to be obedient to His Father, to fulfill prophecy, but also to identify, to stand with the people He had come to save.

Jesus "did not consider equality with God something to be grasped" (Phil. 2:6), and He gave up His glory to become flesh and blood and move into the neighborhood (see John 1:14). John baptized for the forgiveness of sins, yet here was the sinless Christ, waiting in line to be baptized. Why? Because He chose to stand with humanity, with the lost, with the poor, with the wronged. He chose to stand with the people. Jesus was a friend of the poor, and He hung out with sinners and tax collectors. He did not come to "call the righteous, but sinners" (Matt. 9:13). He had compassion on the crowds, cared for the outcasts, had tea with a tax collector, and allowed Himself to be anointed by a prostitute. He stood up to the Pharisees when they blocked the door to God. He stood for the left out and left behind, and we must do the same.

Practicing Mercy and Justice

Our God is a God who acts. His hand still intervenes on behalf of the defenseless. He gets involved.

> The victim's faint pulse picks up; the hearts of the hopeless pump red blood as you put your ear to their lips. Orphans get parents, the homeless get homes. The reign of terror is over, the rule of gang lords is ended (Ps. 10:17-18, *THE MESSAGE*).

We can live out a life committed to kindness, to justice and mercy. It is not an unattainable dream. But a life of mercy and justice requires action. Like Peter, we need to get out of the boat (see Matt. 14:22-36). As I've approached trying to live justly, I've found the following four responses to be helpful.

1. Respond to the Poor

Each Boiler Room asks itself questions: How will the poor be affected by what we do today? Will they be welcome? Will our choices and decisions affect them? Will that effect be positive or negative?

Many consider poverty an issue for the developing world, but in the West, poverty cuts a powerful, often invisible, swathe. In the United States in 2005, 35.1 million people lived below the poverty line (11 percent of the population), and 12.4 million of those were children. That same year, an estimated 24 to 27 million people turned to agencies for help.[7] Poverty is not just a Third World problem.

There are poor people in your community and probably in your church. Maybe unemployment or sickness has contributed to the need, but poverty is there. How will your community of faith respond?

> *Like slavery and apartheid, poverty is not natural.*
> *It is manmade and it can be overcome.*
>
> NELSON MANDELA[8]

2. Respond to Need

Many Boiler Rooms live out this part of the Rule simply by responding to needs that turn up, whether with disadvantaged children in Kansas City, excluded young people in Staines, or First Nations people in Calgary. Boiler Rooms try to help when they're asked.

This can be done in partnership with other organizations. If you feel challenged to feed the homeless in your community, look around you. Someone is already doing it, and perhaps you can partner and support rather than reinvent the wheel. Why not call your local homeless shelter and ask how you can help? It's tempting to start a project ourselves, but sometimes the biggest solution we can bring to the problem is our time. Sometimes, the last thing we need is the limelight.

> *Nurture a love to do good things in secret . . .*
> *be content to go without praise.*
>
> JEREMY TAYLOR, ENGLISH CLERGYMAN[9]

3. Respond with Prayer

Sometimes we can't fix the problem, but our prayers can move mountains. Our actions must be accompanied by passionate and persistent prayer. We must live as though it all depends on us, and pray as though it all depends on Him.

And will not God bring about justice for his chosen ones,
who cry out to him day and night?
LUKE 18:7

4. Respond with Action

We can play a part in changing the world. I'll end this chapter with some personal notes about an issue that is important to me and challenge you to pray for God's leading toward an issue of local or global injustice that will become your passion. When it becomes clear to you, decide to take action and campaign for change.

Over the last year, I have felt challenged to respond to the global arms trade, one of the more hidden injustices in our world. In 2004, one-third of the world's population was at war, which contributes to poverty, human suffering and to many of the social and economic problems faced in the neediest parts of our world. Despite promising an "ethical foreign policy" upon coming to power in 1997, the British government continues to sell arms to 15 of the world's poorest countries.[10]

In December 2001, a deal to sell a $55 million radar system to Tanzania was publicized. This to a country with an average income of about $400 a year! In the face of ongoing global conflicts and the absurdity of poor nations borrowing money for weapons, the five biggest arms dealers are the five permanent members of the UN Security Council: Britain, the United States, France, China and Russia.

I believe this is a justice issue. In countries where people are starving, governments are borrowing money to purchase arms, and the richest nations on the planet make a profit. If I am to practice mercy and justice, I must respond with action, standing with the wronged and opposing those who would extort them.

He has showed you, O man, what is good.
And what does the Lord require of you? To act justly and to
love mercy and to walk humbly with your God.

MICAH 6:8

For Further Thought

Engage with a local issue of justice or mercy. Volunteer for a night at a local shelter for the homeless. Go out with a charity working with needy families. Buy a meal for a street sleeper and sit down to chat with him or her. Commit to research an issue of global injustice. Take time to review both issues after one month to see what you have learned and how you might be able to get involved long-term.

Liturgy

Leader: Lord, You are God of the nations.

All: Let justice roll on like a river and righteousness like a never-failing stream.

Leader: Lord, You place kings and leaders on their thrones.

All: Let justice roll on like a river and righteousness like a never-failing stream.

Leader: Lord, You see the dark places of our cities.

All: Let justice roll on like a river and righteousness like a never-failing stream.

Leader: Lord, You are the defender of the widow and the orphan.

All: Let justice roll on like a river and righteousness like a never-failing stream.

Leader: Lord, we pray for the poor and for the downtrodden.

All: Let justice roll on like a river and righteousness like a never-failing stream. Lord, forgive us when we organize our meetings, only to forget the poor. May justice and righteousness be present in our churches and in the way we live our lives. Amen.

CHAPTER 10

The Practice of Hospitality and Pilgrimage

Offer hospitality to one another.
1 PETER 4:9

The Celtic church reminds us that we were born to quest,
and that pilgrimage is at the heart of our Christian discipleship.
MICHAEL MITTON[1]

Why is the last mile the hardest mile?
THE SMITHS, "IS IT REALLY SO STRANGE?"[2]

Everybody's on a journey.

The Beatles tried to express it in "Long and Winding Road." We are captivated by adventurers such as Everest-climber Edmund Hilary, South Pole-explorer Sir Shackleton, hot air balloon pilots Piccard and Jones, and astronauts like Neil Armstrong and John Glenn. Nelson Mandela traveled his *Long Walk to Freedom,* presidential candidates race on the *Road to the White House* and Olympians run their "road to gold." There are bands that live their entire lives on tour and wanderers that spend years living out of backpacks. Whether real or symbolic, we're all on a journey.

One of my heroines of 2005 was Ellen MacArthur, yachtswoman and now world-record holder for a solo around-the-world trip. On February 8, 2005, she sailed into Plymouth in the UK to break the record. Her diary of the trip speaks of both fear and courage and reminds me strangely of my own life experiences (metaphorically!).

Day 37

Things have been quite tough. My skin was stung by hefty hailstones as I watched the storm pass over. They were banging into me, clattering off the deck, so they must have been hitting hard. I managed a few hours of troubled sleep. I dragged myself off the floor where I was huddled in my oilskins under a fleece blanket and looked at the sky to see yet another demon black cloud. Though the night was hard and exhausting, there was a really beautiful aspect—the sunset was magnificent with the orange glow lighting up the waves. It's amazing to see the darkest clouds blacken the boat before it glowed as if before a winter's fire. It was just stunning.[3]

When I first read that section of her diary, I began to reflect on the many things God had done and spoken to me over the last five years. The theme of "journey" was the loudest and most persistent. My life was a day-by-day journey with God, along difficult paths, through good days and bad. I reflected on the many storms I had faced, of the days when it had seemed like the hailstones were battering me. I began to remember that even in those days, God had revealed shafts of light, which brought great beauty in the midst of sadness.

A Community of Hospitality and Pilgrimage

A Boiler Room Is:
Kind to People by Being a Hospitable Community
Where Pilgrims Are Welcomed, Meals Are Shared
and Where Friendships Can Flourish
Across Boundaries of Race and Culture

It has been said that the longest journey is the journey inward. Like so many of my recent lessons, the inward journey echoes throughout Christian history.

Almost from the beginning of the Christian Church, people have embarked on pilgrimages, which are symbolic of the inward journey. Pilgrims sometimes visited a holy site, as in Geoffrey Chaucer's *Canterbury Tales.* Some travelers embarked on their pilgrimage in fulfillment of a vow by visiting Rome, the epicenter of the Church. Others walked out on a pilgrimage simply in a crazy desire to follow God.

In the summer of 2005, I was excited to spend time with a number of young people heading out on "mobile mission teams." Nomadic in nature, these teams traveled all over Europe, city to city, to connect with friends and churches, to pray for Europe, to meet strangers and to make themselves available for God to use them. Most of all, the goal of these teams was to be led by Jesus—to stay or to go as they felt Him speak. Often they would wake in the morning and pray, asking whether or not it was time to move on. As they reported back to the Boiler Rooms, they told of unexpected encounters, of encouraging believers and of God moving in their lives.

The impetus behind the mobile mission teams was the pilgrimage impulse. In Reading we learned that pilgrimage was a practice that our Benedictine brothers embraced hundreds of years before us, and found that this was yet another practice God wanted to renew.

We would like to rekindle the pilgrimage that occurred as a part of everyday life during the time of the Abbey, by inviting teams from all over the world to work in our town. We would like to receive guests and to offer them hospitality.
FROM THE READING BOILER ROOM'S ORIGINAL BROCHURE
(SEPTEMBER 2001)

A *pilgrimage* is "a journey made to a holy place as an act of devotion."[4] The word comes from the Latin word *peregrinato*, which means "resident alien," and helps us make sense of 1 Peter 2:11, in which Peter describes the Christians he is writing to as "aliens and strangers in the world." Christians are on a lifelong pilgrimage to the Holy Place.

The writer to the Hebrews refers to us as "strangers and pilgrims on the earth" (Heb. 11:13, *KJV*). As "aliens" in the world, we recognize that our home is in another place and that here on Earth we must "stay mobile," traveling toward our real home.

Going on a sacred journey has always been a part of the Christian tradition and is seen regularly in the Bible, even if the word "pilgrimage" became more prevalent later. Abram began his calling with a journey (see Gen. 12:1). After Isaac was born, God called Abraham to journey to Mount Moriah so that God could test him (see Gen. 22:2).

As Israel became a nation, the practice of religious feasts was established, and Jewish families journeyed to Jerusalem to take part. We can read how, as a boy, Jesus accompanied His family on one such journey (see Luke 2:41-42). The ministry of Jesus was characterized by a nomadic and traveling lifestyle, which is a picture (as the Celtic saint Columbanus observed) that "Christians must travel in perpetual pilgrimage as guests of the world."[5] Jesus shared how "the Son of Man has no place to lay his head" (Matt. 8:20). When He sent out His disciples, they too were to travel, relying on others' hospitality. Indeed, the welcome they received would be an indicator of how ready the person was to receive the Good News (Luke 10:5-12). Some traditions have almost forgotten the importance of pilgrimage, but Scripture's "Spirit journeys" show us that God loves mobility—He's always telling us to "Go!"

Hospitality is a much-mentioned topic in the Bible, but an under-taught ministry in our local churches. Paul exhorted the Roman Christians to "share with God's people who are in need" and to "practice hospitality" (Rom. 12:13), but I think we have lost the deep sense of honor associated with the word "hospitality." In Old Testament times, "hospitality" implied care and protection as well as food and a bed. Abraham was a practitioner of hospitality. When three men came to visit him (one secretly being God Himself), Abraham was desperate to help. He acted as a servant to them and gave them a wonderful meal. To Abraham, receiving guests was a favor to *him*.

If I have found favor in your eyes, my lord, do not pass your
servant by (Gen. 18:3).

Hospitality was more than just a ritual. The Israelites saw it as
a sign of their commitment to God (see Job 31:32; Isa. 58:7). Maybe,
as Abraham had done, they would actually be hosting Yahweh (see
Judg. 6:17-23; 13:15-21). In Genesis 19:8, Lot put himself at risk for
the sake of those he had taken in. There are many stories (for example, the Levite in Judges 19:23) where much is sacrificed for the sake
of protecting a guest. *The NIV Study Bible* notes, "ancient hospitality obliged a host to protect his guests in every situation."[6]

In the New Testament, we again find a strong current of hospitality. To some extent, the ministry of Jesus and the apostles was
dependent on the kindness of hosts. Paul's missionary journeys
were possible in large part because of those who cared for him, such
as Gaius, whom he commended in Romans 16:23. We also read
about widows who supported the growing movement of missionaries by offering hospitality (see 1 Tim. 5:9-10; 3 John 1:8).

At its essence, hospitality is about opening doors and hearts to
visitors. It is about a bed and good food. It is about friendship and
protection. And it is a practice that God values highly. Hospitality
and pilgrimage intersect as we look inward to provide for wanderers and travelers, and then outward to God's world.

"I Was a Stranger"
The God of Hospitality

God is hospitable. In Psalm 23, David describes God as a host:
preparing a table, anointing his head with oil, filling his cup.
God's hospitality is so warm, so inviting, that David's desire is to
"dwell in the house of the LORD forever" (v. 6). In Psalm 5, David
delights at being "your invited guest" (v. 7, *THE MESSAGE*), a par-
allel to Jesus' parable of the banquet, in which the King invites the
broken, homeless and hungry to His table.

It is striking that in Jesus' parable of the sheep and the goats
in Matthew 25, He associated Himself with strangers: "I was a

stranger and you invited me in" (v. 35). Jesus identified Himself with a traveler needing care, and was delighted when His followers offered hospitality to "the least of these brothers of mine" (v. 40). It was from this verse that Saint Benedict constructed the element of his Rule declaring that strangers should be welcomed and cared for as though they were Christ Himself.

Ray Simpson suggests that "Hospitality is a sign that a community is alive, that it is not afraid, that it has something valuable to share."[7] It expresses the life and love of Christ by answering the call to care for "the least" who walks through the door.

At his monastery in Derry, Columbanus answered the call by feeding nearly 1,000 people a day. At Reading Abbey, travelers could always find a bed and a meal. Along the famous ways of pilgrimage, like the Way of Saint James in Spain, monasteries sprang up to care for strangers who came to their door each night.

Journeying God

Kanye West sings that "Jesus Walks." According to Scripture, this is true. In Eden, God walked in the cool of the evening with Adam and Eve (see Gen. 3:8). He walked with some of the disciples on the Emmaus Road (see Luke 24:13-35). In Micah 6:8, which we considered in the previous chapter, the prophet called the people to "walk humbly with your God."

It's interesting to note that Micah's call to walk "with your God" is not a call to walk *behind* Him, crawling in the dust at His feet. He invites us to walk *with* Him. God is mobile and calls us to go with Him: to come and follow, to take up our crosses, to go.

The Celts have much to teach us about pilgrimage and the character of the God who invites us to come along. They described the Holy Spirit as the "Wild Goose" because they saw Him as undomesticated and on the move (see John 3:8). Their "Wild Goose chases" were pilgrimages that reflected the wildness of God and the wild abandon He calls us to in following Him.

The story goes that three Irishmen set sail in a tiny boat and were swept across the Irish Sea to Cornwall. When they disembarked, they were captured as suspected spies and taken to the court of King

Alfred. When they were asked their business, they responded that they "wanted for the love of God to be on a pilgrimage, we cared not where."[8]

Legend has it that the Irish monk Brendan jumped in a boat with 14 friends and discovered America eight centuries before Christopher Columbus!

An Irish proverb concludes, "Your feet will bring you where your heart is."[9] The Father of Creation, who made us and delights in leading us to a place of full life (see John 10:10), wants us to journey with Him, to let our hearts be led by His.

The Outward Journey

God has challenged us from day one in our Boiler Rooms to be mobile: to journey *with* God, to journey *after* God, to journey *for* God. Psalm 17:4-5 declares that "I'm staying on your trail; I'm putting one foot in front of the other. I'm not giving up" (*THE MESSAGE*).

Sometimes this mobility means we go out into the local community to serve the poor or share about Jesus. Sometimes it means making connections with other countries. In Reading, it called us to lose our building and become homeless for more than a year. As we journeyed around student houses, church halls and spent time out on the streets, we learned to be mobile.

When we travel, the presence of God is both a comfort and a catalyst. As Moses asked, why should we go if He does not go with us? God's presence with the Israelites in the desert was the power behind and the reason for their journey (see Exod. 33:14-16).

Celtic missionaries believed that they would find God upon their arrival only if He walked with them the entire way. "I shall not find Christ at the end of my journey unless he accompanies me along the way."[10] This model of mobility and journeying has many things to teach us in our postmodern world:

- *Outward journeys can act as symbols of our inward life.* In his thesis "Pilgrimage as a Rite of Passage: A Guidebook for Youth Ministry," Robert Brancatelli suggests pilgrimage as a way of outwardly expressing the change from child to adult.[11] A young person's journey encompasses separation (by leaving home and family; see Luke 15:11-16), an in-between period at a border or frontier (the crossing into adulthood; see Luke 15:17-20) and then reintegration (returning home, sharing stories and embracing changes to character; see Luke 15:20-24).

• *Pilgrimage makes us available for mission.* Four years ago, two of my good friends, Dave and Maz, set off to Australia with their backpacks and a camper van. Their visit wasn't a holiday. Their vision was to be evangelists and pastors among the backpacking community in Australia and New Zealand. Four years later, they returned home with a growing ministry established, a website launched (www.backpackingisit.com), a Backpackers Bible produced and, most important, a large number of people touched and changed by the gospel of Jesus.

• *Pilgrimage answers an inward cry to journey.* We have been staggered by the number of people who have journeyed to visit us in Reading and since at other Boiler Rooms. People from all over the globe have answered a call to *go*, and for most, the *going* is as important as the arrival. We have become more and more convinced that God is reigniting the Celtic passion to pilgrimage "for the love of God, we care not where."

The Inward Welcome

In his wonderful book *Community and Growth,* Jean Vanier champions the principle of welcoming. To welcome people "is to give space to someone in one's heart."[12] Being welcoming is a sign that a community is alive rather than closed (which is, in turn, a "sign that hearts are closing as well"). To be welcoming is a central pillar of the L'Arche community that Vanier writes about: "It is a constant openness of the heart, it is saying to people every morning and at every moment, Come in."[13]

The hardest thing about hospitality is to be welcoming. Sometimes hospitality is a joy. When an old friend or a fascinating new acquaintance arrives, it can be exhilarating to spend time, to have them in your home or your city, to share your time with them. Other times, though, hospitality is hard. A visitor may be overly demanding. Guests may overrun your house when you crave some space. The logistics of preparing meals and providing a bed just don't seem to come together. Vanier writes, "the stranger disturbs because he or she cannot enter into our patterns of thought or our ways of doing things."[14] To the beloved friend and to the challenging stranger, our call is to say they are welcome, to open our doors and our hearts to everyone who comes to our door.

In Luke 7, a "sinful woman" anoints Jesus during a meal at a Pharisee's house. As other guests look on in shock, the woman weeps at His feet, washes them with her tears. She wipes His feet with her hair, kisses them and pours perfume over them. The guests begin to question His behavior: "If this man were a prophet he would know who is touching him and what kind of woman she is—that she is a sinner."

Jesus' response is to acknowledge and affirm the woman's worship. He chooses to show the worth of her actions by honoring the welcome that the woman had given Him contrasted with the lack of welcome His host had shown:

- "*You did not give me any water for my feet, but she wet my feet with her tears and wiped them with her hair*" (v. 44). Washing guests' feet was the minimal form of hospitality at that time. Feet became dusty and dirty from walking and feet were washed as regularly as we offer a visitor a seat or a cup of coffee. To be welcoming involves a practical concern for the guests' needs: a shower, a meal, a bed, information about his or her onward journey . . . whatever is practically needed.

- "*You did not give me a kiss, but this woman, from the time I entered, has not stopped kissing my feet*" (v. 45). A kiss was a usual part of the Jewish greeting, and Jesus' host had failed to greet Him warmly. Paul often encouraged his readers to greet one another with a holy kiss (see Rom. 16:16; 1 Cor. 16:20). To be welcoming, we must open our hearts as well as our doors. We must be prepared to show love, even to the unlovely.

- *"You did not put oil on my head, but she has poured perfume on my feet"* (v. 46). Anointing a guest with oil was a traditional way of honoring a guest (see Ps. 23:5). The host in this case failed to honor Jesus, possibly because he was skeptical of Him. The woman, in contrast, poured oil on His feet and showed honor. How can we honor the needs of our guest before our own? What would bless them? How can we help them feel valued or special to us? How can we communicate to them that they are important to us and to God?

The story of the woman in Luke 7 gives us some important lessons in how to welcome. We should never forget that the Pharisee, the religious leader, was the unwelcoming one while the woman, probably a prostitute, was the one who showed welcome. She let down her hair, something Jewish women only did before making love. She brought a jar of perfume, perhaps a tool of her trade. She wept before Him, in the middle of a highbrow dinner party. And Jesus embraced the whole, seemingly sordid, thing.

Not all guests will be easy. Not all guests will bless you as they visit. Our call, however, is to wash their feet. Our call is to open our hearts, to give them a kiss. Our call is to honor and value them, to anoint them with oil. This is what it means to welcome.

The Practice of Hospitality and Pilgrimage

In this final section, I want to suggest a few practical steps that we've learned in trying to live out the practice of hospitality and pilgrimage. This list is far from exhaustive but gives some basic ideas.

Going on a Pilgrimage

I woke that Easter morning feeling slightly apprehensive. We were ending a weekend of special activities to celebrate Easter: a meditation on Maundy Thursday, a labyrinth, special times of prayer on Good Friday and Easter Sunday. All these events had helped us focus our minds on the cross and resurrection. Now it was Monday, and I was nervous because today we had planned a pilgrimage.

Our aim was to walk from just outside Stonehenge in Wiltshire to Salisbury Cathedral. Pete had assured me it was "only a few miles." When we arrived at our starting point, my nerves increased when I saw that Salisbury was nearly 11 miles away. Had I ever walked that far?

So we walked . . . and walked . . . and walked. By the end of the day, I think I was a few inches shorter. It took me *ages* to recover. But . . . it was strangely amazing. As we walked, we talked. The sense of fellowship was wonderful.

As we walked, we encouraged. It was time to build each other up. It was time to listen and to affirm.

As we walked, we prayed. The sense of God with us was mysterious. What were we doing? Wasn't this some glorified ramble? No. God was there, and I was acutely aware that I wanted to journey with Him. For the last six miles of the journey, we could see the huge spire of Salisbury Cathedral in front of us, drawing us forward. It reminded us of Hebrews 12:2: "Let us fix our eyes on Jesus, the author and perfecter of our faith." As we homed in on the spire, we sensed that we were homing in on Jesus.

As we walked, we journeyed. We took in our surroundings. We met other walkers. We said hello to those we met. We had some conversations. Our pilgrimage took us into the world of journeying. We had an empathy with other walkers. It connected us with a traveling world. The day ended with evening prayer at Salisbury Cathedral and then a pizza together. God was present when we arrived, just as He had been present as we journeyed.

A pilgrimage can take many forms:

- An established or traditional pilgrimage, such as the Way of Saint James in Spain, a journey to Canterbury Cathedral in England, or a journey to World Youth Day for a Catholic teenager

- A mobile mission team, taking an everyday travel route, such as inter-railing through Europe or following a well-used walk

- A virtual pilgrimage: learning about a country, praying for its needs, maybe joining a chat room or discussion to meet some of the people

- An individual pilgrimage to a special site. This could be part of the fulfilling of a vow, a return to a special place or simply a chance for some alone time with God.

- A spontaneous journey. Follow a hunch or calling to visit a place, attend a meeting, or journey somewhere to pray.

Receiving Guests

A central plank of Boiler Room hospitality is providing accommodations, but how does this work in practice? In Reading we were lucky enough to find a building with enough space for visitors' rooms. At a stretch, we could accommodate 16. This was an incredible blessing.

Not every Boiler Room has this sort of space, but we recommend the following:

- Setting aside a couple of rooms to house visitors
- Using a nearby house that is available
- Letting families who wish to provide hospitality take in pilgrims
- Using a nearby bed and breakfast or hostel accommodation

In Manchester, the team equipped a spare room with a bunk bed and received visitors throughout their time in Didsbury. In Calgary, the team spread visitors across their own homes, especially in a community house near the outskirts of the city.

When receiving guests, we find it important to include them in as much of the community's life as possible. We invite them to meals, introduce them to people we work with and take them on mission or mercy projects.

Most important, though, is the task of slowing them down and introducing them to a rhythm of prayer. We ask all our visiting pilgrims to join in with the life of the community and pray for at least an hour a day.

Shared Meals

It has been said that "God is in the details." One of these details, when it comes to hospitality, is meals. I believe in eating. There is something dynamic that takes place when we eat together. There is some sense of connection that takes place when we sit together over a table full of food.

In Celtic monasteries, food was an important part of hospitality. Saint Brigid was famed for her food. Records tell how she sang and prayed in her kitchen as she prepared incredible meals. Saint Hilda reconciled divided leaders by offering them hospitality, food and prayer.

Many current or planned Boiler Rooms are developing a weekly pattern of open or shared meals. The team, resident communities, visiting pilgrims and anyone else are invited to break bread together. It's a pattern I learned from the team in Ayia Napa, where a meal brought together all the threads of the day, and was a place to welcome people into their community. It was amazingly powerful.

Jean Varnier concludes, "A meal is an important community event which has to be well prepared and fully lived."

Opening Our Doors

In the spring of 2005, a new pope was elected in Rome, with the famous white smoke rising from the chimney at the Vatican.

Cardinal Joseph Ratzinger took the name of one of the fathers of hospitality in the Church: Benedict. A few weeks later, we ran across this passage from philosopher and theologian Alasdair MacIntyre:

> What matters at this stage is the construction of local forms of community within which civility and the intellectual and moral life can be sustained through the new dark ages which are already upon us . . . We are waiting not for a Godot, but for another—doubtless very different—Saint Benedict.[15]

Hospitality is making a comeback! At the center of every living faith community are people who have hands open to serve in hospitality and hearts ready to follow God "we care not where." We can do neither if our doors are closed. We must open our doors and hearts.

For Further Thought

Spend some time considering how you might express this element of the Rule in your own community. Experiment by clearing out a spare room and receiving guests. Organize a pilgrimage for your group or plan a mobile mission team.

Liturgy

By day the Lord went ahead of them
in a pillar of cloud to guide them on their way
and by night in a pillar of fire to give them light,
so that they could travel by day or night.

EXODUS 13:21

A Journeying Prayer

Jesus, take me once again on a journey.
Take me to the city,
Take me to the valley and to the mountain,
Take me to the desert.
Take me to the place of wandering,
The place of hunger,
The place of solitude and of pain.
Take me to the place where You seem so far away
Yet only You are there.
Remove my crutches of possessions,
Remove the pillars of my faithless life,
Remove all the thumbs I suck.
And there in that place where nothing is left,
There refine my soul.
Amen.

Not used

Chapter 11

The Practice of Mission

Your message burns in my heart and bones, and I cannot keep silent.
JEREMIAH 20:9, CEV

These [Celtic] communities acted as mission stations
which trained men and women in preaching and healing,
and sent them out on missions.
MICHAEL MITTON[1]

I was on the inside when they pulled the four walls down
I was looking through the window, I was lost, I am found.
U2, "I WILL FOLLOW"[2]

I'm convinced that prayer is a dangerous thing.

Many people throughout history have found out this truth. Hudson Taylor learned it in prayer on Brighton Beach when God called him to China. Martin Luther King, Jr. learned it when he prayed for racial freedom in 1960s United States. Nehemiah prayed for God to save his ruined city and found himself going to do the job. The Church in Acts prayed for boldness to preach the gospel, and as the walls of their meeting room shook, they were catapulted out to the four corners of the earth to establish the Church of Christ.

In September 1999, members of Revelation Church in central London gathered to light a candle and pray nonstop for a month.

Six years later, a worldwide prayer movement has changed the lives of those involved and has touched people all over the earth. Prayer is dangerous.

Beautiful Boys Town

Kelly Greene is one of the people who had her life rerouted by God and became involved with this mad movement called 24-7. Kelly is from Tulsa, Oklahoma. She was in Mexico with a team from her church when, through a series of cancellations and last-minute changes, they found themselves in Reynosa, a largish town near the border. They began to pray around the town, and just as Kelly's mind was beginning to wonder where to go for lunch, they came across Boys Town.

Boys Town is a walled city where drugs, violence and prostitution are the norm. It's said around those parts, "Once you enter Boys Town, you will never leave." The wall keeps the trouble away from the other residents of Reynosa and keeps the thousands of inhabitants in. Boys Town is a drug-tolerance zone. It has one entrance and one exit.

Kelly prayed a prayer, one of those dangerous prayers, that God would send someone to shine a light in this dark and desperate place. A few months later, that someone arrived in Boys Town. The only problem was that the person God sent was the author of that prayer: Kelly Greene.

We first heard from Kelly in early 2005. Arriving in Mexico, Kelly was handed a copy of *Red Moon Rising*[3] and felt God speak to her about a Boiler Room in Boys Town that would be a base of prayer, mercy, hospitality and mission for the residents of the walled city. Kelly began to visit the area regularly, just walking around and praying. No one would talk to her. Some people just stared. But, after months and months of prayerful wandering, things began to happen. She began to form friendships. Openings appeared. God began to work out her dangerous prayers.

In January 2006, Kelly wrote to us again:

The streets of Boys Town are littered with evidence of the previous night's activities (used condoms, empty beer bottles, etc.) and yet, I want to tell you it's beautiful. I'm not sure if words can contain the work of Jesus here. The doorways are darkened by women who have been stripped of their humanity, mere robots who are programmed to do only one thing. They don't feel anything anymore, partly because they're strung out on God knows what, and partly because they have had to turn off their feelings in order to survive another day. But tell them Jesus loves them, and their faces change. Admittedly, some of them struggle to believe it's true, but you can see that they want so badly to surrender to the pull of Jesus' love.

Since then, we have seen God begin to do incredible things in Boys Town. In April 2006, a team from the Kansas City Boiler Room drove down to spend some time with Kelly and see things for themselves. That visit opened new doors, as Kelly was able to go into Boys Town at night for the first time. Juli Cato from Kansas takes up the story:

So much took place in those next few hours. Kelly describes it as one of the most amazing experiences of her life. We had a great time in the bar that night (one of the bars where the federal police allow open drug sales) as Nate Chud, Tim York, Dan Jones and John Arndt went crazy on guitars and drums, with everything from "Twist and Shout" to "Where the Spirit of the Lord Is, There Is Freedom." (By the way, during that song, an older Mexican lady got on the pole and began to dance to it. Don't worry, she had all her clothes on, but I am sure we will never be able to sing that song in worship in the same way again.)

Jacqueline was working behind the bar and began to cry as Kelly walked up to talk to her. She said, "Thank you for coming, thank you for coming here." She told Kelly that the night before had meant so much to her and that her parents had been praying for her and she wanted prayer before we left. So Kelly and I went back to her room to pray with her. Kelly encouraged her to pray first and she told God she wanted to get out of Boys Town, that she wanted to come back to Him and change her life. What an amazing moment to be part of! After a year of diligent prayer and pursuing people, the first prostitute came to Jesus in a real way.

Prayer is dangerous. Look what happened when Kelly Greene engaged in a simple prayer for the people of Boys Town. Her prayer echoed back to her in God's call to go, to be the answer in His strength. Kelly's prayer changed her life and is now changing the lives of others.

If our prayers can be so dangerous, should we pray them? Maybe if we realized their power, we might be a little more cautious before we say our "Amen." Yet prayer without mission is empty. How can we pray for those who are lost in our world without being prepared to go ourselves? Our Incarnate God didn't simply say He loved. He lived out the "Go of God"[4] by coming to us, living with us and dying for us.

Boiler Rooms are communities that pray for the lost and that practice being communities of mission.

A Community of Mission

A Boiler Room Is:
Committed to Taking the Gospel to the World
by Being a Missional Community
Existing for the Incarnation and Proclamation of the Gospel
to All People, to Act as Well as to Pray

Throughout the history of the Christian Church, people have endangered themselves to tell others about Jesus. Into danger, into trouble, into death, these messengers have kept going. They have broken taboos, broken laws, broken boundaries, all in the name of mission.

All authority in heaven and on earth has been given to me. Therefore go and make disciples of all nations, baptizing them in the name of the Father and of the Son and of the Holy Spirit, and teaching them to obey everything I have commanded you. And surely I am with you always, to the very end of the age (Matt. 28:18-20).

Last words are pretty important. You hear of inspiring speeches before a difficult situation. You remember famous last sentences, even when they are layered with irony or tragedy. Here, Jesus is about to ascend to heaven; His time on Earth since His resurrection is complete. Among His disciples, He says His last words: He sends them.

Jesus begins by confirming that "all authority" has been given to Him. Paul fleshes this out in Philippians 2: Jesus had authority before He came to Earth as a human, yet "being in very nature God, did not consider equality with God something to be grasped, but made himself nothing" (vv. 6-7). Jesus chose to be a servant, to be restricted within a human body. Paul goes on to say that "being found in appearance as a man, he humbled himself and became obedient to death—even death on a cross" (vv. 7-8). Jesus Himself was sent; He had a mission. The Father said, "Go," and He did, to reveal the Father, to care for the sick, to seek out the lost sheep, and eventually to die and rise again, His mission accomplished.

Verses 9 to 11 tell us that because of His willingness to go, God exalted Him to "the highest place" (v. 9) and declared that "at the name of Jesus every knee should bow" (v. 10). When Jesus reminds His disciples of His authority, we remember that this authority was given up for us and then reclaimed because of His obedience to His mission.

Jesus then gives His instruction to *go*. This was not a new call. The Bible uses the word 1,514 times! The Gospel of Matthew alone uses the word 54 times, ending with the risen Jesus saying, "Go and make disciples of all nations." As with all the other practices we have looked at, our beginning point is Christ Himself.

Jesus was on a mission. Jesus talked about mission. Jesus is missional now, calling the people of the world to Him. And out of that place He calls us to go:

In the same way that you gave me a mission in the world, I gave them a mission in the world (John 17:18, *THE MESSAGE*).

The disciples were called to go to a variety of situations: to their neighborhood in Jerusalem, to their nation Judea, to their enemies in Samaria, and to "the ends of the earth" (Acts 1:8).

Mission is about being sent. "Mission" is not a three-week trip to Africa; it's a life lived because Jesus has sent us . . . across the street, just as much as across the seas. Mission is an echo of Christ's mission to us. It is beating in time with the heart of God, longing to be in relationship with the peoples of the world. It is a response to the repetitive call to go and is a natural response to finding Jesus. Mark records that "the disciples went out and preached everywhere" (Mark 16:20), and Luke wrote an entire book (Acts) that chronicles the disciples' response to the call to go.

Mission flows from God Himself. Our love for Him sends us to love others. God sends, Christ was sent to us and now we are sent out to "make disciples."

Watching for the Prodigal Son

Jesus told good stories. They were set in the ordinary, in the everyday lives of His listeners. They were unexpected, they had twists and turns and they often surprised or even shocked. His story of the Lost Son (Luke 15) is no exception.

Jesus told of a son who wished his father were dead. He demanded his inheritance, the money he was due when his dad passed away. Amazingly, his father agreed to give him the cash. That in itself was probably enough to enrage Jesus' audience. *How could the father be so stupid? He should stand up to this unruly son!* But the father agreed and off the son went for several months of fun.

Luke, in typical understatement, tells how he "squandered his wealth on wild living." You can imagine the parties, clothes, jewels and entertainment that he would have indulged in. Soon all the son's money was gone and then a famine came. He had to feed pigs (the crowds would have gasped at this detail—working with unclean animals was the most demeaning job imaginable for a Jew) just to avoid starving.

Then the son has a brainwave: He'll return home and work for his dad! He knows he's no longer worthy to be called a son, but the life of a hired hand would be loads better than what he's enduring now. So off he goes.

Most of us already know the outcome of this incredible story, but those first hearers would have been staggered. *The father welcomes him!* He runs to the wayward son, something considered undignified for a Jewish man. He gives him a signet ring and a long robe, signs of honor. He places shoes on his feet, a signal of his move from slave to son (slaves went barefoot) . . . and then *he throws a party.*

It must have been a shocking story—the indignant reaction of the second son may be a mirror of the listeners' reaction—yet this is the welcome we receive when we come back to God. My favorite line highlights the love that God has for those who are as yet outside His global family of love, those who are "lost":

But while he was still a long way off, his father saw him and was filled with compassion for him (Luke 15:20).

How did the father see the son so far off? Was it just luck? Did the father just happen to be looking to the horizon that day and there his son was? Maybe. In my imagination, I see the father's daily ritual of looking to the horizon, searching and hoping that his son would be there at the end of the road. For months, maybe years he had gone out each day, only to return disappointed. But *that* day when he made his daily trek, there was a figure out there on the horizon. It was his son! He ran to greet him. (Speculation on my part maybe, but the two parables that precede this one encourages an understanding of the Father constantly looking for the lost: the shepherd who seeks out one lost sheep and the woman seeking and finding her lost coin.)

Charles Spurgeon put it like this: "The third parable would be likely to be misunderstood without the first and second. We have sometimes heard it said—here is the prodigal received as soon as he comes back, no mention being made of a Savior who seeks and saves him. Is it possible to reach all truths in a single parable? Does not the first one speak of the shepherd seeking the lost sheep? Why need repeat what has been said before?"[5]

We have a heavenly Father who is constantly looking, constantly seeking out those who are lost in hopes that they will return. Even when people across the world are still a long way off, He is running to them, loving them, honoring them and celebrating them. God loves the lost. Our witness, our mission is a response to God's heart of love for those who don't know Him. And this can lead us to some unlikely places.

Ask Brian and Tracey Heasley and their family. In February 2005, we stood in Saint Mary's Church in Marylebone, London, for a 24-7 gathering to commission and send them off to Ibiza. Several months before our gathering in London, God had begun to speak to Brian and Tracey about this island He loved. The two sensed a call to move there with their kids, Ellis (9) and Daniel (6), and to build a Boiler Room on the island.

The Heasleys had always had a heart for the nations, but this move was big and it was different. Brian and Tracey were leading a dynamic and successful church in Norfolk, England. Their kids were settled and everything seemed set. Now they were hearing the "Go" of God.

As we prayed for them and washed their feet, I was struck again by how bizarre it was to send missionaries to Ibiza. And then I remembered that our God of love was already there, in a place written off as godless. It just made sense. It was the heart of God for the lost that called Brian and Tracey's lives and catapulted them from Norfolk to Ibiza.

In April 2005, just before their departure, they told 24-7's website, "It's so encouraging that we are being asked to play a small part in a massive dream that many have had for years. At times it's both scary and exciting, but we want our time in Ibiza to be used in building the team and in establishing the base so thousands will be touched and changed for good."

Christ's Call and Command

Mission is about story. Jesus called the disciples to be witnesses, a commission to "Go and tell the story." To be witnesses, we must tell how *our* stories intersect with God's story.

Jesus spent much of His ministry sharing life in conversation and relationship, around meal times, in squares and synagogues, with people. The life of the Father burst out of Him in the most ordinary of settings. Jesus' mission was based in His love for His Father—it was a message that flowed out of Him and revealed God.

In the same way, we go with our story of Christ's call to us. Mission tells the story of His work in our hearts, but we also go because He has commanded us. We cannot hide away. Christ has called us—He has met with us and called us by name. The task is immediate. Jesus threw Himself into the world, in the midst of His enemies. We must do the same. In *Life Together,* Bonhoeffer reminds us that the place of the Christian is not "in the seclusion of cloistered life" but in the world. "Jesus Christ lived in the midst of His enemies."[6]

When one of the members of the early mission teams to Ibiza reflected on her journey there, she discovered this same desire to go:

> I knew it would stretch me beyond anything I had done before and it would take me out of my comfort zone, but I couldn't deny that Jesus was calling me to "go." I guess God was changing my heart. I didn't want to pray from the sidelines anymore. I wanted to pray in the midst of the hurting and the lost, to let my prayer be active, to let my actions be the answer to some of my prayers. We were

going to Ibiza to take the power of prayer beyond church buildings and meetings and into the streets.

I'm beginning to understand that when I pray, I don't change God, but God changes me and radically touches my life and the lives of those I touch. When we pray, we cannot remain passive, because God stirs us to be active and to love the people we are praying for with our actions. Ibiza is a high place for the emerging generation. It's high time that we left our godly ghettos to invade and inhabit such places for Jesus.

Saint Francis of Assisi was someone whose movement embodied this commitment to respond to the call and command of God. He loved and cared for lepers, something that would have been one of the severest of tests in the Middle Ages. He gave to the poor and cared for widows; he showed love to anyone in need. But compassion for the poor was only one strand of this outward life. He was just as committed to mission and to preaching, and it came from a base of inward devotion:

> The preacher must first draw from his secret prayers what he will later pour out in his holy sermons; he must grow hot within before he speaks words that are cold in themselves.[7]

What I like most of all about the story of Francis is the way that prayer, mission and mercy were so intertwined. He did not have weeks of mission or projects to work with the poor. He simply approached life with a commitment to pray and serve God, and to do so outwardly by loving those he met and sharing the source of that love, his faith in Christ.

Responding to Christ's Sacrifice

As we learn to adopt Christ's mission, we can also learn His method—the way God went about this journey of salvation: sacrifice. Peterson writes, "sacrifice is God's way of dealing with what is wrong in history, which is to say, what is wrong with us, individually and collectively. It is God's way of dealing with sin."[8]

Salvation and sacrifice have always been closely linked. We see Abraham called to sacrifice Isaac, only to be given a lamb at the last minute. We see sacrifice in the Passover and salvation in the flight from Egypt. We read about the cost and sacrifice paid by the prophets, many of whom faced persecution for the words they spoke. We read about the rituals of priestly sacrifice for sins, then see it mirrored in what Christ did on the cross.

This biblical overture of sacrifice echoes through the Old Testament and points to the Messiah, to the Christ and to the sacrifice He will pay for salvation. Isaiah's songs tell us again and again of the suffering that the Messiah will endure and the central part it will play in God's plan:

> Yet it was the LORD's will to crush him and cause him to suffer, and though the LORD makes his life a guilt offering, he will see his offspring and prolong his days, and the will of the LORD will prosper in his hand. After the suffering of his soul, he will see the light of life and be satisfied (Isa. 53:10-11).

Sacrifice and suffering were central to Christ's mission. This was the method of outreach that God had chosen. His sacrifice took our place and our pain, "nailing [them] to the cross" (Col. 2:14). As the apostle John put it, He was "the atoning sacrifice for our sins, and not only for ours but also for the sins of the whole world" (1 John 2:2). God so loved the world, and sacrifice was the key that restored relationship between Him and His creation. As we set out on our mission to take the gospel to others, we cannot avoid the road of sacrifice.

> If anyone would come after me, he must deny himself and take up his cross daily and follow me (Luke 9:23).

In Western culture, we have been guilty of sanitizing evangelism. In seeking out how to share Christ with relevance, we have forgotten that Christ crucified is a "stumbling block" to some and "foolishness" to others (see 1 Cor. 1:23). In desiring a relational approach to mission, we have embarked on "friendship evangelism"; only we have forgotten how to make friends, at least with anyone different than us. Living in such a comfortable and tolerant culture, we have forgotten the cost of sharing faith. In the midst of our sermons on "success theology," we have forgotten the place of sacrifice.

We started this chapter by considering the "go" of God in Matthew 28. He has sent us out because "you are witnesses of these things" (Luke 24:48). The most common Greek word used for "witness" in the New Testament comes from the Greek verb *matyreo*. It looks familiar, doesn't it? It's where our word "martyr" comes from, and martyrdom is what the word meant for many early believers. The martyring of all the apostles except John (he survived being boiled in hot oil), and the countless deaths of people sharing the gospel of Christ, meant that a witness was someone who chose to suffer or even to die rather than renounce Christ and His mission. Witnessing was serious, sacrificial business.

Throughout history, to tell others about Jesus meant suffering. Jesus warned us it would be so, telling us of the blessing that would come to us "when people insult you, persecute you and falsely say all kinds of evil against you because of me" (Matt. 5:11). Read any good book on Christian martyrs and you'll learn about the early bishops, some of them so scared that they "seemed like living martyrs."[9] The Coptic Church endured "the era of the martyrs." You can read about the pre-Reformation reformers like Jan Huss, who was burned at the stake for heresies that many of us now accept as sound doctrine. You can find out about the Christian victims of major wars, such as the countless Hungarian priests murdered during and immediately after the Second World War, first by Nazi occupiers and then by Soviet liberators.

And martyrdom happens today, in greater and greater numbers. Release International estimates that 200 million Christians in more than 60 countries are denied fundamental human rights because of their faith. Parvez Masih, a Christian head teacher from Lahore, Pakistan, endured incredible hardship after his arrest for "blasphemy": "On the day of his arrest—April 1, 2001, he was taken to a river, had a gun put to his head and told to renounce Jesus. He refused."[10] The sacrifice and cost of mission cannot be ignored. But what does this mean for us? Maybe our lives are far too comfortable for us to begin to live uncomfortably. Maybe we are too shy of the gospel's challenge to be a challenge to others.

My greatest fear for the Boiler Rooms developing around the world is that they will become comfortable, that the sacrifice and cost will become minimal. Our Boiler Rooms should be in the hardest places. Boys Town and Ibiza should not be the occasional stories that we cheer from the sidelines. Among the poorest of the poor, among those who are lost beyond what we can imagine, we should be in Christ's name, becoming a fragrant "sacrifice of praise" (Heb. 13:15) as we lay down our lives as "living sacrifices" (Rom. 12:1). It is there that the Kingdom will come.

The Practice of Mission

In Acts 2, we see a community of believers committed to mission. The explosive mix of Christ-centered living, the power of His Spirit and a willingness of the people to boldly go and share had a massive effect on Jerusalem society. It started with 3,000 finding faith when Peter spoke at Pentecost, but Acts records that "the Lord added to their number daily those who were being saved" (2:47).

Boiler Rooms seek to be missional communities. Based around a lifestyle of prayer and a willingness to welcome and to love others, Boiler Rooms practice *in-reach*, when people come through their doors to find Christ. Based around a willingness to go and to engage with the world around them, Boiler Rooms also practice *outreach*, moving out of their venues and going where people are. These two concepts form the basis of missional practice within 24-7 Boiler Rooms.

We have to develop a rhythm of working within our communities that allows for intense outreach, connections, friendship and involvement in very dark places to work alongside a lifestyle that is reflective, recharged and intimate.

BRIAN HEASLEY, IN A 24-7 IBIZA PLANNING DOCUMENT

In-Reach

On October 18, 2002, we organized a special birthday party in
Reading. It was the first birthday of the Reading Boiler Room. We
gathered in Saint Laurence's Church, one of the few remaining
abbey buildings, to celebrate everything that God had done. By
then, the Reading Boiler Room's clientele had changed and our
gathering needed to reflect that.

Phil Baldwin, who worked for 24-7 at that time, takes up
the story:

> That Friday night was one of the best nights in ages. I think
> I enjoyed the meeting more than any meeting I've been to
> for as long as I can remember. It was just fun and felt like
> what church should be. I was sitting behind a kid with a
> Marilyn Manson hoody on, surrounded by kids with
> Slipknot and Korn hoodies. They were talking, sometimes
> joking about the people putting their hands in the air and
> saying "Amen." A little fight broke out a few rows in front
> of me at one point! Mobile phones were going off and peo-
> ple answered them. Kids walked in and out. The majority of
> the congregation was probably under 16 years of age.
>
> Amidst all the joking, they were really serious, too. I
> was really surprised when they were all silent to pray for
> that boy's family or their friends or themselves. They were
> getting into the music, and the offering bit really surprised
> me! How many churches have a kid coming up to the front
> to celebrate because he managed a whole week at school!

We had a wonderful night and it was truly reflective of the people who had made up our first year. Why had so many unchurched
young people connected with the Boiler Room? To this day I still
don't really know. But many found Christ by coming in, finding a
welcome in the prayer room and in those gathered there.

- *In-reach is a good welcome*, a warm cup of tea, free Internet
  access, or even just a comfy chair and a willingness to talk.

Some of our best conversations came from people drop-
ping in. The biggest challenge is simply to open the
doors and welcome people in. How can you open your
doors to your community? Community meals, free tea
and coffee, art galleries or open days can all help with
this sense of welcome.

- *In-reach can be through the prayer room.* In Reading, we
  found that people of no faith would often use the prayer
  room. In Ibiza, the prayer room became the focal point
  for the team's mission. It's worth considering how accessible our places of prayer and worship are to those who
  wouldn't normally come to church. Is the language easy
  to understand? Is there a cross to ensure people know
  Jesus is the center of what we're doing? How easy is it for
  a non-Christian to pray there?

- *In-reach can be through a service or kindness.* In San Antonio
  (Ibiza), Brian's aim was for a venue where people could
  feel welcome and receive care. He dreamt of a van to
  transport people home who were too drunk to get there
  on their own. The base could be a place where people
  could learn to DJ or paint, but most of all it would be a
  place of friendship. How can you and your community
  of faith meet the needs of those around you?

- *In-reach can be about the community itself.* While living in
  Dresden, Markus Laegel and the prayer community
  there held music nights in their house, welcoming people in. How can you open the doors of your community
  and give space for others to join you?

Outreach
"Outreach" has become a very familiar term in the Church. I wonder, though, whether it is as significant if it's not balanced by in-
reach. The sense of breathing, of an in-and-out rhythm for each of

these practices, is vital to our living out the Rule. Outreach is about going out of our doors, onto the streets, into the dark places to the light of Jesus.

- *Outreach can be about leaving your city.* Many Boiler Rooms are beginning to find that they can provide short-term help or mission in other places or nations. Whether responding to a crisis or going to share the gospel, this is a vital part of outreach. For example, after praying for the city of New Orleans, the team from Kansas City went to Houston to help with the relief after Hurricane Katrina. After meeting Kelly Greene, they packed their bags and headed for Boys Town. How can your community be ready to respond and to go?

- *Outreach can be prayer on the streets.* I have grown to love the model of outreach in places like Ibiza and Ayia Napa. Teams often just head out onto the streets to ask people whether they can pray for them. In the summer of 2006, street teams in Ibiza took prayer requests from (and prayed for) 1,100 people, both workers and tourists. What would this look like in your community or your city?

- *Outreach can be in a particular culture.* Just as ancient missionaries took the gospel to unreached cultures, we need to discover and apply what the gospel looks like in skate culture, in hip-hop culture, in club culture, in football stadiums, in the shopping mall. In Southampton, where a 24-7 community is emerging, many go out into the clubs to pray and make friends there. One of the leaders told me of three break-dance crews organized by Christians. Thanks to their willingness to engage with a culture they love, Christians are now accepted as part of that culture.

- *Outreach can be about words and preaching.* Sharing our faith with words may be seen as old school, but it still has a massive part to play. It's often the hardest for us. Are we willing to give an answer to questions when they're raised? Are we willing to speak about Christ "in season and out of season" (2 Tim. 4:2)?

As with most of the lessons we've learned through Boiler Rooms, these principles of in-reach and outreach are based around our experiences with real people, like Emily.

Emily's Story

Emily got involved in the Reading Boiler Room through our work in the Forbury Gardens Park. As she visited the venue, she began to make friends. "I kinda liked it. I liked the people," she told me when I interviewed her in 2003.

She wasn't too put off by all the God stuff all over the walls, either: "I'd been to a Catholic school, made to go to Mass, that sort of thing, so the God stuff wasn't new to me, but it was different."

When we sat down and talked, I asked her why so many young people come down to the Boiler Room. "I came for the free food," Emily admitted, "but I think it's more than a place to hang out, for most of us who come down. I think most people know something's here—subconsciously maybe." It was amazing how many people walked through our doors saying they sensed God, even though many didn't believe. That was Emily's experience, too.

In August 2002, something unexpected took place in Emily's life. "Loads of my friends had gone down to a summer camp called Junction 12," she told me. "They all said how amazing it was and that lots of people had turned Christian." Emily thought that was a bit weird, but also quite cool. "In a way, I felt jealous. I wanted to see why people had changed."

Emily went along to the last night of the camp and heard a talk about Jesus. "Then they did the whole 'If you want to be a Christian stand up' thing. So I did." Emily stood with her friend who'd gone too. "I felt this massive rush. I burst into tears. Then a lady prayed for me and gave me a Bible. It was amazing."

As she walked out of the venue, Emily met her first challenge. Her friends said to her, "Have you been brainwashed, too?"

"That was hard," she told me, "because I tended to be a follower. My mates told me to put my Bible away, but I didn't."

Emily spent the following year down at the Boiler Room, praying more regularly than most. When we closed, she got connected with a local church for a while before eventually leaving Reading. When we spoke, she reflected on the sense of connection she felt in the Boiler Room. "If the Boiler Room wasn't here, I would have lost my faith in seconds."

"Why?" I asked.

"The people here, the stuff on the walls, seeing God worshiped . . ."

The worship element was important for her. "I knew about worship from Mass, and that still teaches me. I can't get too relaxed with God, but I've learned you can worship God in many ways, not just the formal way. I love to make collages, write poems and listen to music. Using all of them helps me pray and worship."

In-reach and outreach worked in harmony to draw Emily to God. Are we willing to open our doors so that our community can come in? Are we willing to go out those same doors to the dark and lonely places of our world?

For Further Thought

Organize an open meal for those who live around you or for those with whom you and your community mix. Try inviting the homeless man who sleeps in the park or your friends from the club you go to or the elderly lady who lives down the street. Cook them a wonderful meal and make them feel welcome. Be willing to move forward with whatever comes out of it.

Liturgy

Leader: The whole earth is wrapped in darkness. All people are sunk in deep darkness.

All: Come to us, Lord Jesus. We will go with You, Lord Jesus.

Leader: But God rises on you; His sunrise glory breaks over you.

All: Come to us, Lord Jesus. We will go with You, Lord Jesus.

Leader: Get out of bed! Wake up! Put your face in the sunlight. God's bright glory has risen for you.

All: Come to us, Lord Jesus. We will go with You, Lord Jesus.

Leader: Not long ago we were despised, out of the way, unvisited, ignored. But now God has put us on our feet. The outcast has become the great tribe, the weakling has become strong. He promises, "I am God. At the right time I will make it happen."

All: Praise You, Lord. You come to us when we call on You. You call each one of us to follow You. You send us to the world. You are faithful; we will follow You.

(Liturgy based on Isaiah 60.)

CHAPTER 12

The Practice of Learning

Let the wise listen and add to their learning,
and let the discerning get guidance.
PROVERBS 1:5

I don't think much of a man who is not wiser today than he was yesterday.
ABRAHAM LINCOLN

And the lesson today is how to die.
THE BOOMTOWN RATS, "I DON'T LIKE MONDAYS"[1]

I've known Martha a long time now. I first met her in May 1995, on the steps of Saint Paul's Church in Salisbury, on my first day in the city. I had moved there as a fresh-faced 25-year-old, about to start my first paid job as a youth worker. I remember how scared I was. I remember how much it helped that Martha teased me when I arrived. She was 15.

I spent three years in Salisbury, with Martha and the rest of the youth group. She helped me lead the 11 to 14 age group. We chatted about a Youth For Christ summer team. I helped her with her application to work with Oasis in South London. She moved to Reading in 1999—I had moved a year earlier when I began at Greyfriars Church. Martha had come to spend a year with us.

And she's still here. After a year's internship, Martha took a post at a local school called Meadway working with excluded young people—a job that had come off the back of our mentoring work there. She's now a key employee at Connexions (a service organization for young people), a fully qualified and trained youth worker.

In 2003, it was my privilege to speak at Martha's wedding to Luke, an amazing man from the Greyfriars youth group I led years ago. In 2005, after the two of them had joined the small church plant (New Hope) that Karen and I are also a part of, Martha gave birth to Alfie, their wonderful son. Her family now lives about 100 yards away from us.

I thank God for Martha. Our friendship has evolved from young person and youth leader, to worker and mentor, to friends, colleagues and now neighbors. Recently, as I worked with Martha and some young people from our church, it became evident that Martha's skills as a youth worker have blossomed. She has so much to give, and she leads in a way completely different from me—she has skills I could only dream of.

I cannot take a lot of credit. There were many occasions when Martha grew in spite of, not because of, me. She is God's work and I thank Him for what He has done, because through Martha, I've learned what I believe are two of the most important principles about learning and discipleship.

First, learning is a lifelong process. Learning comes through relationships and long-term living far more than it does through courses or programs. Life and practice have discipled Martha.

Second, the commitment of a teacher, leader or mentor is often for life—we must share our lives as we teach and be prepared to continue that shared life past contracts or year-long plans. The commitment to teach and the commitment to learn go hand in hand, and friendships and life provide the ideal classroom.

A Learning Community

A Boiler Room Is:
Committed to Sharing the Gospel by Being a
Learning Community of Training and Discipleship
Where People Are Growing in Their Faith, Their Life-Skills
and Their Ability to Lead

"Learning," "training" and similar words weren't a frequent part of our vocabulary in the early days of 24-7. We all understood the important place of discipleship and that it was a key part of what we were doing. But when it came to 24-7 prayer rooms, the move of God seemed so natural and organic that we simply didn't want to touch it. In any case, 24-7 wasn't forever—right? Soon God would tell us it was time to stop.

As 24-7 came into its fifth year, we began to worry a little. So often our problem in the church is that we over-train and under-release. We want people to do a course or two, learn from others and then slowly release them into leadership. But God was doing something very different with 24-7. Men and women in their late teens and twenties were taking on key roles of leadership around the world. It was, and is, amazing what they achieve. Yet was it time for us to give some support, some training? Had we over-released and under-trained?

The issue of learning also arose as we began to sense that God's plans for 24-7 were somewhat longer than we had thought. While the movement had begun in prayer rooms and as a means of providing blessing to churches, movements and cities, now we were finding missions creating Boiler Rooms and building for the longer term. From Reading to Belgrade and from Ibiza to Kansas City, people were settling in for the long haul, and we needed to spend some time learning and training so that we would be ready to walk the road God had paved.

The *Penguin Concise Dictionary* defines "learning" as "acquired knowledge or skill, especially knowledge acquired by study and education."[2] Whether in academic study or in the "school of hard knocks,"[3] learning (or discipleship) is vital to our walk with God. We study the Bible to understand who God is, how He operates, what He thinks about us and how we should follow Him. Jesus was often referred to as "Rabbi" or "Teacher" because that is what He was to His followers—He taught them by revealing God the Father (see John 14). Wise King Solomon exhorted, "Let the wise listen and add to their learning" (Prov. 1:5). We need to be people of study and depth.

The Church has never been short on places of academic study, but if following Christ is not learning's aim, we hit problems. Remember, the Pharisees were educated and learned, but they did not understand God enough to see Jesus for who He was. In *The Spirit of the Disciplines,* Dallas Willard questions why it is that "for at least several decades, the churches of the western world have not made discipleship a condition of being a Christian."[4] The primary purpose of learning in the Boiler Room Rule is discipleship, which can simply be defined as being a student of Jesus. We learn language and gain understanding as children at school, and as we grow, we learn skills for success in our jobs, our families and marriages, even for our leisure activities. But learning also comes from life, from listening to others, from observing the world around us. This is how we gain our worldview. Our understanding of how the world works is mostly based on our experiences and the culture we have lived in. This can be a good or a bad thing. Sometimes we need to unlearn things we have always assumed before we can truly learn.

For the disciple who is willing to question his or her assumptions, communities can be the most effective place of study—the university of life. In *Leadership and the New Science,* Margaret Wheatley argues, "We all construct the world through the lenses of our own making and use these to filter and select. We each actively participate in creating our worlds. Observation, then, is a very complex and important issue."[5] In communities, we can:

1. *Learn to understand others.* We are called to love others as ourselves, so surely we must take an interest in them and their lives.

2. *Learn to understand ourselves.* Why do I do the things that I do? Why do I feel this way? What are my gifts? What aren't my gifts?

3. *Learn to apply and live the things we learn.* I can theorize and understand the issues around poverty, but until I make friends with a man or woman who is poor, I cannot *learn.* Until I love, I cannot truly understand what love means.

4. *Learn to understand our world.* Can we see God in the shopping mall as much as in our study groups? My journal is full of songs, notes about films, newspaper stories and observations, because I believe Creator God is evident in my world, and I want to learn from Him.

The Fear of the Lord

The primary principle of Christian learning must be that it begins and ends with God. Learning cannot be about us. Though we gain *knowledge*, we only *learn* things that God Himself reveals. Though many books, websites and seminars have been dedicated to teaching, we will never reach the point where we don't need to sit at the feet of God to learn from Him. He is our teacher; we are His disciples.

The proverbs and psalms remind us that "the fear of the LORD is the beginning of knowledge" (Prov. 1:7) and that "the fear of the LORD is the beginning of wisdom; all who follow his precepts have good understanding" (Ps. 111:10). Fear of the Lord is not terror or some sort of slavish cowering. "Holy fear . . . is God-given, enabling men to reverence God's authority, obey his commandments and hate and shun all form of evil."[6]

This fear—the recognition of the greatness of God, the gaze in wonder and awe—this is the beginning of our journey toward learning. It must be the foundation for our study and discipleship:

> Fear-of-the-Lord is the cultivated awareness of the "more and other" that the presence or revelation of God induces in our lives. I am not the center of my existence; I am not the sum-total of what matters; I don't know what will happen next.[7]

Learning and Doing

In his New Testament letter, James laments the kind of discipleship that majors on listening and minors on action:

Do not merely listen to the word, and so deceive yourselves. Do what it says. Anyone who listens to the word
but does not do what it says is like a man who looks at his
face in the mirror and, after looking at himself, goes away
and immediately forgets what he looks like (1:22-24).

Learning without action is false—it makes no sense. I must
admit there are times when I look in the mirror and don't really
take in what I see (if I had more hair on my head, looking tidy
would be more of a problem!), yet the absurdity of James's word
picture makes his point: You look in a mirror to see *yourself* . . .
it serves no other purpose!

Monastic history is littered with many who chose learning
and ritual without action and devotion. Yet at their radical beginnings and more militant margins, monastic movements have practiced techniques of learning and meditation with a desire for God
and a commitment to obedience at their core:

> While the Desert Fathers chanted, recited and chewed on
> biblical texts, they saw scripture less as something to be
> talked about and more as something to be done.[8]

In September 2005, the first 13 students on the UK 24-7 Transit
course arrived at Sunbury Court, and their induction into a year
with our Boiler Rooms began. Transit had begun as a leadership
course in Kansas City, and as our relationship with the team and
a vision for the Boiler Room there grew, we were impacted by
Transit and what it might mean for us in 24-7. We recognized the
need for training and wondered whether Transit might be part of
the answer.

In some ways, Transit is similar to other training schemes
in that we ask students to come for a year to be involved in the
movement. But in other ways, Transit is quite different. It's about
a deliberate mix between classroom teaching and practical application. We're convinced that lessons learned academically must be
applied practically in the Boiler Rooms.

*The idea of experiential learning that is incorporated in Transit
deals with all the different learning styles. It's like how everyone
always says that university teaches about life because you get
taught about looking after yourself, studying and social life.
Transit similarly deals with the reflective, the active and the
questioner by engaging a lifestyle of learning as opposed to sitting
in a session. Learning is constant and consistent. To learn about
being kind really gets practiced in a community that shares life
together! We learn in the living room. And not just during the
teaching times—from picking up the crumbs that are tossed out
by experienced practitioners of the gospel, such as Eva Sarsa,
Simon Batchelor and Paul Wegenast.*

ANDY WILSON, TRANSIT STUDENT, MAY 2006

This is how Jesus put it: "Therefore everyone who hears these words of mine and puts them into practice is like the wise man who built his house on the rock. The rain came down, the streams rose, and the winds blew and beat against that house; yet it did not fall, because it had its foundation on the rock" (Matt. 7:24-25).

Listening to Others

In *Life Together*, Bonhoeffer argues that we "can never know beforehand how God's image should appear in others."[9] The incompleteness of our knowledge should affect the way we treat others, what we expect from them and what we are prepared to give to them. It should also affect how we listen and our openness to learn from each human being we meet. "The first service one owes to others in the fellowship is to listen."[10]

A community should be a place of learning as brothers and sisters connect and share. It "builds itself up in love" (Eph. 4:16). Learning is not a commodity for the leader to dispense and the members to absorb—it should be mutual, as each member brings the wisdom of his or her own experience. "As iron sharpens iron, so one man sharpens another" (Prov. 27:17).

One of the things that continually amazed me during the first years of the Reading Boiler Room was how much I learned from the young people who came in. Can unchurched young people teach me about God? Can the poor or the homeless or even those of other religions lead me toward Jesus in my learning? The answer, of course, is yes.

> *I've learned to see the face of Jesus in everyone, in the Boiler*
> *Room or on the streets. What is their potential? Who could they be?*
> *How is Christ at work in their lives?*
>
> HANNAH LEES, TRANSIT STUDENT, MAY 2006

One such person who taught us was Adam Cooley. During his short life, Adam taught me much about the faithfulness of friendship. He taught about the value of life and about God, even though I suspect he would have been shocked that such a thing was taking place.

In the summer of 2002, Adam died of a drug overdose. Sitting in a squat in central Reading, he lost his life because he lost the battle with a substance he had fought against. At the time, I tried to make sense of his death in my journal:

> The funeral bowled me over . . . wasn't expecting it to, but it did. That stuff from Ecclesiastes kept ringing round my head: "Everything is meaningless." Lots of questions going round my head. Is it all meaningless? What's the point of anything we're doing? Which of these kids will be in a coffin next? How do we know? Will God help us share with the urgent cases first or is it just potluck? I feel like the Boiler Room is some kind of spiritual ER, cases flooding in all the time. But it's not, is it? We can't do prayer triage and find the urgent ones . . . We just have to take them one by one, and often they don't want our help. Often we're not in any place to give anything, except God.
>
> Today I feel more adrift, more hopeless than I think I have since all this began . . . and yet I feel more determined than ever not to give up. Maybe it's only one more prayer away. Maybe the person I talk to or care for

today might be dead tomorrow. It's that real. There are no rehearsals anymore.

C'mon—we were desperate to go beyond the normal, to grab on to the coattails of God. He was among the hurting and bleeding—we knew that—now He's among the dead. What will our response be? How much deeper can we go? Maybe all we have left to give is our very lives. Maybe all we can do is to spend ourselves in the name of God. Maybe just in our weakness, where we are, in pain, maybe that's where God's voice is its loudest. Maybe the place we've spent years trying to run away from is the very place God wants us to be.

In our desire to share about Jesus, we have to remember that the lost are people, loved and designed by the Creator. In our urgency to care for the poor, we have to remember that the poor are poor *people*, people who have dignity and beauty, who were designed in the image of God. We must desire friendship first and never treat people as a program. We realize there is much to learn: from the beggar and the businessman, from the priest and the pill-popper.

> *I am defeated, and know it, if I meet any human being from whom*
> *I find myself unable to learn anything.*
> GEORGE HERBERT PALMER (1842-1933),
> AMERICAN SCHOLAR AND AUTHOR

The Practice of Learning

So what does the practice of learning look like in our Boiler Rooms? In some ways this is the hardest practice to pin down, because it happens in so many unseen ways. Learning takes place every day as visitors enter, as people pray, as conversations take place. We believe in the meditative learning of the Benedictines and study at university or college, but also in the classroom of the coffee shop, where we chat, listen and learn from each other. That being said, there are a few common strands.

The Word of God

In a Boiler Room, the Bible is important. Massively important. As you enter, you may see Bible verses on the walls. In the prayer room, you'll find Bibles available. You'll see people meditating Scripture and read verses that God has impressed on others scrawled on the walls or painted in intricate designs. Scripture inspires the prayer stations, and many of the prayers themselves flow from the Word of God.

Most of the creative ways we pray or learn are based around Scripture. We ask God to highlight particular verses or passages that may help us in our journey. We often use a reading series and discuss Scripture as part of our gatherings and prayer times.

Transit approaches its teaching of the Bible as God's Story—that is, that God's work of salvation began in Creation, has traveled through the whole of the Old and New Testaments, and carries on today, where we take our place in God's Story of salvation. We learn Scripture with the understanding that we are part of its story, and it has much to say to us today. The aim is to grow storytellers.

One tool we use is liturgy (written responsive prayers) for daily times of prayer. Liturgy based on Scripture was a practice begun by the Desert Fathers and is still used by many today. In Reading, we found *Celtic Daily Prayer* by the Northumbria Community[11] immensely valuable and used it for morning, midday and evening prayers. In time, we began to write and use our own liturgy, forming prayers around Scripture that was important to us or that God had spoken to us about, such as Isaiah 61. (You have seen examples of our liturgies at the end of each chapter.) We have found liturgy a valuable tool in learning Scripture. Benedictine monk Jean LeClercq commended liturgy as the ritual around which the whole of a monk's life rotates: "In liturgy, love of learning and desire for God find perfect reconciliation."[12]

Another practice we have found helpful is biblical meditation, or *lectio divina*. Also begun by the Desert Fathers, "sacred reading" was established by the Benedictines, who made it part of their Rule and way of life. *Lectio divina* is a simple discipline of reading and rereading a passage of the Bible to allow the Holy Spirit to speak to us. "The *Lectio Divina* assumes that by entering deeply into the text of God's Holy Word, God will be made known to us, speak to us and direct our lives."[13]

The third tool we use regularly is journaling. It is interesting to note that for monastic traditions in which there was often a vow of silence, writing was the only way to communicate reflections about the Word of God. Traditions such as the Benedictines have reams of beautifully written reflections about the Bible.

Journaling allows us to record our thoughts, reactions and fears. It allows us to express what is on our minds or in our hearts and helps us consider our journey thus far. Each student in Transit has a journal that is the tool that holds together all he or she experiences and learns during the year. Students share regularly from their journals, "teaching back" the training they have received.

Spiritual Direction

Spiritual direction is, in reality, nothing more than a way of leading us to see and obey the real Director—the Holy Spirit hidden in the depths of our soul.

THOMAS MERTON[14]

I believe spiritual direction is also vital to learning within Boiler Rooms, although probably most of the Boiler Rooms don't know they are practicing it.

Spiritual direction is a process of discipleship and learning that depends on a man or woman being prepared to be a co-traveler in someone else's Christian journey. It is not counseling, not heavy on teaching or on imposing doctrine—spiritual direction is hearing and helping in the context of a friendship. Will we travel alongside rather than seeking a shortcut through a sermon or reading list? Will we commit to help a person find God in each step he or she takes?

A friend loves at all times, and a brother is born for adversity (Prov. 17:7).

Spiritual direction is also about listening to the Holy Spirit, about being prepared to discern on behalf of someone else and about developing that person's relationship with God. Like all other forms of learning we have looked at, it is about finding God at a deeper level.

From Jesus' relationships with Peter and John to Paul's relationship with Timothy, from the leadership of Early Church leaders like Smyrna and Polycarp to Benedict, the Dominicans, Ignatius Loyola and to many traditions today, spiritual direction has always been a part of following Christ in our world.

An example is John Cassian (A.D. 350-435), one of the earliest recorded proponents of spiritual direction. Influenced by the Early Fathers, Cassian introduced a distinctive process of mentoring a novitiate into the monastic life. He put every novitiate under the guidance of an older and more experienced monk and gave great thought to who would be given the responsibility of leading in this way. Benedict was so impressed by how Cassian wove these principles into monastic life that his Rule lifted much of Cassian's ideas verbatim. By the end of the seventh century, spiritual direction was a key component of Western monasticism.

In Boiler Rooms, this ancient Christian practice took shape naturally in the emerging communities. Just by nature of the Boiler Room itself, we often found ourselves in informal mentoring relationships, listening, praying, seeking God and then aiding people on their journey. The direct teaching that has emerged through Transit is the exception rather than the rule—most people who come into a Boiler Room are just looking for guidance from God.

Can we adjust our lives to listen, to be slow to speak, using questions to unlock a person's mind to potential areas of growth and journey? Can we be prepared to journey *with* people who come through our doors? In our Boiler Rooms, we've found that no matter what words people say, the question they're most often asking is, Will you walk with me?

A Rhythm of Learning

A commitment to practice of learning is not easy. When we build in regular prayer, study time and work duties, we can easily find our time eaten up. Our response to this dilemma has been to build a rhythm of life and activity that aims to balance each of the six practices and gives time for God to teach and speak to us.

The ancient Celts divided their day into work (often manual and practical), study, regular prayer and rest. All four of these ingredients are vital, and we seek to keep them in balance as we find a rhythm for each Boiler Room. During Transit in Reading, we lived in a bi-weekly rhythm. Each day began with at least an hour of prayer, sometimes more. There would be time for individual and corporate study, a morning of solitude time, and weekly mentoring. Space would be made for time together to review what had been going on, as well as for regular meals with each other and some meals where the local community was invited. There would be practical work such as a food run to the homeless, mission work in the town center and manual work around the Boiler Room. There would also be a fortnightly retreat for more intensive training. A rhythm of life provides a disciplined environment where a balance of life can be achieved and where space is given for God to teach.

Gathering

An invaluable time of learning is when we gather together as a larger community. In Kansas City, the Boiler Room operates in concentric circles of community, with a core, a group of advisers, those who attend regularly and a fringe. Within these different spheres, groups coordinate and implement the Boiler Room's Practices. With such a diverse group, times of gathering are vitally important.

> Let us not give up meeting together, as some are in the habit of doing, but let us encourage one another—and all the more as you see the Day approaching (Heb. 10:25).

I've written before that we are a little too good at meetings in the Church, so it's important to be fresh and creative when we gather. In our early Boiler Rooms, unhappiness with meetings caused us to swing too far away from organization, to fluidity and unpredictability. This had its benefits, but also its limitations. As we've journeyed on, it's become evident that learning and growth take place when people meet others from outside their normal sphere of friends, and if we are to facilitate this, we have to be intentional. On a deep level, intentional gatherings are vital to the life of the community.

In Kansas City, the community gathers every Wednesday to pray, worship and receive teaching. These gatherings are central for imparting vision and direction. In a monastery, an abbot or abbess often teaches each morning about the Rule, and in the same way, Boiler Rooms need directing toward the key aspects of the Rule and its Practices.

> *Leaders of communities must continually announce the vision and remind members of the call of God.*
> THOMAS MERTON[15]

Gatherings in Kansas City also take the shape of parties (they party very well!), meals and even watching the Super Bowl. Meals are particularly important in the learning process because meals give a chance for conversation, listening, encouragement, and space for every member to contribute. If we are subscribers to "the ministry of all believers," we should also be subscribers to the teaching and contribution of all believers. "People are touched by the simplest words—the ones that come with humility, truth and love."[16]

For Further Thought

Ask God to teach you in unlikely places for at least a week. Enter into conversations, willing to listen and expecting to learn. Ask the Holy Spirit to speak to you as you listen to the radio, watch a movie or live your life. Take a humble and teachable attitude into each day—then journal about the results.

Liturgy

Great are the works of the Lord;
they are pondered by all who delight in them.
PSALM 111:2

Leader: I will extol the Lord with all my heart.

All: The fear of the Lord is the beginning of wisdom. Teach us, God.

Leader: Great are the works of the Lord; I ponder them and delight in Him.

All: The fear of the Lord is the beginning of wisdom. Teach us, God.

Leader: Your deeds are glorious, Your ways majestic.

All: The fear of the Lord is the beginning of wisdom. Teach us, God.

Leader: I remember Your wonders, the works of Your hands.

All: The fear of the Lord is the beginning of wisdom. Teach us, God.

Leader: I understand that You are compassionate and gracious. You provide for me; You remember Your covenant of love.

All: The fear of the Lord is the beginning of wisdom. Teach us, God.

Leader: You are steadfast, You are faithful and You redeem our souls.

All: The fear of the Lord is the beginning of wisdom; all who follow His precepts have good understanding. To Him belongs eternal praise. Teach us, God. Amen.

(Liturgy based on Psalm 111.)

CHAPTER 13

Punk Monks and Rescue Shops

*If anyone would come after me, he must deny himself
and take up his cross daily and follow me.*

LUKE 9:23

*Jesus Christ lived in the midst of his enemies . . .
so the Christian, too, belongs not in the seclusion of cloistered life,
but in the thick of foes.*

DIETRICH BOENHOEFFER[1]

In the city there's a thousand things I wanna say to you.

THE JAM, "IN THE CITY"[2]

It's mid-morning and I take a break from the talk I'm preparing. I look out the large window and see the roof of the Naughty-But-Nice porn shop next door. I can see the minivan from the Scientologist Church parked across the street, just down from the theater and a bar. I see a guy in a Snoop Dogg T-shirt talking on his mobile phone.

I walk out of the office and follow the smell of freshly baked bread that's calling me out to the kitchen, where Miller is taking huge loaves and flat breads out of the oven. Over on the couch, I see Linnea, who has been praying and reading for a while before returning to her latest art project. She switches on an Elbow CD and creates wonders on canvas—I can see an amazing green picture with intricate designs peeking through the door of the studio. As I reach the kitchen, I smell the freshly made fair-trade coffee and pour myself a cup. I wander over to the prayer area and read some of the prayers on the wall. In the distance I can hear Ben working with an electric saw—he's creating a new prayer room at the other end of the building. As I read, I hear the door open and see some of the Transit students returning from their morning at Operation Breakthrough, a huge pre- and after-school program for Kansas City kids. John tells me about the kid with whom he spent time today—he was so full of medication that he just wanted to sleep. We sigh and offer up a little prayer. A police siren breaks through the moment of silence.

Welcome to one of our newest Boiler Rooms: Kansas City.

It's February 2006, and I am visiting Kansas City for the commissioning of their new building just outside the downtown area of the city. Later that night, as David, Molly, Wendy, Mary, Adam, Nathan and Marisa sit before us, we will wash their feet and pray for them, and I will trip out at how much God has done—more than I can comprehend.

Coming Back to Dietrich

As I reflect on the new Boiler Room communities emerging in the United States, the UK, Germany, and other places all over the world, I can't help but come back to Dietrich Bonhoeffer, who would have celebrated his one-hundredth birthday in 2006:

> The restoration of the church will surely come from a sort of new monasticism, which has only in common with the old an uncompromising attitude of life lived according to the Sermon on the Mount in the following of Christ. I believe it is now to call people together to do this.[3]

The monastic movements of the past began because their Church was in compromise. We find ourselves in the same place. The Church was catapulted to the center of culture when the Roman

Empire converted to Christianity. We are now in a different place, with the Church on the margins, just one voice among many—yet the danger for compromise is the same. The call of the Desert Fathers, of Francis, of the Celts, of Benedict, comes back to us. Will we live out this gospel of ours, without compromise, without fear? Will we center our lives on Jesus through prayer? Will we be kind to others, by seeking mercy and justice in our communities and our world? Will we share the gospel, passionately and purposefully, to a world that is lost?

In *The Cost of Discipleship*, Bonhoeffer highlighted three challenges that confront us as Christians at the beginning of the twenty-first century. Whether you plan to start a Boiler Room, intend to live by the Boiler Room Practices or are simply interested in monasticism and the story told in this book, these challenges are at the core of serving Christ in our world today. It's my dream that a new "confessing brethren" might emerge for this new millennium.

1. Jesus-Centered Living
Jesus is the only significance. Besides Jesus nothing has any significance. He alone matters.[4]

I'm tired of strategies, of keys to growth or models of building church. I'm tired because usually they don't work. I'm tired because they put me and others in boxes. I'm tired most of all because they're centered on us and not on Christ.

If there is one overwhelming message that Bonhoeffer brings, it's that Christ is the key—nothing and no one else can replace Him.

We've thought about the idea of community, of shared lives, of mission-minded individuals gathering together around a rule of life. Yet the place we aim for cannot be attained without Christ. Jesus has to be the center of all we plan, all we live out, all we do, all we are.

My dream is to see Boiler Rooms that gather around Jesus. My dream is to find daily rhythms of Christ-centered prayer. I dream of lives shared not around culture or race or class, but around Christ. I dream of mobile teams praying and sharing the light of Christ in the world. I dream of new music, new poetry, new art, all holding Christ at the core. And I dream of an army of disciples who love each other, love the world they are placed in and, ultimately, love Christ, even to death.

> May I never boast except in the cross of our Lord Jesus Christ, through which the world has been crucified to me, and I to the world (Gal. 6:14).

2. Costly Discipleship
Cheap grace is the deadly enemy of our church.[5]

In his preface to *Cost of Discipleship*, John de Grochy highlights the plight of the modern-day Church. He writes that we "have gathered like eagles around the carcass of cheap grace, and there we have drunk of the poison which has killed the life of following Christ."[6]

Let's face it, Christianity is much easier, much more palatable and frankly a whole lot better for us (in the short-term) if suffering and cost are removed. We like a gospel that offers us health, wealth and prosperity, and conversion is a lot more appealing if we can promise all of the above.

But we follow the gospel of Christ, a gospel that's a story of incarnation, in which God "became flesh and blood and moved into the neighborhood" (John 1:14, *THE MESSAGE*). It's the story of a Christ who was rejected and oppressed. It's the story of Christ who led a homeless, nomadic existence where "foxes have holes and the birds of the air have nests, but the Son of Man has no place to lay his head" (Matt. 8:20). It's the story of a Christ who suffered and died to achieve our salvation. It's the story of a Christ who, even when resurrected and victorious, still bore the wounds of His crucifixion (see John 20:27).

If the Good News is that we can become a part of Christ's story, we should not expect to have it any easier! If we "live easy," we spit on Christ's suffering and sacrifice and treat it as garbage. This is what Bonhoeffer called "cheap grace." In contrast, he called monasticism "a living protest against the secularization of Christianity and the cheapening of grace."[7] Monastics embrace a life of suffering and of difficulty, and they do so to keep alive the flame of Christ and His gospel.

Cheap grace causes us to hide the lost, because we don't want to mess up our lives or to offend or confront by sharing the gospel with others. Cheap grace causes us to hide the poor, because it is costly to befriend those who have nothing. Cheap grace leads us in the footsteps of the Levite and the Priest, who walked away from the dying man and crossed to the other side of the road (see Luke 10:25-41).

The gospel of Christ sets us in the footsteps of the Samaritan. It tears up our plans and schedules and demands that we stop by the roadside, give up our time and spend our money. As Bonhoeffer concluded, "Suffering . . . is the true badge of discipleship."[8]

I dream of Boiler Rooms that live this costly grace, where the poor are truly welcomed and loved and where hospitality is shown even to the most unlovely. I dream of Boiler Rooms where the gospel is proclaimed fearlessly, where injustices are challenged loudly and where life is championed freely. I dream of a people who don't waver in the face of suffering, but walk forward, knowing that as they suffer, they are joined with others around the globe, and joined with Christ, who suffered on our behalf.

3. Visible Communities
Flight into the invisible is a denial of the call. A community of Jesus which seeks to hide itself has ceased to follow Him.[9]

At the beginning of this book, we considered thin places, the Celtic idea of locations where the divide between heaven and Earth is narrowed. We were initially led to investigate this idea because of our smelly prayer rooms, which reeked of incense and reminded us of the "prayers of the saints" (Rev. 5:8). The presence of God was there.

As we thought about what God was doing, we were inevitably drawn to the notion of incarnation—Christ dwelling with us—and then to consider what it would mean for *us* to incarnate *our* prayers:

to be prayerful communities in the midst of our cities. We knew we were called not just to pray, but also to *be* the answers to some of our prayers. It was this breakthrough that led us to the seeds of the Boiler Room Practices and eventually to the Rule.

Bonhoeffer's third challenge is about communities: We cannot be hidden in our world. Communities must be visible, to be "cities on a hill" that can't be hidden (Matt. 5:14). The Incarnation is our blueprint as we seek to plant visible communities.

- The Incarnated Christ took His place in the world. He occupied space and engaged with the world around Him. In the same way, we must take our place in the world, occupying space and engaging with the world.

- The Incarnated Christ lived among people, but lived differently. We are called to live differently among—not apart from—others. This will make an impact and possibly lead to persecution, just as it did with Christ.

- The Incarnated Christ came to call the poor, the despised, the broken and the forgotten. Many of them embraced Him. He challenged the rich, the powerful, the comfortable and the self-righteous. Many of them rejected Him. As we seek to live Jesus-centered lives, we should expect the same reactions.

I dream of Boiler Rooms that are involved in social care and that challenge injustices publicly. I dream of Boiler Rooms that host meals for the poor and the downtrodden. I dream of Boiler Rooms that challenge the rich and the powerful. I dream of visible communities that display the light of Christ in the place where they are.

We cannot hide away—*we must not.* We cannot hide in our Christian cultures, bookshops or conferences. We cannot hide in our gated communities or comfortable streets. We must be a visible community, incarnating the Good News.

Rescue Shops

The birth, development and expansion of Boiler Rooms over the last five years has been quite a journey, and I must confess that it's been hard to distill it down into just one book! I am sure much more is yet to come. As long as God has redemption on His mind and in His heart, He will continue to draw His people close and then send them out, full of His love and purpose. C. T. Studd, the former cricketer who became a missionary, put it like this: "Some want to live within the sound of church or chapel bell—I want to run a rescue shop within a yard of hell."[10]

In the end, a Boiler Room is just such a "rescue shop." In the rhythm of life with God and each other, Jesus teaches us how to save.

For Further Thought

Grab yourself a coffee and spend some time in reflection. Journal any final thoughts you have after considering this book, and if it's appropriate, ask God to help you put into practice what He's speaking to you about.

Liturgy

Now to him who is able
to do immeasurably more than all we ask or imagine,
according to his power that is at work within us,
to him be glory in the church
and in Christ Jesus throughout generations,
forever and ever! Amen.
EPHESIANS 3:20-21

Leader: Father, we remember Your faithfulness to us.

All: You give good gifts, more than all we ask or imagine.

Leader: Father, we invite Your Spirit into our hearts afresh.

All: Power of God, be at work within us. Convict us of our sins. Heal us of our infirmities. Give us peace in our hearts. Give us passion in our souls.

Leader: Glory to You, God.

All: Glory to You in the church and throughout generations, forever and ever. Amen

Centers of *Shalom*

Pete Greig

*I told them how the hand of my God had been favorable to me
and also about the king's words which he had spoken to me.
Then they said, "Let us arise and build."
So they put their hands to the good work.*
NEHEMIAH 2:18, *NASB*

In my introduction, I admitted that Andy Freeman and I have more in common with Napoleon Dynamite (the ludicrous nerd) than Napoleon Bonaparte (the military hero). I rather regret that the ensuing chapters probably proved this point.

In a vain attempt to break out of geekdom, I decided a couple of years ago to visit a very fashionable store in town in search of a pair of trousers. This particular shop sells urban street wear for skaters, snowboarders, power-kiters and jugglers, and the guy behind the counter isn't so much a shop assistant as a one-man definition of Cool. I stepped nervously across the threshold, noticing the small cluster of pierced-up dudes hanging around the counter talking slowly as if they were stoned. They eyed me up and down with evident disdain and returned to conversation. Apologetically, I snuck past them to the trouser rail and began flicking through the extensive range of voluminous, multi-pocketed, camouflage pants.

Suddenly, a voice from the check-out: "Yo, dude!"

"Um, hello," I replied—adding a very unconvincing "dude."

"Need any help over there?" It was the guy with the shaggy hair and pierced eyebrow.

Secretly, I felt like I was 10 years old and the coolest kid at school had just deigned to talk to me on the playground.

"I'm fine thanks, erm . . . dude." *I have to stop saying that word.* Then the assistant with the pierced eyebrow said the most surprising thing possible: "I saw you at church last night."

I was speechless. Was it a wind-up? Had he hated it? What had I said? Why had he come? *If this guy is a Christian,* I figured, eyeing him nervously, *he is deep undercover.*

"How did you like it?" I asked, probing for clues.

"Yeah, church was *fat!*" came the reply.

I have a confession to make at this point—a confession that will, I suspect, condemn me for all time to the Nether Realms of Uncool in the minds of many. Standing in that shop, staring like a bewildered octogenarian at that disheveled paragon of all things youthful, I had absolutely no idea whether "fat" (or *phat* as I later discovered) meant bad, good or indifferent. Had he loved church? Had he despised it? Flailing for answers, I tried another angle.

"W-what did you think of our building?" (We had recently moved into a large converted warehouse and tricked it out with video screens and a state-of-the-art sound system.)

"Man," came the answer, "it made me *sick.*"

While I was unsure about the merits of *phat,* I was quite certain that vomiting was fundamentally undesirable, and with that realization, it became clear to me that he had hated church. He had despised our pastel sweaters, our under-pocketed trousers, our value footwear, our jeans with elasticized waists, our inability to dance let alone to juggle, skate or surf. He had been turned off Jesus forever by our soft-rock singing, our unpunctured anatomies and our misguided notion that kites are merely a bit of harmless fun for small children on a Sunday afternoon. He and his friends, I now realized, were laughing at me.

With mounting indignation, I decided I didn't want any of his stupid trousers. What was so cool about paying double for pockets only an orangutan could reach without stooping? Why on earth had I been considering the merits of a pair of militarily camouflaged trousers in a quaint, English cathedral city? Hurriedly I breezed out of the shop but, as I did so, the guy behind the counter called after me:

"Maybe I'll catch you again on Sunday . . . later, dude!"

I looked back in surprise—he wasn't joking! He was smiling enthusiastically. He had liked his visit to church after all. And slowly it dawned on me that—for this particular human being—if a thing was *phat* it was good and if it made him *sick* it was even better.

Communication is never easy, but when it comes to prayer—which is to say, when it comes to conversing with a divine, invisible, inaudible Being whose very existence is questioned by many—communication is even harder.

We know that the first disciples (who went on to have very significant prayer lives) found prayer difficult, because one day they welcomed Jesus back from one of His regular prayer times with a confession of need: "Lord, teach us to pray" (Luke 11:2). In response, Jesus gave them The Lord's Prayer as a model, saying "This, then, is *how* you should pray" (Matt. 6:9, emphasis added).

New Wine

I'm writing these closing words on an icy knife of a day in the snow-covered city of Madison, Wisconsin, where a hundred people have gathered from all over North America to strengthen our relationships and thus grow together in our understanding of the Boiler Room journey, depicted by Andy so beautifully in this book. The prophets of doom may be writing our generation off in large block letters on the sanctuary walls, but here in Madison, looking around the room at all these amazing people—some bound for Iceland, Mexico and the Middle East, artists and activists, thinkers and blue-collar pragmatists—it's evident that God is pouring new wine on this generation.

Last weekend I had the privilege of speaking to several hundred students in Phoenix, Arizona. You should have seen the passion with which they worshiped, how intently they listened and

how wholeheartedly they responded! More than 100 attended a
seminar designed for just 20 people on the subject of community.
More than 400 students prayed continually, night and day, for
56 days before Christmas.

God is pouring out new wine on our generation, but where,
I wonder, are the new wineskins that can contain and convey
God's many blessings while the wine matures and grows in poten-
cy and depth? Jesus cautions us like this:

> No one pours new wine into old wineskins. If he does, the
> new wine will burst the skins, the wine will run out and
> the wineskins will be ruined. No, new wine must be
> poured into new wineskins (Luke 5:37-38).

Jesus says that if we do not change to embrace the new thing
God is doing, there may well be a double tragedy. First, the old
wineskins may be damaged as they try to contain something that
cannot fit for long within our present cultural protocols. Second,
blessings God is pouring out on our generation may be wasted if
they are not given the flexible space necessary for new wine to
mature into a vintage.

Of course, everyone wants the passion and energy of younger
people to prop up their own status quo. I had a cup of tea with a
young guy named Eno who had literally led hundreds of his
friends to Jesus when he converted from a nominally Muslim
background. At the weekly rehearsals of his band and at gigs, Eno
began to read the Bible to friends and fans, and many responded
to the gospel without having had any prior contact with traditional expressions of church. Eventually, however, a local pastor heard
about this mini-revival and (with excellent motives, I'm sure)
sought to temper the wildness and immaturity by fitting each new
Christian into his church cell-group structure. Sadly, this forced
action killed the momentum, sidelined the wild young leaders and
within a year, most of those baby Christians had fallen away from
the faith. By seeking to squeeze new wine into an old wineskin,
that pastor did damage to both.

We see thousands of young people worshiping with all their hearts to wonderful new songs. Will that passion mature or subside when suffering comes? We live on the cusp of an unprecedented wave of possibilities as the world is changed forever by information technology. Will the Church be changed too, or will we use new technology to prop up the old way of doing and seeing things? Small communities of people are seeking to plant simple expressions of church in pubs, clubs and cyberspace. Will we bless and support such initiatives or haggle for members and ownership of the word "church"? Businesses are being launched by those with a desire to minister in the marketplace by bridging the sacred-secular divide. Will we encourage entrepreneurial Christianity and morph to resource its pioneers in spite of the mess, or will we sue to maintain a monopoly on ministry within the walls of Sunday morning and the incumbent priestly elite?

The Church Is Bigger Than You Think

In his book *The Church Is Bigger Than You Think,* missiologist Patrick Johnstone argues that there have been at least three major expressions of Christian community down the ages. We are most comfortable, he says, with the *congregational* model that (by definition) gathers people in certain places at certain times and therefore tends toward an emphasis on buildings and programs. Congregations will probably always be the predominant expression of church, functioning effectively as a wineskin for many of God's blessings and as an agency for the advancement of the kingdom of heaven.

However, Johnstone also identifies two noncongregational models of church that, he says, have been vitally important throughout Church history and that we cannot afford to ignore. First, there is the *apostolic* (missional) expression of church. An example of this is a mission agency like Youth With A Mission, which does not function as a congregational model and ardently resists the idea that it might be a "church," even though it has established many wonderful, dynamic communities of prayer, discipleship and evangelism (called Bases) all over the world. Second, Johnstone recognizes the *monastic* tradition of communities that minister to God and to the world in prayer. The apostolic and the monastic models, he says, are vital expressions of God's Church, raised up in every generation to perform functions that congregations cannot.[1]

I remember calling a relatively small meeting at the first Boiler Room venue in Reading one day, only to discover that they didn't have the basic components for a meeting of 30 people. Andy Freeman was embarrassed that there weren't enough chairs and no audio-visual equipment—but I was delighted! This community had, at that time, been praying together continually for a year, reaching out evangelistically and doing much that is reminiscent of the Early Church . . . and had done so without the kinds of meetings we consider essential to church life!

Boiler Rooms are an experiment in the apostolic and monastic expressions of Christian community, because we feel that the congregational model is very well represented in most parts of the Western world. We believe that the outward apostolic impulse of simple communities centered on mission and the inward monastic instinct toward prayer and solitude might be deeply attractive to a globalizing, tribalizing post-Christian culture in which congregations do not always fit as meaningfully or as naturally as they once did.

Centers of *Shalom*

One of Jesus' most common greetings was *Shalom Aleichem,* which means "peace be with you," and one of God's names revealed in the Bible is *Jehovah Shalom.* The dream of the people of God has always been for *shalom,* a profound and integrated peace expressed not just in inward tranquility but also outwardly in righteous relationships and glorious community. It's a dream we see outworked in the Early Church and in the Celtic monasteries with their holistic mission and authentic, redemptive lifestyles. It's a dream we still cherish.

When Chairman Mao expelled all Christian missionaries from China in the 1950s and established Communist collectives across the nation, many people feared for the wellbeing of the Church in that land. Under oppression and persecution, it thrived and the residual Christian communities often modeled the aspirations of Communism more effectively than the Communist enclaves themselves. In a delightful little book called *The Jesus Family in Communist China* written in the 1960s, there is a moving depiction of the way that these Christian villages blessed their environment and baffled the government inspectors by outdoing the Communists in sharing resources for the greater good.[2] Often as you approached one of these Christian villages, you would notice that the quality of the roads was steadily improving, as was the irrigation in the fields and the standard of living of the surrounding villagers. The Christian villages were so well run because the Christians spent all their spare resources (their "tithe") on their neighbors, helping those outside the village in practical ways. What a great picture of the "colonies of heaven" described by Dietrich Bonhoeffer when he dreamed of a new form of monasticism centered on the Sermon on the Mount! How wonderful it would be to see such communities within contemporary society, generously radiating the blessings of the Kingdom to their immediate neighbors.

On October 2, 2006, a small, introverted Amish community called Nickel Mines suddenly found itself as headline news all over the world in the most tragic circumstances possible. A 32-year-old milk truck driver named Charles Carl Roberts broke into a one-room schoolhouse in Pennsylvania and killed five girls aged 7 to 13 before killing himself. The reaction of that Christian community speaks powerfully about the radical power of *shalom* to transform a broken world.

First, some Amish elders visited Marie Roberts, the wife of the murderer, to offer forgiveness. I remember seeing this on television and gasping—did they really mean it? Wasn't it a bit too quick?

Next, the families of the five dead girls invited the widow to their own children's funerals. I struggle to imagine anything more painful than attending the funeral of one's own child. If the child had died unnaturally—if he or she had been killed—the pain would surely fuse with seething anger against the perpetrator. I struggle to comprehend how those families could seek out the wife of their children's murderer to request her presence at the funeral, as an act not of bitterness, but of forgiveness.

Before the media could dismiss the invitations as emotionally deluded or religiously fanatical, the villagers publicly requested that all relief monies intended for the bereaved families be shared equally with Marie Roberts and her children. She, they pointed out, was also grieving.

Finally, in a breath-taking act of peacemaking, more than 30 members of the Amish community quietly attended the funeral of the killer to stand with his family and join in the prayers.

"Their actions," concludes the bestselling author Diana Butler Bass, "not only witness that the Christian God is a God of forgiveness, but they actively created the conditions in which forgiveness could happen . . . Forgiveness is, as Christianity teaches, the prerequisite to peace. We forgive because God forgave us; in forgiving, we participate in God's dream of reconciliation and shalom."[3]

The Amish witness was not just an unusually forgiving response to terrible tragedy from a somewhat eccentric people. Deep down, we know that their response was profoundly and even shockingly different from anything to which we are accustomed. One might describe it as heroic. And it was not just one individual who mustered the courage to extend grace as sometimes happens in such situations (almost invariably from Christians)—it was five extended families and an entire community who chose to forgive. Their forgiveness was not just a matter of a few brave words and a gracious smile to the cameras. It was outworked at multiple, practical levels.

I believe that the world is crying out for communities like Nickel Mines that are truly and defiantly Christian. They are the hope of the world (see Col. 1:27). Through tragedy, the Amish reminded us that to be Christian in our present context is not merely *sub*-cultural—it is *counter*-cultural. We may, of course, find the Amish customs and clothing quaint, but many of their

convictions provide extraordinary answers to the clichéd question "What would Jesus do?"

Whether we look at this startling Amish act of forgiveness, the
Chinese villages that outshone the Communist ideal, the Celtic
monastic settlements that brought gospel-fuelled transformation
to entire regions of Northern Europe, or the world-changing witness of the Early Church, we see the power of Christian communities to live so that the world itself is transformed.

Looking Forward

Andy and I are dreaming of such "centers of shalom"—priestly
communities with a heartbeat of prayer—interacting symbiotically
with the wider culture and modeling something truly redemptive.
We're not advocating fleeing society in order to establish holy
enclaves, and neither are we envisaging staying within society to
function as a religiously inclined subculture that requires techniques and programs to bridge the divide. Our vision is for dynamic communities of faith outworked counter-culturally within cities,
workplaces and on campuses. These will be marked out by being:

- *Passionately and unashamedly abandoned in their love for Jesus.*
  We want to prioritize the ways and the worship of Jesus
  Christ above all else.

- *Corporate, not individualistic.* While it's probably impossible for anyone on their own to live an entirely perfect,
  ethical lifestyle (because when you get one area right you
  will probably be neglecting something else), together we
  can model something prophetically hopeful to a world
  in need of answers. Such communities can provide grace
  for the changing seasons of life. As Eugene Peterson says,
  "I am not myself by myself."[4]

- *Holistic, not fragmented.* We seek to live integrated lives that
  balance work, rest and prayer sustainably and that engage
  with society politically, economically and spiritually.

• *Qualitative.* Boiler Room communities will not be defined, verified or justified by their size or productivity but by their character—their love. While we believe that fruitfulness is both desirable and inevitable, our values are more important than our practices (although they are inseparable, in practice, as are faith and works). To put it another way, we do not believe that the end always justifies the means.

• *Fun.* We believe that a lifestyle of *shalom* is delightful, celebratory and life-affirming. While pain is inevitable, joy and playfulness are not, and the message of the kingdom of heaven demands that we seize opportunities to savor life's goodness whenever we can.

• *Generous.* Boiler Room communities are not competitive and miserly with vision and resources. We seek to be generous with our lives (sacrificial), with our salvation (missional), with our resources (merciful) and with our time. We believe that worship calls us to give and to live generously.

• *Experimental.* We believe that innovation is more likely to be good than bad. We suspect that it's better to change for the sake of change than to stay the same for the sake of staying the same. We want to create cultures in which there is an entrepreneurial spirituality and an implicit freedom to fail.

In other words, we want to establish communities that are like Jesus, because He modeled these ideals and did so lavishly. He was passionately and unashamedly abandoned to the will of His Father, regardless of personal cost. He was, and is, corporate rather than individualistic—Trinitarian in nature and communal in vocation. Jesus is also holistic, profoundly relevant to every aspect of life (not just the religious bits). He too was qualitative rather than quantitative, leaving behind just 11 representatives and a legacy of simple stories about mustard seeds and little children. Jesus was celebratory, magnetically attractive to children, a storyteller who poked fun at the pretentious and pompous, and who's first miracle took place at a party. Jesus is the true innovator, Creator of all things! Finally, Jesus Christ is, as we know, eternally generous, giving His likeness to humanity, His life on the cross and His love unconditionally.

This, then, is our story and our vision. Communities of prayer, mission and justice centered on Jesus have touched and transformed the world before, and our prayer is that it might happen again. We're busy forming such greenhouses of *shalom*, intentional communities centered not on meetings or buildings, but on a disciplined and delightful rhythm of prayer and focused outward on those who are poor materially and spiritually. Join us!

Lord, I have heard of your fame;
I stand in awe of your deeds, O Lord.
Renew them in our day,
in our time make them known;
in wrath remember mercy.
HABAKKUK 3:2

𝕿he Boiler Room Rule

The 24-7 Boiler Room Rule:

The Purposes, Principles, Practices and Customary
Requisite of a Licensed 24-7 Boiler Room Community

What Is a 24-7 Boiler Room Community?

A 24-7 Boiler Room is a Christ-centered community that practices
a daily rhythm of prayer, study and celebration while caring actively for the poor and the lost.

I. The Two Purposes

A 24-7 Boiler Room exists to love God *in prayer*
and to love its neighbors *in practice*. These purposes are contextualized in community and
expressed in a defined location.

II. The Three Principles

At the heart of every Boiler Room is a living community committed to being:
1. *Authentic:* True to Christ.
2. *Relational:* Kind to People.
3. *Missional:* Taking the Gospel to the World.

III. The Six Practices

Every Boiler Room Community applies these three principles practically through Six Practices.

1. A Boiler Room Is True to Christ by Being:

- A *prayerful* community, practicing a daily rhythm that includes all kinds of prayers on all occasions.
- A *creative* community where artistic expressions of prayer and worship take the form of art, sculpture, new music, poetry, dance, fun and a celebratory lifestyle.

2. A Boiler Room Is Kind to People by Being:

- A *just and merciful* community where the practical needs of the local poor are met and where liberation is championed.
- A *hospitable* community where pilgrims are welcomed, meals are shared and where friendships can flourish across boundaries of race and culture.

3. A Boiler Room Is Committed to Taking the Gospel to the World by Being:

- A *missional* community existing for incarnation and proclamation of the gospel to all people. To act as well as to pray.
- A *learning* community of training and discipleship, where people are growing in their faith, their life-skills and their ability to lead.

Practical Customary

The ancient monastics would often add a customary to their Rule as an explanation of how their values were to be worked out in practice. We sensed the Lord calling us to write a simple customary for our Boiler Rooms, giving guidelines about how to outwork the two purposes, three principles and six practices day to day.

1. The Practice of Prayer

Model #1: The Laus Perennis. Ideally, Boiler Rooms will pray continually night and day (known in the monastic traditions as the *laus perennis*). However, we do not see this as the only model of persevering prayer and do not require it of every Boiler Room unless the Lord has clearly given such a call.

Model #2: Rhythmic Prayer. Should a Boiler Room choose not to practice the *laus perennis*, we do expect there to be a disciplined *daily* rhythm of prayer. At least one of these daily gatherings should be held in the Boiler Room venue itself (unless the community is temporarily without such a base). There are many historical precedents for such a rhythm:

- Scholars tell us that the ancient Temple in Jerusalem conducted three fixed prayer meetings a day (at 9 A.M., noon and dusk) and we know that Early Church leaders endorsed this rhythm of prayer with their presence.

- The Benedictine Rule, practiced since the fifth century A.D., lays out a vigorous schedule of daily prayer including vigils (middle of the night), matins (pre-dawn), vespers (just before sunset) and compline (night).

- In addition to the daily rhythm of prayer practiced by all Boiler Room communities, we also expect them to establish regular seasons of 24-7 (night and day) prayer. For instance, our West London Boiler Room currently prays nonstop for one week in every six.

2. The Practice of Mission

Boiler Rooms are missional communities, which means that our prayer times must never become insular or disembodied from practical engagement with those who do not share our Christian faith. The Boiler Room is both a launch pad for outreach (sending Christians out) and a center for in-reach (gathering people in).

- *Outreach*: Boiler Rooms are encouraged to partner annually with 24-7 Mission (or an equivalent agency) in mobilizing short-term teams to engage cross-culturally in kind and creative evangelization. They are also encouraged to engage in local expressions of ongoing mission, such as Alpha Courses and student missions.

- *In-reach*: Our sacred space must never become so rarefied that it seems inaccessible to those unaccustomed to church culture. Rather, we want our culture and our buildings to be welcoming and inclusive places in which people can feel safe and unconditionally accepted. We believe in becoming an answer to our own prayers for the poor and the lost.

3. The Practice of Mercy and Justice

We expect our Boiler Rooms to be agencies of mercy and justice. We ask them to help people engage actively with the poor and oppressed: practically at an inter-personal level, prayerfully for the local community and even politically at a global level.

- *Personally*: There should be at least one opportunity a week for people to join in with a reputable project that helps the poor, excluded or disadvantaged.

- *Locally*: We encourage Boiler Rooms to pray purposefully for statutory bodies such as the police and social services and also for Christian ministries working locally with the marginalized.

· *Globally*: Boiler Rooms in free societies are also encouraged to campaign intelligently and prayerfully on behalf of the poorest people on Earth.

4. The Practice of Hospitality and Pilgrimage

Boiler Rooms are required to offer simple hospitality to strangers wishing to stay and pray. They must have the ability to provide—or at least have easy access to—short-term accommodation, even if this is not possible in the venue itself. Where possible, there should be a warm welcome for people visiting, a place to drink coffee and chat, and a regular open/shared meal. Boiler Rooms may also organize annual opportunities for pilgrimage, either within their own country or overseas.

5. The Practice of Creativity

Boiler Room communities are called on to encourage and enjoy creativity in all its forms. While some Boiler Rooms will be stronger than others in this area, we expect the creative arts to be a key component of every Boiler Room. Artists should be welcomed and encouraged and artistic expression and communication with God should be open to all. To create an environment for this, Boiler Rooms should have space set aside in their venues and money in their budgets for facilitating the arts—this can be anything from a recording studio to a pottery kiln, a garden to a dance studio, a dark-room to a gourmet kitchen!

6. The Practice of Learning and Discipleship

All Boiler Rooms are learning communities committed to mutual discipleship, study and the ongoing spiritual formation of the community and its individual members. Some Boiler Rooms are recognized by 24-7 as Training Centers, thus benefiting from a regular influx of trainees.

Within the core team at the heart of every Boiler Room community, we expect there to be a climate of relational accountability and mutual submission. An abbot or abbess is appointed to lead this team lovingly and with recognized authority, accountable ultimately to God and temporarily to 24-7 alongside locally appointed structures.

Many Boiler Rooms practice a daily rhythm of prayer, work, study and rest, something that the early Celtic monasteries lived out and that inspired us in our early days as Boiler Rooms. Whenever Boiler Rooms multiply we expect the sending community to offer strong initial support and oversight to these new communities they have planted.

Not Buildings but Community

Although the term "Boiler Room" evokes the image of a room within a building, a Boiler Room is *not* a building—it is a community committed to the purposes, principles and practices of the lifestyle outlined above. A Boiler Room community is neither defined by, nor dependent on, the use of a fixed base, just as a human family continues to be a family even if it loses its home. The first task of a group seeking to start a Boiler Room is to build a local praying community—there is no way a Boiler Room can be carried alone.

Having said this, just as a home is helpful for a family, a home is helpful for a Boiler Room. Having such a base (or a series of buildings within walking distance of each other) can greatly enhance the Six Practices of the community by providing:

- A dedicated place for prayer
- A studio for artists
- A hostel for pilgrims
- A mission station for outreach
- A launching pad for acts of mercy
- A training base for the learning community

In theory, a building is not essential, but the reality in practice is that no Boiler Room can be expected to continue fruitfully for very long without such a center.

To learn more about the Rule and to obtain a study guide called "Signs of Life" written by Phil Anderson, visit www.philanderson.org/signsoflife.

So, You Want to Start a Boiler Room?

If you're interested in starting a Boiler Room where you live, here are our top five tips for getting started.

1. *Organize a 24-7 prayer week.* This is always the best starting point. Organize a room and get people praying; see what God does and how people react. It will give you a much clearer picture of where things are locally. Most existing locations have run several prayer weeks before even considering starting a Boiler Room. You can find details about prayer weeks and register at www.24-7prayer.com.

2. *Gather friends around you.* Do others share a vision for a Boiler Room? We suggest you get together informally, chat, pray, eat a meal together. Good Boiler Rooms always build from friendship.

3. *Get in touch.* If your prayer weeks go well and you still sense God prompting you about Boiler Rooms, get in touch with us. There is a dedicated Boiler Room website at www.boiler-rooms.com that can tell you how.

4. *Go and visit a Boiler Room.* The Internet site has details about commissioned Boiler Rooms globally, and the next step is to go and have a look. The vision of Boiler Rooms is better caught than taught, so we suggest you

spend as much time as possible in existing Boiler Rooms. See also the following section on 24-7 Transit, which enables you to spend nine months in leadership training at a Boiler Room.

5. *Live out the Rule.* The Boiler Room Rule is designed to work in big venues or small groups. If things continue to progress, we suggest you begin to live out the rule among your friends/community. Meet regularly to pray, practice hospitality and serve the poor. If the Rule works well among you when you're under the radar, it will serve you well if a Boiler Room is eventually launched where you are.

24-7 Transit Course

For those considering beginning a Boiler Room, we strongly recommend our Transit Course. The course is based around the dual processes of (1) the inward journey of spiritual formation and (2) the outward journey of social transformation. More information about Transit can be obtained from the website, www.24-7 prayer.com, or by post:

UK 24-7 Transit
Tim Rose
c/o 24-7 Transit
City of London Boiler Room
The Basement
4-14 Tabernacle Street
London EC2A 4LU
tim@e2w.org.uk

USA 24-7 Transit
24-7 Prayer USA Office
3829 Main Street, Unit 2
Kansas City, MO 64111
usa@24-7prayer.com

Germany 24-7 Transit
Ralf Neumann
Dorfstrauss 62/Alte Scale
04565 OT Ramsdorf
Regis-Breitingen, Germany
ralf.neumann@24-7prayer.com

To read about stuff we couldn't fit in this book
and to discuss and comment, visit
http://punkmonk.typepad.com/.

Recommended Reading

There have been many books that have helped and influenced us while the Boiler Room communities have developed. The following is a summary of those titles we drew heavily on and found consistently helpful.

Missional Community

Bonhoeffer, Dietrich. *The Cost of Discipleship*. New York: Touchstone, 1995. Bonhoeffer's call to new monastic communities echoes throughout this book.

———. *Life Together*. New York: HarperSanFrancisco, 1978.

Foster, Richard. *Streams of Living Water*. New York: Harper San-Francisco, 2001. Foster explores the six great traditions of Christian spiritual practice (contemplative, holiness, charismatic, social justice, evangelical and incarnational) through biblical and ancient lenses and case studies of people who expressed them.

Johnstone, Patrick. *The Church Is Bigger Than You Think*. Darlington, UK: Evangelical Press, 1998.

Peterson, Eugene. *Christ Plays in Ten Thousand Places*. Grand Rapids, MI: Eerdmans Publishing Company, 2005. Peterson's "conversation in spiritual theology" has become one of the central books for our Transit training year and helped us think about incarnational communities.

Vanier, Jean. *Community and Growth*. London: Darton, Longman and Todd, 1976. Written by the founder of the L'Arche Community, this book is one I regularly return to for its insights about living out simple community. Chapters about meals and hospitality are especially helpful.

Celtic Spirituality

Bradley, Ian. *Colonies of Heaven: Celtic Models for Today's Church.* London: Darton, Longman and Todd, 2000. Ian Bradley's book taught us a great deal about how the Celts approached communities and church.

Mitton, Michael. *Restoring the Woven Cord.* London: Darton, Longman and Todd, 1995.

Simpson, Ray. *Exploring Celtic Spirituality.* London: Hodder & Stoughton, 1995.

Monasticism and Rules of Life

Bessenecker, Scott. *The New Friars.* Downers Grove, IL: InterVarsity Press, 2006.

Chesterton, G. K. *Saint Francis of Assisi.* London: Continuum Publishing, 2001. Chesterton's biography was by far the most insightful into the life of Saint Francis and most helpful to me. It's honest, straight-talking and a great read.

Dunn, Marilyn. *The Emergence of Monasticism.* Oxford: Blackwell Publishing, 2000.

Gregg, Robert C. *Athanasius: The Life of Antony.* New York: Harper-SanFranciso, spiritual classics ed., 2006.

Jamison, Abbot Christopher. *Finding Sanctuary* (Collegeville, MN: Liturgical Press, 2006). Written by the abbot of Worth Abbey (featured in the BBC show *The Monastery*), this is a helpful, readable and practical journey through monasticism and the Rule of St. Benedict.

Talbot, John Michael. *Hermitage: A Place of Prayer and Spiritual Renewal.* New York: Crossroad Publishing, 1988.

Prayer and Practice

Celtic Daily Prayer: Prayers and Readings from the Northumbria Community. New York: HarperCollins, 2001. Used by many Boiler Rooms as part of their rhythm of prayer, we have continually found this a helpful resource.

Claiborne, Shane. *The Irresistible Revolution.* Grand Rapids, MI: Zondervan, 2006. A profound and challenging book written by a man who is practicing new monasticism in the heart of real life. A friend recently wrote to tell me how this book had "done some major damage to her life."

Greig, Pete. *Red Moon Rising.* Orlando, FL: Relevant Books, 2003.

Schaeffer, Francis. *Art and the Bible* (L'Abri pamphlet). Downers Grove, IL: InterVarsity Press, 1973.

Sider, Ronald. *Rich Christians in an Age of Hunger.* Nashville, TN: W Publishing Group, 2005.

Endnotes

Punk Monk

1. The American Heritage® Dictionary of the English Language, Fourth Edition, Houghton Mifflin Company, 2004, s.v. "punk." http://dictionary.reference.com/browse/punk (accessed January 2007).
2. WordNet® 2.1, Princeton University, s.v. "monk." http://dictionary.reference.com/browse/monk (accessed January 2007).

Introduction: Colonies of Heaven

1. Ian Bradley, *Colonies of Heaven: Celtic Models for Today's Church* (London: Darton, Longman and Todd, 2000), pp. 55-56.
2. Leonard Sweet, in an address to the United Methodist Association of Communicators' annual meeting, January 11-13, 2001, in San Diego, California, USA.
3. Robert Cahill, *How the Irish Saved Civilization* (London: Sceptre, 1995), p. 148.
4. Jerry C. Doherty, *A Celtic Model of Ministry: The Reawakening of Community Spirituality* (Collegeville, MN: The Liturgical Press, 2003), pp. 29-31.

Chapter 1: Revolution: Evolution

1. G. K. Chesterton, *Saint Francis of Assisi* (New York: Doubleday and Company, 1924).
2. Tracy Chapman, "Talkin' Bout a Revolution," EMI April Music, Inc. for Purple Rabbit Music, New York, NY.
3. Thomas à Kempis, *The Imitation of Christ* (New York: Vintage Classics, 1998).
4. U2, "New Year's Day," Universal Polygram International, Los Angeles, California.
5. Karl Marx, *Critique of Hegel's Philosophy of Right* (Cambridge, MA: Cambridge University Press, 1977).
6. From Bono's introduction to "Helter Skelter" on *Rattle and Hum:* "This song Charles Manson stole from the Beatles . . . we're stealing it back."
7. Chambers Reference Online (*Chambers Dictionary*), s.v. "revolution." http://www.chambersharrap.co.uk/chambers/features/chref/chref.py/main?query=revolution&title=21st (accessed January 2007).
8. The Clash, "Hate and War," Universal Polygram International, Los Angeles, California.
9. The Campaign for Nuclear Disarmament (CND) campaigns nonviolently to rid the world of nuclear weapons and other weapons of mass destruction and to create genuine security for future generations (see www.cnduk.org); Amnesty International advocates on behalf of others for issues of human rights (see www.amnesty.org).
10. Dietrich Bonhoeffer, from a letter written to his brother Karl-Friedrich Bonhoeffer from London on January 14, 1935, published in *A Testament to Freedom: The Essential Writings of Dietrich Bonhoeffer* (New York: HarperSanFrancisco, 1995), p. 424.
11. Paul Bond, "Obituary of Joe Strummer," World Socialist Website. http://www.wsws.org/articles/2003/jan2003/stru-j13.shtml (accessed January 2007).
12. Ed Leidel, "Awakening a Grassroots Spirituality" paper, section 3, "Searching for an Integrated Lifestyle: Breathing In and Breathing Out." http://www.eastmich.org/awakening/Section3.htm?FCItemID=S000D597F (accessed January 2007).

Chapter 2: Beginnings in Thin Places

1. Ray Simpson, *Exploring Celtic Christianity* (London: Hodder and Stoughton, 1995).
2. Siouxie Sioux, quoted in Simon Goddard, "Interview: Siouxie Sioux," *Uncut*. http:// www.uncut.co.uk/music/siouxsie_sioux/interviews/32 (accessed February 2007).
3. Jack Hayford, cited in Gerard Kelly, *Spring Harvest Study Guide* (Sussex: Spring Harvest, 2003).
4. Susan Hines-Brigger, "Finding God in the 'Thin Places,'" *The American Catholic*, March 2001. http://www.americancatholic.org/messenger/Mar2001/feature1.asp#F3 (accessed January 2007).
5. "Consecration and Dedication of a Building," Portsmouth Anglican Diocese. http://www.portsmouth.anglican.org/info/bishop/liturgy/diocesan_liturgical_re sources/consecration_and_dedication_of_a_building/ (accessed January 2007).
6. Marcus Borg, *The Heart of Christianity* (New York: HarperSanFrancisco, 2003).
7. I first read about incarnational youth ministry from *Youth Work and the Mission of God* by Pete Ward (London: SPCK, 1997). The idea may have been someone else's, but I have to credit Wardy for helping me with this.
8. Eden Project, Manchester, part of the ministry of The Message Trust. http://www. message.org.uk/edenproject.cfm (accessed January 2007).

Chapter 3: History Speaks

1. Alfred Lord Tennyson, "Ulysses," first published in *Poems* (London: Edward Moxon, Dover Street, 1842).
2. John Lennon and Paul McCartney, "The Long and Winding Road," Sony/ATV Tunes LLC/Beatles, Nashville, Tennessee.
3. "Reading from God's Perspective," Tilehurst Free Church. http://www.curve. org.uk/RFGP/RFGP.htm (accessed February 2007).
4. *The Rule of Saint Benedict in English* (Collegeville, MN: The Liturgical Press, 1982), 22:5.
5. The main sources used for the history of Reading Abbey were Dr. Jamieson B. Hurry, *Reading Abbey* (London: Elliot Stock, 1915) and Rev. E. Scantlebury, *The Story of Reading Abbey and the Catholic Church in Reading* (Reading, 1938).
6. John Wesley, *A Plain Account of Christian Perfection* (Kansas City, MO: Beacon Hill Press, 1966).
7. Compline is an ancient form of liturgical night prayer used in many traditions. Simon and his friends who led Compline each Friday for a season at Reading Boiler Room used a Celtic form of Compline from *Celtic Daily Prayer: Prayers and Readings from the Northumbria Community* (London: HarperCollins, 2001).
8. *The Rule of Saint Benedict in English,* 53:1.
9. Ibid., 53:16.
10. Translations by Catherine Misrahi, *The Love of Learning and the Desire of God* (New York: Fordham University Press, 1982).
11. Author unknown, cited in Dr. Jamieson B. Hurry, *Reading Abbey*.
12. Steve Stockman, *Walk On: The Spiritual Journey of U2* (Orlando, FL: Relevant Books, 2002).
13. *The Rule of Saint Benedict in English,* 37:2.
14. Ibid., 58:24.
15. From "The Legend of the Three Companions," thought to be written by Brother Angelo, *Saint Francis of Assisi: English Omnibus of the Sources of the Life of Saint Francis,* edited by Marion A. Habig (Quincy, IL: Franciscan Press, 1991).

16. From a story on www.24-7prayer.com.
17. If you would like to find out more about the order and explore the practical outworking of their Rule for today, I recommend Pete's book *The Vision and the Vow* (Orlando, FL: Relevant Books, 2004) and a biography of Count von Zinzendorf called *The Lord of the Ring* by Philip Anderson (Ventura, CA: Regal Books, 2007).

Chapter 4: From Buildings to Communities

1. Pete Greig, *The 24-7 Prayer Manual* (Colorado Springs, CO: Cook Communications, 2005).
2. Ibid.
3. Robert Lacey and Danny Danziger, *The Year 1000* (New York: Back Boy Books, 2000).
4. Jean Vanier, *Community and Growth* (London: Darton, Longman and Todd, 1976).

Chapter 5: The Ancient Art of Breathing

1. Karl Barth, *Prayer and Preaching* (London: S.C.M. Press, 1964), p. 19.
2. Bono, quoted in Michka Assayas, *Bono: in Conversation with Michka Assayas* (New York: Riverhead Books, 2005), p. 272.
3. David Adam, *Walking the Edges: Living in the Presence of God* (London: SPCK, 2003), p. 66.
4. John O'Donohue, *Anam Cara: A Book of Celtic Wisdom* (New York: Cliff Street Books, 1998), p. 109.
5. Benedicta Ward, cited in Henri J.M. Nouwen, *The Way of the Heart* (London: Darton Longman and Todd, 1999), p. 34.
6. Christopher Jamison, *Finding Sanctuary: Monastic Steps for Everyday Life* (Collegeville, MN: Liturgical Press, 2006), p. 5.
7. Adam, *Walking the Edges: Living in the Presence of God*, p. 66.
8. Ian Bradley, *Colonies of Heaven: Celtic Models for Today's Church* (London: Darton, Longman and Todd, 2000), p. 56.
9. Ibid.

Chapter 6: The Boiler Room Rule

1. Count Nicklaus Ludwig von Zinzendorf, *Rules of the Order of the Mustard Seed* (Budingen, 1740).
2. Thom Yorke, "Exit Music (for a Film)," WB Music Corp., Los Angeles, California.
3. Roy Hattersley, *The Life of John Wesley* (New York: Random House, 2003).
4. "The Spirit of the Foundry," a lecture by Lord Leslie Griffiths at The Healthy Church Event in Houston, Texas, January 2005.
5. John Wesley, *A Plain Account of Christian Perfection* (Kansas City, MO: Beacon Hill Press, 1966).
6. Christopher Jamison, *Finding Sanctuary* (Collegeville, MN: Weidenfeld and Nicolson, 2006).
7. Much of my inspiration to look at Zinzendorf's vow has come from *The Vision and the Vow* by Pete Greig (Orlando, FL: Relevant Books, 2004). The original vow was taken by a handful in the Moravian community led by Zinzendorf.
8. "The Throne of God," a talk given by Fr. Timothy Radcliffe O.P., for the World Conference of Abbots, Saint Anselmo, September 2000.
9. Ibid.
10. Ibid.

11. John Stott, *Between Two Worlds* (Grand Rapids, MI: Eerdmans, 1994).

12. Adrian House, *Francis of Assisi* (Mahwah, NJ: Paulist Press, 2003).

13. Pete Greig, *The Vision and the Vow* (Orlando, FL: Relevant Books, 2004).

14. Fr. Timothy Radcliffe, OP in "The Throne of God," prepared remarks for the Conference of Abbots, San Anselmo in September 2000.

15. House, *Francis of Assisi.*

16. Cardinal Basil Hume, *To Be a Pilgrim* (Slough, UK: Triangle, 1994).

Chapter 7: The Practice of Prayer

1. Richard Foster, *Celebration of Discipline* (London: Hodder and Stoughton, 1998).

2. The Flaming Lips, "The Sound of Failure/It's Dark . . . Is It Always This Dark?" W. B. Corp., Los Angeles, California.

3. Heinrich Zimmer, *The Irish Element in Medieval Culture* (New York: Putnam's Sons, 1891).

4. J.M. Clark, *The Abbey of Saint Gall as a Center of Literature and Art* (Oxford: Cambridge University Press, 1926).

5. Ray Simpson, *Exploring Celtic Spirituality* (London: Hodder and Stoughton, 1995).

6. Ibid.

7. Bede, *Ecclesiastical History of the English People* (New York: Penguin Classics, 1991).

8. Andreas Davis Pinkey, *Abraham Lincoln: Letters from a Slave Girl* (New York: Winslow Press, 2001).

9. The Westminster Catechism (1642-47).

10. Richard Foster, *Prayer* (London: Hodder and Stoughton, 1992).

11. Bill Hybels, *Too Busy Not to Pray* (Downers Grove, IL: Intervarsity Press, 1998).

12. P. T. Forsythe, *The Soul of Prayer* (Vancouver, B.C.: Regent College Publishing, 1997).

13. Pete Greig, *The 24-7 Prayer Manual* (Colorado Springs, CO: Cook Communications, 2005).

14. Ibid.

15. Robert Lacey and Danny Danziger, *The Year 1000* (New York: Back Bay Books, 2000).

16. Richard Foster, *Streams of Living Water* (San Francisco: HarperSanFrancisco, 2001).

17. Simpson, *Exploring Celtic Christianity.*

18. Matthew Henry, quoted by Arthur Wallis, *In the Day of Thy Power* (Columbia, MO: Cityhill Publishing, 1990).

19. Pete Greig and Dave Roberts, *Red Moon Rising* (Orlando, FL: Relevant Books, 2003).

20. Check out Pete's book *God on Mute: Engaging the Silence of Unanswered Prayer* (Ventura, CA: Regal Books, 2007) for an in-depth exploration of this struggle.

21. Matthew Henry, *Commentary on the Whole Bible* (Peabody, MA: Hendrikson, new ed., 2006)

Chapter 8: The Practice of Creativity

1. Francis Schaeffer, "Art and the Bible," L'Abri pamphlet (Downers Grove, IL: InterVarsity Press, 1973).

2. Paul Bond, "Obituary of Joe Strummer," World Socialist Website. http://www.wsws.org/articles/2003/jan2003/stru-j13.shtml (accessed January 2007).

3. Esther de Waal, *The Celtic Way of Prayer* (London: Hodder and Stoughton, 1996).

4. Ray Simpson, *Exploring Celtic Christianity* (London: Hodder and Stoughton, 1995).

5. Shaeffer, "Art and the Bible."

6. Eugene Peterson, *Christ Plays in Ten Thousand Places* (Grand Rapids, MI: Eerdmans Publishing Company, 2005).

7. Michael Card, *Scribbling in the Sand* (Downers Grove, IL: InterVarsity, 2002).

8. Shaeffer, "Art and the Bible."
9. Card, *Scribbling in the Sand.*
10. Hans Rookmaker, "Letter to a Christian Artist," August 23, 1966, cited in Michael Card, *Scribbling in the Sand.*
11. Elbow, "Grace Under Pressure," W. B. Music Corp., Los Angeles, California.
12. Harold Best, *Music Through the Eyes of Faith* (New York: Harper Collins, 1993).
13. Herve de la Martiniere, quoted in the preface of Yanns Arthur Bertrand, *Earth from Above* (New York: Henry N. Abrams, Inc., 2005).
14. Noel Dermot O'Donoghue, *The Mountain Behind the Mountain* (Edinburgh: T&T Clark Books, 1993).
15. Brother Aidan, *Catholic World Report,* March 1993, quoted in Ray Simpson, *Exploring Celtic Christianity.*
16. Steve Turner, *Imagine: A Vision for Christians and the Arts* (Downers Grove, IL: Inter-Varsity Press, 2001).
17. "Global Worship Report," Worship and Arts Network, vol. 2, no. 8, June 2000. http://www.ad2000.org/tracks/worship/gwrv2n8.htm (accessed February 2007).
18. Turner, *Imagine: A Vision for Christians and the Arts.*
19. Margaret Wheatley, *Leadership and the New Science* (San Francisco: Berrett-Koeler, 2001).
20. C. S. Lewis, *The Lion, the Witch and the Wardrobe* (New York: Harper Collins, 2005).

Chapter 9: The Practice of Mercy and Justice

1. Martin Luther King, Jr., "Letter from a Birmingham Jail," April 16, 1963.
2. Simple Minds, "Wall of Love," EMI Virgin Music Inc., New York, NY.
3. Ray Simpson, *Exploring Celtic Spirituality* (London: Hodder and Stoughton, 1995).
4. W. R. Chambers, *Chambers English Dictionary* (Edinburgh, UK: Chambers Harrap Publishers, Ltd., 1998).
5. J.R.R. Tolkien, *The Fellowship of the Ring* (London: George Allen and Unwin, 1968).
6. William Temple, *Christianity and Social Order* (London: Shepheard Walwyn, Ltd., 1976).
7. Statistics based on 2005 U.S. Census Data, cited at "Hunger Facts: Domestic," Bread for the World website. http://www.bread.org/learn/hunger-basics/hunger-facts-domestic.html (accessed February 2007).
8. Nelson Mandela, from a speech at the Make Poverty History Launch, February 2005.
9. Jeremy Taylor, *The Rules and Exercises of Holy Living and the Rules and Exercises of Holy Dying* (Whitefish, MT: Kessinger Publishing, LLC, 2006).
10. Robin Cook, former U.K. Foreign Secretary, from a speech on May 12, 1997.

Chapter 10: The Practice of Hospitality and Pilgrimage

1. Michael Mitton, *Restoring the Woven Cord* (London: Darton, Longman and Todd, 1995).
2. The Smiths, "Is It Really So Strange?" Warner Music, Ltd., London.
3. Ellen MacArthur, "Taking on the World," *Daily Telegraph,* February 8, 2005.
4. *Chambers Reference Online,* s.v. "pilgrimage." http://www.chambersharrap.co.uk/chambers/features/chref/chref.py/main?query=pilgrimage&title=21st (accessed February 2007).
5. Ray Simpson, *Exploring Celtic Spirituality* (London: Hodder & Stoughton, 1995).
6. *NIV Study Bible* (London: Hodder & Stoughton), notes for Judges 19:23.

7. Simpson, *Exploring Celtic Spirituality*.
8. Esther de Waal, quoted in *The Celtic Way of Prayer* (London: Hodder & Stoughton, 2003).
9. Ibid.
10. Ibid.
11. Robert Brancatelli, "Pilgrimage as a Rite of Passage: A Guidebook for Youth Ministry," a thesis for Catholic University of America, Washington, D.C., 2001.
12. Jean Vanier, *Community and Growth* (London: Darton, Longman and Todd, 1976).
13. Ibid.
14. Ibid.
15. Alasdair MacIntyre, *After Virtue: A Study in Moral Theology* (Notre Dame, IN: University of Notre Dame, 1984).

Chapter 11: The Practice of Mission

1. Michael Mitton, *Restoring the Woven Cord* (London: Darton, Longman and Todd, 1995).
2. U2, "I Will Follow," Universal Polygram International, Los Angeles, California.
3. Pete Greig, *Red Moon Rising* (Orlando, FL: Relevant Books, 2003).
4. Nicky Gumble, *Questions of Life: A Practical Introduction to the Christian Faith* (Elgin, IL: David C. Cook Publishing Company, 2002).
5. C. H. Spurgeon, "The Lost Silver Piece," cited in *The Treasury of the New Testament* (Grand Rapids, MI: Zondervan, 1951).
6. Dietrich Bonhoeffer, *Life Together* (San Francisco: HarperSanFrancisco, 1978).
7. Thomas of Celano, "The Second Life of Saint Francis," cited in Marion A. Habig, ed., *Saint Francis of Assisi: Omnibus of the Sources* (Quincy, IL: Franciscan Press, 1991).
8. Eugene Peterson, *Christ Plays in Ten Thousand Places* (Grand Rapids, MI: Wm. B. Eerdmans Publishing Co., 2005).
9. William Harmless, *Desert Christians: An Introduction to the Literature of Early Monasticism* (New York: Oxford University Press USA, 2004).
10. From Release International website, www.releaseinternational.org.

Chapter 12: The Practice of Learning

1. Bob Geldof, "I Don't Like Mondays," Music Sales Corp., New York.
2. *Penguin Concise English Dictionary* (London: Penguin Books, 2001), s.v. "learning."
3. The *Oxford English Dictionary* (New York: Oxford University Press USA, 2nd ed., 1989) cites a 1912 work by the American writer George Ade, *Knocking the Neighbors*, as the origin of this phrase.
4. Dallas Willard, *The Spirit of the Disciplines* (New York: HarperSanFrancisco, 1991).
5. Margaret Wheatley, *Leadership and the New Science: Discovering Order in a Chaotic World* (San Francisco: Berrett-Koehler Publishers, 2006).
6. I. Howard Marshall, A. R. Millard, J. I. Packer and Donald J. Wiseman, eds., *IVP New Bible Dictionary*, 3rd edition (Downers Grove, IL: InterVarsity Press, 1996).
7. Eugene Peterson, *Christ Plays in Ten Thousand Places* (London: Hodder and Stoughton, 2005).
8. William Harmless, *Desert Christians: An Introduction to the Literature of Early Monasticism* (New York: Oxford University Press USA, 2004).
9. Dietrich Bonhoeffer, *Life Together* (New York: HarperSanFrancisco, 1978).
10. Ibid.
11. Northumbria Community, *Celtic Daily Prayer: Prayers and Readings from the Northumbria*

Community (San Francisco: HarperSanFrancisco, 2002).

12. Jean Leclercq, *Amour des Lettres et le Désir de Dieu: Initiation aux Auteurs Monastiques du Moyen Âge*. English translation by Catherine Misrahi, *The Love of Learning and the Desire of God* (New York: Fordham University Press, 1982)

13. Tony Jones, *The Sacred Way* (Grand Rapids, MI: Zondervan/Emergent YS, 2005).

14. Thomas Merton, *Spiritual Direction and Meditation* (Collegeville, MN: Liturgical Press, 1960).

15. Ibid.

16. Ibid.

Chapter 13: Punk Monks and Rescue Shops

1. Dietrich Bonhoeffer, *Life Together* (New York: HarperSanFrancisco, 1978).

2. Paul Weller, "In the City," Polydor Ltd., UK.

3. Dietrich Bonhoeffer, taken from a letter written to his brother Karl-Friedrich Bonhoeffer from London on January 14, 1935, published in *A Testament to Freedom: The Essential Writings of Dietrich Bonhoeffer* (San Francisco: HarperSanFrancisco, 1995), p. 424.

4. Ibid.

5. Ibid.

6. Ibid.

7. Ibid.

8. Ibid.

9. Ibid.

10. Norman Grubb, *C. T. Studd: Cricketer and Pioneer* (Cambridge, UK: Lutterworth Press, 2003).

Epilogue: Centers of *Shalom*

1. Patrick Johnstone, *The Church Is Bigger Than You Think* (Darlington, UK: Evangelical Press, 1998).

1. D. Vaughn Rees, *The Jesus Family in Communist China* (Carlisle, UK: Paternoster Press, 1967).

3. Diana Butler Bass, "What If the Amish Were in Charge of the War on Terror?" Beliefnet, October 11, 2006. http://www.beliefnet.com/blogs/godspolitics/2006/10/diana-butler-bass-what-if-amish-were.html (accessed February 2007).

4. Eugene Peterson, *Christ Plays in Ten Thousand Places* (Grand Rapids, MI: William B. Eerdsman Publishing, 2005).

Additional Resources

*Red Moon Rising: The Adventure of Faith and the
Power of Prayer*
By Pete Greig and Dave Roberts
The amazing story of the birth of the 24-7 Prayer movement.
(Relevant/USA, 2003; Survivor/UK, 2004;
Brockhaus/Germany, 2005; Päivä/Finland, 2005; Torch
Trust for the Blind [audio]/UK 2006)

The Vision and the Vow: Rules of Life and Rhythms of Grace
By Pete Greig
A contemporary call to discipleship
exploring the words of Pete Greig's poem "The Vision,"
which has touched more than one million people.
(Survivor/UK, 2004; Relevant/USA, 2004)

*The 24-7 Prayer Manual: A Guide to Creating and Sustaining
Holy Space in the Real World*
Everything you need to know to set up and run
a night-and-day prayer room.
(Survivor/UK, 2003; Cook Communications/USA, 2005)

The Lord of the Ring: A Journey in Search of Count Zinzendorf
By Phil Anderson
A fascinating biography of the little-known man
who inspired modern prayer and missions movements.
(Survivor/UK, 2006; Regal/USA, 2007)

God on Mute: Engaging the Silence of Unanswered Prayer
By Pete Greig
Pete Greig, writing out of the pain of his wife's
fight for her life and the wonder of watching the prayer
movement they founded touch lives, wrestles with the
dark side of prayer and emerges with a hard-won
message of hope, comfort and profound biblical
insight for all who suffer in silence.
(Regal/USA, 2007, Survivor/UK, 2007)

[24-7 TITLES]
WWW.24-7PRAYER.COM

Engaging the Silence of Unanswered Prayer

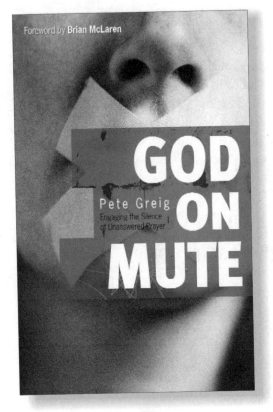

God on Mute
978.08307.43247

Pete Greig, the acclaimed author of *Red Moon Rising*, has written his most intensely personal and honest book yet in *God on Mute*, a work born out of his wife Samie's fight for her life. Greig asks the timeless questions of what it means to suffer and to pray and to suffer through the silence because your prayers seem unanswered. This silence, Greig relates, is the hardest thing. The world collapses. Then all goes quiet. Words can't explain, don't fit, won't work. People avoid you and don't know what to say. So you turn to Him and you pray. You need Him more than ever before. But somehow…even God Himself seems on mute. In this heart-searching, honest and deeply profound book, Pete Greig looks at the hard side of prayer, how to respond when there seem to be no answers and how to cope with those who seek to interpret our experience for us. Here is a story of faith, hope and love beyond all understanding.